LORD NORTH

——

THE PRIME MINISTER
WHO LOST AMERICA

Lord North. North clutches a document, and stands as if addressing the House of Commons. *(British Museum)*

LORD NORTH

THE PRIME MINISTER
WHO LOST AMERICA

PETER WHITELEY

THE HAMBLEDON PRESS
LONDON AND RIO GRANDE

Published by The Hambledon Press 1996
102 Gloucester Avenue, London NW1 8HX (UK)
PO Box 162, Rio Grande, Ohio 45674 (USA)

ISBN 1 85285 145 7

A description of this book is available from
the British Library and from the Library of Congress

Typeset by York House Typographic Ltd

Printed on acid-free paper and bound in Great
Britain by Cambridge University Press

Contents

Illustrations

Between Pages 104 and 105

Acknowledgements

The author and publisher are grateful to the following for permission to reproduce illustrations: Arthur Ackermann & Peter Johnson Limited, pl. 3; the Rt Hon. Kenneth Baker C.H., M.P., pp. 117, 213; the Bodleian Library, Oxford, pl. 10, p. 55; Bruce C. Bossom Esq., pl. 6; the British Museum, pp.ii, 37, 69, 76, 102, 139, 143, 159; the Earl of Dartmouth, pl. 17; the Duke of Grafton, pl. 19; the Earl of Guilford, pls 1, 2, 4, 5, 7, 9, 21; the House of Commons, pl. 14; the Borough of Richmond upon Thames, Local Studies, pl. 13; the National Portrait Gallery, pls 1, 15, 16, 20; the Board of Trustees, the Victoria and Albert Museum, pl. 18. The author and publisher also wish to express their thanks to the Courtauld Institute for supplying photographs and advising on permissions.

Preface

I would first like to thank the staff of the Bodleian Library's Department of Western Manuscripts. The library holds by far the largest collection of papers relating to the North family available for research, and this book could not have been written without the efficient and courteous access to them that the Bodleian and its staff provide.

I also wish to acknowledge my deep debt to the London Library and to all who work there. In the course of writing this book it has often seemed a second home, and I join a whole throng of authors, past and present, in expressing my admiration and gratitude for this incomparable institution.

On a more personal level I especially wish to thank three people. First, Philip Howard, who kindly read some of my earlier, unpublished attempts at historical biography and encouraged me to persevere. Secondly, Anthea Secker, whose constructive and detailed comments on my original typescript led to some much-needed rewriting. Thirdly, and most importantly, Angela, my wife, without whose patient support and understanding this book would never have been completed.

To Angela

Introduction

The England into which Lord North was born in 1732, in the fifth year of the reign of George II, King of Great Britain and Elector of Hanover, was a country growing in self-confidence and prosperity. The 1707 Act of Union had achieved a practicable (though not universally popular) partnership with the kingdom of Scotland, adding some one million people to the six million in England and Wales already governed directly from Westminster.[1] The Union lanced a potential source of discord, and released opportunities for commercial enterprise and cooperation, benefiting trade on both sides of the Border.[2] Ireland, with its population of perhaps one and a half million,[3] and a system of indirect rule exercised through the Irish Parliament in Dublin, remained an unsolved problem. Yet, after James II's defeat at the Boyne in 1690, it offered annoyance, rather than any serious threat to the stability of the British state during the following century.

In addition to resolving (or at least containing) the centrifugal tensions within the British realm, England had acquired by the time of Lord North's birth a substantial overseas empire in India, North America and the Caribbean. These possessions were generally the outcome of chance, emigration or the pursuit of trade, rather than of deliberate conquest, but their existence engendered a sense of national self-confidence. This empire was protected by a navy often starved of funds, and partially dependent on the resentful products of the press gang, but capable of successfully challenging the fleets of France, Spain and Holland. It was regarded by the nation with pride; both *Rule Britannia* and *Hearts of Oak* date from the 1740s.

This picture of assurance can be overdrawn. If from one perspective England and Scotland were two of the oldest nation states in Europe, from another they were countries that had been torn apart in the civil wars of the previous century, and had only recently achieved stability with the Glorious Revolution of 1688–89, the Act of Union of 1707 and the accession of the Hanoverians in 1714. At first hand (or at most at one or two removes), these events continued to shape the political outlook of Lord North's elders and contemporaries. When he was born his great great uncle, the biographer and historian Roger North, was still alive.[4] Roger had been a successful lawyer in the reign of Charles II, and under his successor became Attorney-General to the Queen, Mary of Modena. He refused to transfer his allegiance to William and Mary, spending the rest of his long life as an obscure country gentleman on his estate in Norfolk. Another relation, Lord North's first cousin twice removed, Lord North and Grey, fled to the court of the Old Pretender at Saint-Germain, accepting the empty honour of an earldom in the Jacobite peerage.[5] The future Prime Minister, in contrast, was more typical of his class and generation: he distrusted anything that might disturb the hard-won peace and security of his own times.

At the time of the final attempt at a Stuart restoration in 1745, the English aristocracy and gentry showed little enthusiasm for the adventure; their Scottish counterparts not a great deal more. The upper and middling levels of society had too much to lose from a further upheaval. They may not have loved the first two Hanoverian kings but, by the middle of the century, this line offered the best prospects for established order and continuing prosperity.

Many statistics for the increase in trade, agriculture and manufacturing output during the eighteenth century are inevitably estimates. Nevertheless, it is not in doubt that it was a period of rising (if unevenly distributed) prosperity; a figure in the region of 40 per cent has been hazarded for the expansion in the main sectors of the economy during the first forty-five years of Hanoverian rule. During the 1760s the pace of growth was slower; disruption from the Seven Years War, ended by the Treaty of Paris in 1763, was followed by a run of bad harvests from 1764 to 1767, both having an impact on economic activity. The final decades of the century, however, again saw an upward trend.[6]

Growth was partly the result of technical innovation. In 1712 Newcomen's atmospheric engine (the forerunner of the steam engine) was first employed to pump out mines, a development that allowed more efficient extraction of ores and coal.[7] Around the same time the problems of smelting lead, copper and tin with coal were solved, and by the middle of the century iron ore could be processed with coke; foundries no longer needed to be near a source of woodland fuel. In the textile industry inventions such as James Hargreave's spinning jenny, introduced in 1766,

enormously increased productivity.[8] Better road and water transport reduced carriage costs, and agricultural output grew as improved strains of
corn, cattle and sheep were bred. Organisational changes also contributed
to growth. Enclosure during the eighteenth century, of both common land
and land previously reserved for open-field systems, allowed a much more
efficient use of resources, and the success of many landowners in con-
solidating small tenancies into larger units served a similar purpose.[9] At the
same time credit and banking techniques were becoming increasingly
sophisticated, providing the finance necessary for the expansion of trade
and manufacture. If fear of instability, even of constitutional collapse, was
never far from the minds of the propertied classes, it did not inhibit a
determined, almost exhuberant, confidence in what the future offered.

The eighteenth century has been aptly named the 'Aristocratic Century'.[10] For a comparatively brief time in English history, a non-royal
hereditary elite was the predominant political force in the country, ready to
justify its position in terms of a barrier to royal absolutism, on the one
hand, and to potential 'democratic' anarchy on the other. This claim must
not, however, be pushed too far; it does not offer a comprehensive guide to
political structures under the first three Georges. It is not even easy to
define the term aristocracy with precision. It is reasonable to regard it as
comprising all holders of hereditary and courtesy titles, together with their
near relations, but it is hard to draw any clear line dividing it from the
upper echelons of the landed gentry.[11] At its centre was the peerage,
exercising formal, constitutional power through membership of the House
of Lords. This power was limited, however; taxation was in the hands of the
Commons, and the peerage itself was small in numbers. In the middle years
of the century English peers usually totalled around 190, to which must be
added the twenty-six episcopal peerages and, after 1707, the sixteen
Scottish Representative Peers. The actual voting strength of the House of
Lords was usually much lower, diminished by peeresses in their own right,
minors and Roman Catholics, and by others who through miscellaneous
circumstances, such as illness, madness or poverty, were unable or in-
eligible to attend. Even including proxies (which were permitted in the
Lords), voting numbers in the Upper House seldom exceeded 120, and
were often far less.[12]

The size of the peerage may have been relatively small but many
members of it were extremely rich, an asset in an age when the distribution
of favours played an important part in the political process. There was,
however, something more subtle underpinning aristocratic power in the
eighteenth century than the existence of a rich hereditary peerage. The
British aristocracy formed a class rather than a caste.[13] The belief that the

peerage itself enjoyed a constant refreshment of middle-class talent has been largely abandoned;[14] the close association of the aristocracy with other strata of propertied society was not solely due to upward mobility. There were three reasons why the dividing line between this class and those immediately beneath it was blurred, and thus for an influence by the aristocracy that was well beyond what its comparatively small size might have been expected to offer.

First, unlike many continental nobilities, British aristocrats enjoyed no special tax privileges.[15] Their concern, for instance, to keep the land tax low was shared by the humblest squire. Secondly, the absence from English surnames of the 'de' or the 'von', together with strict conventions for the inheritance of courtesy titles, deprived commoners who were of noble lineage of any automatic mark of distinction. The son of the younger son of a duke was usually plain Mr, and his sister, unless she made a good marriage, was Miss or Mrs. Thirdly, respect for primogeniture (as well, possibly, as the increasing use of the strict settlement),[16] left many younger sons of the aristocracy to make their own way in the world. Trade was mostly regarded as unsuitable, so they made their careers in the law, the church, the armed forces or government service. In these spheres they met men from different backgrounds, many of whom became their friends, and some of whose sisters they married. The aristocracy, especially the richer members of the peerage, remained a self-conscious elite, but its culture and assumptions were shared with a wider circle. Although it provided the bulk of the ruling class in the eighteenth century, that class also included the richer country gentry, together with small numbers of well-connected lawyers, service officers and bankers. Wealth and wordly success were accepted qualifications, even if birth always offered the surest route to position and influence.

Lord North was a fully-qualified member of this extended circle. He was descended from a line of aristocrats that stretched back 200 years; his mother was the daughter of a Montagu Earl of Halifax. His father's second and third marriages linked North with the Earl of Dartmouth and (more distantly) the Marquis of Rockingham, but these grand associations did not prevent him from choosing as his own wife the daughter of a Somersetshire squire. When the time came for his eldest son to consider marriage, North was more than happy to welcome the possibility of a match with the daughter of James Egerton, a very rich but little-known gentleman from Yorkshire.[17] North was not indifferent to social position. After the elopement in 1764 of Lady Susan Fox-Strangways with the Irish actor William O'Brien, he told his father that 'every year, &, one may say, every month of late has produced an instance of some unequal, improper, unaccountable & unhappy match',[18] but he never allowed considerations of class to dominate his understanding of the world. His position as both aristocrat and commoner (his title was a courtesy one as the elder son of an Earl) was central to his political success. He was on terms of easy familiarity with the most blue-blooded in the land, but his powerbase was the House of Commons, and especially the country gentlemen of England who occupied its backbenches.

The workings of this aristocratic (and cultivated) society were oiled by two key elements: patronage and good manners. Patronage has acquired unfortunate connotations; the term is normally avoided today when describing the system by which modern Ministers appoint paid members to unelected quangos. In the eighteenth century it was the accepted method by which posts were filled (not always unworthily), services acknowledged and livelihoods secured for all manner of people. One person's preferment to position, honours or paid employment usually depended on another and more influential person's goodwill or sense of obligation. Patronage extended also to the use of the royal prerogative to bestow titles, often at the request of senior Ministers; it could well be a cheaper form of reward than appointment to a salaried office. It is not necessary to defend every aspect of the system to see that on the whole it worked. Moreover, it bound together in a network of mutual obligation a diverse range of people, giving them a common interest in continuing national stability.

Patronage was one of the responsibilities that Lord North least enjoyed exercising; he never found it easy to say 'no', frequently an inevitable response in a world where petitioners were likely to exceed places. Many of the requests which took up North's time were concerned with quite lowly positions. In an undated letter from Downing Street he told his father: 'I have never yet heard of the place called Sweeper of the Rooms mentioned in Mrs Wright's letter; at least, I am sure no such place is in my gift'.[19] A rich or successful man's own relations were naturally the first who expected to benefit, either directly or in an intermediary capacity, from his patronage. It would never have occurred to North that he ought not to help his family if he reasonably could. He was perfectly willing to arrange the appointment of one of his wife's needy clerical relations to a comfortable living,[20] and, at a rather more exalted ecclesiastical level, to further the career of his half-brother, Brownlow. Brownlow's meteoric rise from a humble canonry, through the deanery of Canterbury, then via the bishoprics of Lichfield and Worcester to the plum see of Winchester, took place within the twelve years of his brother's premiership. It caused a few raised eyebrows even at the time, but Lord North was not simply favouring the interests of a close relation; he was also providing himself with a committed supporter in the House of Lords and, as it appears, appointing a man to the bench who took his diocesan responsibilities seriously.[21]

In much the same way, when North's eldest son, George, was selected to stand in 1778 for the safe Treasury seat of Harwich,[22] presumably on his father's initiative, it was not just a case of unprincipled nepotism. With the arrival of the Prime Minister's son in the Commons the administration was assured of another reliable vote. No doubt it would have been considered rather remiss of North if he had not helped the young man to embark on a political career, but the motive behind it was self-interest as well as family loyalty. Patronage did not just provide a handy form of outdoor relief for needy relations or deserving old retainers. Throughout the political world, the armed forces, the church and government service, the right of appointment was a valuable asset but, particularly with regard to important positions, it was used with an eye to possible reciprocal benefit more than simple family aggrandisement.

'A nation of freemen, a polite and commercial people' was the description the greatest eighteenth-century jurist, William Blackstone, used of the English of his time.[23] Good manners served to make the patronage system less demeaning for both the petitioner and the dispenser; the former could wrap his request in expressions of overblown respect, while the latter, particularly if he was compelled to return a refusal, embellished his reply with compliments on his correspondent's unrivalled qualifications for the job he was not getting. At times a dislike of plain English could lead to absurd euphuisms. After Charles Townshend's resignation as Secretary at War in 1762, North wanted to tell his father that the ex-Minister had still been well-received at court, but he conveyed this information by writing: 'A Great Lady, & a Greater Man talked with him at a great house in a great company near half an hour apiece'.[24] The circumlocution in this case seems pointless, but the convention of an oblique approach to contentious or potentially embarrassing subjects allowed scope for the unruffling of feathers and the maintainance of civilised personal relations.

On plenty of occasions, particularly when dealing with their social inferiors, members of the upper and middling classes could be brutally frank but, in general, politeness was observed within their own circles. In the eighteenth century political divisions reflected the individual and collective pursuit of power more often than profound philosophical differences, but good manners (at least outside Westminster itself) helped to keep the various players – and their families – on speaking terms. North's own father showed the importance he attached to ensuring that political divisions did not jeopardise social intercourse when he declined to become involved in the preliminaries to the bitterly contested Oxfordshire election of 1754, although he was one of the most important men in the county and, moreover, his son was about to stand for the first time for the borough seat of Banbury. He had, he said, 'many worthy neighbours who think differently from me in politicks, with whom I have a great deal of satisfaction in living upon good terms'.[25]

Politeness, or perhaps its near synonym deference, was also the solvent that allowed the newly-rich to join the ranks of the already-established. As mentioned above, the eighteenth century saw a substantial rise in national wealth, and hence in the number of wealthy individuals. Many of the new arrivals had begun as farmers, traders and manufacturers. On achieving a greater degree of prosperity they, and even more their wives and daughters, wanted to become part of the social world they had only before seen from the outside. Particularly important as neutral meeting-grounds were the popular spas of Bath, Tunbridge and elsewhere; if a man and his family appeared well-bred (a phrase that referred to behaviour far more than to ancestry) they were acceptable at the assemblies and other public entertainments that were the staple offering of the watering-places. From there a more general integration into polite society followed naturally, providing additional cohesion to that section of the population that valued continuing stability so highly.

Although deference might involve exaggerated respect for people higher up the social scale, as a man climbed the ladder he had the satisfaction of demanding an equal measure of deference from the increasing numbers he now found beneath him. The system had an interior logic that gave it strength. The larger part of the nation, which could never expect to receive any support from it, took its vicarious revenge through the enjoyment of a flood of some of the most undeferential and scatological cartoons ever printed.[26]

This brief look at the world in which Lord North moved would be incomplete without a glance at an aspect of technical progress that made its social cohesion easier to achieve: the enormous improvement in communications that took place, especially in the second half of the eighteenth century. Bath and other resorts became crucibles for the assimilation of new money into polite society partly because they became so much easier to reach. In earlier centuries the upkeep of the roads had been largely the responsibility of the parishes in which they lay, with little control over the standards applied. The eighteenth century saw the rapid development of the turnpike trusts under which, in return for the right to levy tolls on passing traffic, money could be raised for the maintenance of existing, and the building of new, roads.

The first turnpike Act had been passed in 1663, but the process only gathered momentum in the second and third decades of the next century, reaching a climax in the 1750s and 1760s.[27] By the time George III ascended the throne there was a basic national road network, and travel had improved in both speed and reliability. Whereas the journey between London and Bath could, at the beginning of the century, take two or three days (assuming the weather did not close the road altogether), sixty years later stages coaches on a regular schedule completed the journey within the hours of summer daylight.[28] The new method of financing road construction also allowed improvement in the quality of the surface, although it was not till the last thirty years of the century that the dramatic changes associated with engineers such as Thomas Telford and James Macadam were achieved.

Gentlemen who could afford it travelled in their own light post-chaises, making use of horses available at the post-houses along the route; averages of seven miles per hour or more were achieved without difficulty. In a letter to his father in May 1769, Lord North told him: 'Nothing could be more pleasant or more easy than my journey yesterday: I was at Eton between five and six o'clock of the afternoon'. His father was staying with relations south of Salisbury, where North had evidently just left him, so he had covered a distance of at least sixty miles in the day.[29] On another occasion, Lady North, writing from her own family home at Dillington in Somerset, tells her father-in-law that North would be leaving for London on Monday and would be back on Saturday.[30] Road travel, at least for the privileged, was becoming routine.

Another result of the improvements in the road network was a corresponding upgrading of the postal services. A properly efficient and inexpensive service had to await the introduction of the first mail coach in 1784;[31] before that most public mail was carried by mounted post-boys, often handicapped by bad roads. This service was supplemented by 'expresses', intended primarily for Ministers and government business; instead of heavy mailbags, only individual letters were carried, and their passage had to be given priority by postmasters.[32] Within roughly a radius of one hundred miles, Ministers in London could write to their colleagues on their country estates and expect a reply within two days. The service available to the public may have been rather slower, but the vast number of letters from the eighteenth century which have survived – which can only be a tiny fraction of those written – attest not only the importance members of polite society attached to keeping in touch with one other, but also to the ease and reliability with which it could be done.

The eighteenth century, particularly for those at or near the top of society, was a period when the enjoyment of life ranked high in the scale of priorities. Attitudes to pleasure were no longer inhibited by the ethical (though divisive) certainties of the previous century, and the moral earnestness and bleak Sundays of the next were still just a gleam in the eyes of Dissenters. Lord North's life as a servant of his country was full of trials and tribulations, and he never tried to disguise from himself – or from others – his recurrent sense of his own inadequacy in meeting them, but his reflections are always refreshingly free of guilt. Despite his cares, and his occasional bouts of depression, North's enjoyment of life was seldom impaired for long. His family, his friends, good food, the classical Latin authors, a hand of whist at Whites, the vegetable garden at his country retreat at Bushy Park, all these were things he valued. When he was Chancellor of the Exchequer, and the probability of becoming Prime Minister was already apparent, he found time to express his thanks in his own hand to his father: 'Your Lordship could not make me a present more acceptable to my taste, than the basket of bloated herrings, which we received safely yesterday. I prefer them greatly both to red & white herrings. We eat one yesterday & found it excellent'.[33]

Politics in the eighteenth century, as in most other periods of history, was a serious business, sometimes (as the unfortunate Admiral Byng discovered) a lethal one, but the enjoyment of life was valued as possibly never before or since in English society. It is against this background, a world of pleasure-seeking, leavened with self-confident patriotism, that Lord North's career as a statesman unfolded.

1

Background and Upbringing

The Honourable Frederick North was born in London on 13 April 1732 in the family home in Albemarle Street off Piccadilly. His father was Francis, Lord Guilford, a member of an old, distinguished but not particularly important family whose rank in the peerage had never risen above that of baron. His ancestor Edward North had been a sure-footed functionary in Henry VIII's government, who as Chancellor of the Court of Augmentations had played a central role in laundering the assets of the dispossessed monasteries. Partly as a result of this activity and partly through marrying a rich widow, he was able to buy as his London residence the Charterhouse in Finsbury near St Paul's, previously a principal house of the Carthusian Order, and in Cambridgeshire the estate of Kirtling where he rebuilt the house on a magnificent scale.[1] Edward North was one of Henry VIII's executors and in that capacity became a member of the Regency Privy Council intended by the King to oversee the minority of his son Edward VI. When King Edward died North's political acumen briefly deserted him and he supported Lady Jane Grey, but he quickly came to his senses and made his peace with the new regime of Queen Mary. She was sufficiently impressed by his abilities and his loyalty to call him to Parliament in 1554 as Lord North of Kirtling.[2] On her death in 1558 he changed step once more and welcomed the succession of her half-sister Elizabeth, who graciously spent her first six nights in London as Queen under his roof at the Charterhouse. Thereafter he increasingly withdrew from public affairs and died in 1564. He was buried in the family chapel he had built in the church at Kirtling, in a tomb only exceeded in magnificence by that of his son, the second Lord North.

Edward North's successors were courtiers, lawyers, politicians and writers. At the end of the seventeenth century a younger son of the fourth Lord North became Lord Keeper of the Great Seal under Charles II, and was raised to the peerage by James II as Lord Guilford.[3] His grandson, who succeeded to the title in 1729 when he twenty-five, was the father of the Prime Minister. Five years later he also inherited the North barony from a childless and exiled Jacobite cousin, and for the next eighteen years confusingly styled himself Lord North and Guilford. In 1752 he was raised to the rank of Earl and reverted to the use of Guilford on its own, and that is the name under which he will appear in this book, while his son will be referred to as North.

At the time of the future Prime Minister's birth the Norths were not rich in comparison with many of their fellow aristoctrats. The third Lord North had dissipated much of the wealth amassed by his ancestor by cutting a dash at the court of James I, and the position had only been partially retrieved by the first Lord Guilford, the Lord Keeper, who had both made money and married it. His wife was the heiress daughter of the last Earl of Downe; through her he acquired, from Trinity College, Oxford, a perpetual lease on the house and estate of Wroxton near Banbury.[4] This property descended to Francis, Lord Guilford, and Banbury became the family pocket borough, the one for which Lord North himself sat unopposed for thirty-six years. After the death of his cousin in 1735, Guilford also inherited the North estates at Kirtling. Yet, as he had a number of family claims to meet and a position to uphold, there is no doubt that in his early days the Prime Minister's father considered he had to live very carefully to make ends meet. No figures have been found for Guilford's income when he was first married, but accounts in his own hand from thirty years later (which do not include the very large sums by then coming from his third wife's Kent estates), show his 'clear revenue' from his own properties at between £4000 and £5000 a year.[5] To this something must probably be added for income from investments, together with his official salary for the fairly brief periods in his life when he held court appointments. It seems that the parsimony learnt when young persisted throughout his life, despite the increases in wealth brought by his three marriages.[6] When Guilford was thirty-three George II is reported as describing him as 'close fisted and domineering';[7] nearly forty years later Horace Walpole wrote he was 'very rich but very covetous'.[8] This meanness extended to the way he treated his eldest son. It is of course true that in the days before death duties rich men did not necessarily hand over their estates or investments to their heirs before they died; and if the old man lived to eighty-six as Lord Guilford did, dying only two years before his son, that was just bad luck. Guilford unquestionably regarded his eldest son with affection and admiration but his refusal to provide him with more than the barest financial help throughout his long parliamentary career shows

Guilford in an unsympathetic light. More importantly it probably influenced North at critical points in his life. He needed office and the sinecures the King could offer because he needed the money that went with them.

Lord Guilford was also a bully, though like many bullies he was not particularly courageous. George II described him to Lord Hervey as 'a very poor good creature but a very weak man'.[9] In 1771 Guilford bitterly criticised his step-son the Earl of Dartmouth for declining the office of Privy Seal under North, but Dartmouth stood his ground and forced Guilford into a humiliating climb-down.[10] Nevertheless there was a more attractive side to Guilford's character and one that no doubt strengthened his hold on his family's respect. He was not devoid of humour and he was conscientious in both his private and public duties. On his appointment in 1730 as governor of the Prince of Wales's two eldest sons, Mrs Delany, a well-informed but kindly eighteenth-century gossip, commented: 'I am extremely glad of this piece of news; so excellent and so agreeable man must be of infinite service to any youth that is capable of receiving good from precept and example'.[11] Moreover, his parental concern was not confined to his own sons and daughters but extended to his step-children. When his second wife Elizabeth died in 1745 he found himself with her two children from her previous marriage to Lord Lewisham on his hands. He wrote to their grandfather the Earl of Dartmouth:

> The unspeakable loss the poor Children have sustained is an infinite aggravation to my sufferings, as I fear it will be impossible for me to make them any degree of reparation. Yet all the affection, care & attention that it is possible for me to show, shall never be wanting. As I have never made any distinction between your Lordship's grandchildren & my own children, so I never mean to do it. I hope they will always look upon my house as their home, & me as a father, and that you will be so good as to consent that they shall (this summer at least) remain with me at Wroxton. There is such fondness among our children that a separation would almost break their hearts.[12]

This was not mere hyperbole and it is evident that his affection was appreciated and returned by his family, even if they must sometimes have grumbled at his possessive ways. Many years later, in 1779, he was again the subject of Mrs Delany's correspondence: 'Lord Guilford gone to his house in Kent, expecting Lord and Lady North [son and daughter-in-law], their two daughters, and two eldest sons, just returned from their travels, Lord and Lady Willoughby [son-in-law and daughter], and Mrs Keene [step-daughter]. He is like the old patriarch entertaining all his family'.[13]

Filial deference was, however, especially pronounced in the case of his eldest son, who never quite broke free from his father. This is how North wrote to him when he was thirty-five and already Chancellor of the Exchequer and a member of the Cabinet: 'I hear the clock striking eight, and am prevented by it from expressing the gratitude that I feel for all the tenderness and affection which breathes through your Lordship's letter. But I will write tomorrow whatever I have no time to say now. I am, My Lord, Your most dutiful son, North'.[14]

Lord North's mother was Lady Lucy Montagu, only child by his first marriage of George, Earl of Halifax. Lucy's mother had also been an only child; through her, Lucy inherited property in Northamptonshire which after her death passed to her husband Lord Guilford.[15] They were married when he was twenty-five and she was nineteen. It is reasonable to assume the match had the blessing of both families, as she was marrying a member of the old aristocracy and he was acquiring what he undoubtedly regarded as a much needed boost to his finances, though it is hard to believe Guilford had much in common with his father-in-law. After the death of Halifax in 1739, Lord Egmont described him as 'A squanderer of money . . . [who] loved horse-racing and kept a mistress'.[16]

There is a portrait of Lucy attributed to Ramsay in which she appears attractive rather than beautiful, possibly a little humourless, but beyond the bare details of her short life little is known of her. She bore Guilford two children and died from smallpox after the birth of the second, a daughter also called Lucy, in May 1734.[17] No scandal attached to her name during her lifetime, and none can be found in contemporary memoirs or correspondence. Some years later, however, a rumour surfaced that she had had an affair with the Prince of Wales, father of George III, and that the King and Lord North were half-brothers.

In 1730, two years after his marriage, Guilford had been appointed a Lord of the Bedchamber to Frederick, Prince of Wales, at a salary of £600 a year.[18] The Prince had had an unfortunate upbringing. He was only seven when his grandfather George I succeeded to the English throne in 1714 but he was left behind in Hanover when the royal family moved to England. He saw neither of his parents nor any of his brothers and sisters until he was summoned to London fourteen years later and made Prince of Wales. Unfortunately absence does not always make the heart grow fond and relations between the Prince and his parents, George II and Queen Caroline, rapidly deteriorated into a state of open warfare, which continued more or less unabated until Frederick's death in 1751. There were faults on both sides but he was not a very sympathetic character. This is how a reasonably unbiased observer, the first Earl of Egmont, described him in his diary:

The character of the Prince is this: he has no reigning passion, if it be to pass the evening with six or seven others over a glass of wine and hear them talk of a variety of things, but he does not drink. He loves play, but plays to win, that he may supply his pleasures and generosity, which last are great, but so ill-placed, that he often wants wherewith to do a well-placed kindness, by giving to unworthy objects. He has had several mistresses, and now keeps one, an apothecary's daughter of Kingston; but he is not nice in his choice, and talks more of feats this way than he acts. He can talk gravely according to his company, but is sometimes more childish than becomes his age. He thinks he knows business, but attends to none; likes to be flattered.[19]

The Prince of Wales, a bachelor till 1736, was a libertine of a rather unimaginative sort and, like all the Hanoverians, he had appalling taste in mistresses. Horace Walpole wrote 'His chief passion was women, but like the rest of his race beauty was not a necessary ingredient'.[20] He compelled his Keeper of the Privy Purse to call on the best known of his mistresses, Anne Vane, a Maid of Honour to the Queen. The reluctant visitor got his revenge by describing her to Egmont, who recorded the comments in his diary: 'This fat, and ill-shaped dwarf, has nothing good to recommend her that I know of; neither sense nor wit, and is, besides (if report be true) the leavings of others, and among the rest of my Lord Harrington, who was last year to have married her, but he forsook her, having gained his ends without it'.[21] As was to be expected, Anne Vane had a child, but what really upset Lord Egmont was that thirteen months later her maid also had a child and the Prince of Wales was father to both. This was the man whose household the virtuous, rather priggish Guilford joined in 1730.

In 1736 the Prince of Wales married Princess Augusta of Saxe-Coburg. Two years later in June 1738 she gave birth to their second child and first son, the future George III. The new Prince was therefore six years younger than Frederick North. Comments reputedly made in jest by the Prince of Wales to Lord Guilford about the physical similarities between their respective eldest sons must be treated with scepticism. This story, and with it the implication of shared paternity, first appeared in print in the pages of Sir Nathaniel Wraxall's *Memoirs* but, as he was not born till 1751 (the year the Prince died), he cannot be taken as a reliable witness. Wraxall is, however, more credible when in the same passage he describes the resemblance the King and his Prime Minister bore to each other in later life. He also drew attention to the coincidence that both men went blind.[22] Wraxall knew North towards the end of his premiership, sat on the same parliamentary committee and visited him at Bushy Park, where North normally resided when not at Downing Street.[23]

It seems Wraxall attached little credence to the story of North's royal paternity; indeed it is hard to find anyone else who took it seriously. Charles Townshend, North's predecessor at the Exchequer, once referred to him as a 'seeming changeling', but it is difficult to regard that as important evidence.[24] The most prolix correspondent and memorialist of the age, Horace Walpole, did not believe the rumour,[25] and there appears to be no reference to it in the course of his extensive and often waspish commentaries. It has been argued, nevertheless, that even if the story is untrue its very existence affected public interpretation of North's apparent reluctance to gainsay George III, particularly after he became Prime Minister.[26] If this was the case it would surely have been a popular topic with political satirists. Yet of the 550 or so cartoons in the British Library for which the catalogue entry gives North as the main or subsidiary subject, only two of them, published in 1773 and 1782 respectively, appear to allude to a blood relationship with the King.[27]

One hundred years later a story was published that (with a good deal of circumstantial evidence) indirectly cast doubts on the chastity of Guilford's first wife, Lucy Montagu, but it had no direct bearing on the paternity of North himself. It is impossible to dismiss completely the idea of consanguinity between North and George III, but North's lifelong closeness to his father implies that – even if he had heard it – he himself did not believe the story. There is hence no reason to think that the gossip had any bearing on his dealings with the King, or on political sentiment while he was First Minister.

In January 1736, less than two years after his wife's death, Guilford remarried. His new wife was Elizabeth, Viscountess Lewisham, widow of the Earl of Dartmouth's son and the daughter and heir of the late Sir Arthur Kaye, a Yorkshire baronet and MP. She brought her new husband some increase in wealth but, quite apart from that, it is clear the entire North family entered on a very happy period in their lives. The new Lady Guilford was a considerable correspondent, a number of whose letters have survived. They suggest a pleasant, lively woman, and one who enjoyed her husband's company.[28] Elizabeth had had three children by her first husband, a son William, later the second Earl of Dartmouth, aged five at the time of her second marriage, and two daughters. As the letter already quoted from Guilford to the old Lord Dartmouth shows, these stepchildren were welcomed into their new home and, despite occasional political differences, William became Frederick North's life-long friend. They went on the Grand Tour together and, thirty years later, when they were both in their fifties, a biographer of North describes them 'like two schoolboys released for a holiday, set off together on an excursion that ended with a visit to their sister and her husband, Lord Willoughby de Broke, at Margate'.[29] North's own family life was to prove extremely happy and his capacity for friendship and easy personal relationships was one of his most noted characteristics. It is not stretching speculation too far to assume that this trait originated with his formative years in his father's household. While North may have suffered from his failure ever to break entirely free from parental dominance, Guilford is entitled to credit for much that was warm, attractive and upright in his son's way of life.

Over the nine years following her marriage Elizabeth bore Guilford a son and three daughters, but the years of happiness came to an abrupt end in 1745. First one of their daughters died, then Elizabeth herself died in childbirth, being followed three months later by another daughter.[30] Guilford's motherless household now consisted of his own three children and three step-children. He told Dartmouth that 'I know this heavy affliction is laid upon me by Divine Wisdom that cannot err',[31] but his grief was not allowed to interfere with his reponsibilities for his remaining family.

At the age of twelve, shortly before his step-mother's death, Frederick North was sent to Eton. Although he was the first member of his family to be educated there, one of the major public schools was increasingly seen as an 'appropriate preparation for that public life which was the destiny and the duty of the upper classes'.[32] According to a contemporary, North was 'often careless and absent [but he] was, in general, at the head of his form'.[33] The suggestion of abilities marred by indolence and lack of application was to be echoed many times during his years of office. A more flattering picture comes from the Lower Master, Dr Dampier, who writing to Guilford about his son's health said: 'He deserves the Commendation and Love not only of his Relations, but of everyone about him'.[34] In another letter Dampier was even more complimentary: 'I am pleased to see in many instances how both the masters and the boys love him, and that he really, by his behaviour, deserves it from both, which is not often the case. I think he has greatly contributed to the very good order the school is in at present'.[35] The model schoolboy who is equally loved by masters and fellow students invites scepticism but, even if allowance is made for Dampier's wish to enlist Guilford's support in his campaign to become Head Master of the school,[36] the picture in this case sounds honest. All through his career North had a great capacity for attracting affection even if it was sometimes tempered by exasperation, and few of his political opponents found it easy to hate or even to dislike him.

After North left Eton his father wrote to him: 'My dear Man, or rather Boy: It gives me great pleasure to find you have left a very good name behind you, & I hope you will preserve it at Oxford ... Believe me, my Dear, Your Very Affectionate Father'.[37] In the autumn of 1749 at the age of seventeen he went up to the university to Trinity, the college endowed by his ancestor the Earl of Downe, where his step-brother Lewisham had already matriculated the previous winter. If his father's letter betrayed any concern that his son might misuse his time at university or acquire bad habits it proved unnecessary. North seems to have been a model undergraduate no less than he had been a model schoolboy, attending punctiliously to his religious and scholastic duties. His tutor, the Revd James Merrick, referred in a letter to Guilford to 'the great honour they [North and Lewisham] have done us by their publick example'.[38] On another occasion, writing to North himself, he spoke of his 'Uniform attention to the minuter points of duty'. He continued:

> It is an unspeakable satisfaction to me that you have by God's blessing been made sensible of the importance of religion before your entrance upon public life. Your improvement in piety, at this season of your life, will be the best preparation for every future scene of it; and your preserving that cheerfulness of temper and desire for knowledge which you now have, may be of excellent use in recommending the example of your piety to others.[39]

As befitted an eighteenth-century gentleman, North's religion was undemonstrative and devoid of 'enthusiasm', but his loyalty to the established church, its existing institutions and its way of doing things was rock-like. Nowhere was North's fundamental conviction that change was usually for the worse more evident.

As well as attending to spiritual matters, North was a conscientious student acquiring a reputation as an accomplished classical scholar. While still a schoolboy he had composed a number of polished Latin odes in the style of Horace, which were later published in an Eton anthology,[40] and this interest in classical literature remained with him and sometimes consoled him till he died.[41] Nathaniel Wraxall said that not only was he a fluent French speaker but that he 'was equally well versed in the great writings of antiquity'.[42] He left the university in the same golden glow as attended his departure from Eton, the President of Trinity in a letter to Guilford referring to North and Lewisham as those 'most amiable young gentlemen whose residence was a very great advantage as well as ornament to the College', a compliment that Guilford returned by presenting Trinity with a fine silver basin and ewer.[43]

North's time at school and university can clearly be considered well-spent, but there is something lacking. There is never any hint of rebellion or wish for independence, a trait that appears at least briefly in most adolescents. He seldom found it easy to challenge authority whether represented by his father or the King. His precocious virtue, however, never turned stale or tiresome as he grew older; it was fortunately leavened with a ready wit. He had an unpompous ability to accept jokes at his own expense and to respond to humour in others. When he was Prime Minister a Mr Speke, an impecunious clergyman who was a relation of Lady North's, preached a sermon before North which took as its text 'promotion cometh neither from the east, nor from the west, nor yet from the south'.[44] North enjoyed the joke and a little later the King accepted his recommendation for a clerical preferment for Mr Speke, who found himself vicar of a comfortable parish near Lady North's family home.[45]

When they came down from Oxford, in the spring of 1751, North and Dartmouth (as Lewisham had now become on the death of his grandfather) prepared to set out on the Grand Tour. Guilford fussed over the arrangements like a mother-hen. After an earnest correspondence with Dr Dampier at Eton, a Mr Golding was hired as a chaperon-cum-tutor for their travels. Dampier described him:

> I am well acquainted with Golding's character in many particulars myself & know him personally, but what we both were most in doubt about were his Politics. As to that point Lewth had given me full satisfaction. He assures me he is perfectly loyal and anti-jacobinical & that for his politics he will be answerable. He is a learned, sensible, honest man and as awkward a broad-faced fellow of a College as any I know. So that in some respects he might be of great use to them, and in others an errand [sic] Incumberance. He would look will after their brains and homes, but be a drawback upon their progress in company and the manners of the countrys they go to.[46]

According to Dr Dampier this rather unexciting choice was endorsed by the two young men themselves.[47] It is ironic that Guilford should have been so concerned at the possible risks abroad to his son's political views when most of North's career was spent defending the status quo. Unconventional or rebellious ideas never appealed to him. It is almost equally comical to envisage Mr Golding keeping a watchful eye on the behaviour of North's companion. Dartmouth was to become renowned for his piety,[48] being dubbed 'The Psalm-Singer' by his political opponents.[49] He was later a follower of Selina, Countess of Huntingdon, whose 'Connexion', a kind of upmarket Methodism, was established to save the souls of the aristocracy from perdition.

Before they could embark on their tour, North and Dartmouth must have been present at an event of some importance for the North family fortunes. At St Anne's church Soho, on 17 June 1751, Guilford married for the third time, choosing as his bride Katherine, Countess Dowager of Rockingham, widow of Lewis the second Earl. She was so fat and the weather so hot that it was cattily suggested she had been kept on ice for three days before the ceremony to stop her melting;[50] of much greater importance, she was extremely rich. Her grandfather, Sir Henry Furnese, had been a successful City merchant and had bought the estate of Waldershare in east Kent. Although Katherine was his son's second daughter, she had inherited most of his wealth through her brother, who had died childless, and was reputed to have an income of £6000 a year.

2

Coming of Age

By the end of July 1751 everything was ready and the two amiable, privileged and slightly earnest young men set off with their bear-leader for the fleshpots and galleries of Europe. The Grand Tour was an expensive operation, and the fathers and guardians who financed it expected a social and cultural return for their money. No doubt few parents would object if there was a small scattering of wild oats because there was, after all, something to be said for sowing them on the Continent rather than at home. Nevertheless the main purpose of the Tour was to broaden the minds and outlook of men who would take their places in polite society; whose vocations were to govern as legislators at Westminster or as magistrates in their own counties. North and Dartmouth were not unusual in taking their travels seriously. Whether they extended their experience in less virtuous directions it is impossible to say but, given the known characters of both of them, it seems unlikely that Mr Golding was too often expected to turn a blind eye.

When they arrived on the Continent the party set out for Leipzig, travelling through Holland and calling at The Hague and Hesse Cassel on the way. On reaching their destination, Dartmouth wrote a long letter to his Oxford tutor, Dr John Huddersford.[1] He reported that the journey had not been as inconvenient as expected, though while passing through Westphalia they had had to spend two nights in their coach as the accommodation was so bad. At The Hague they had kissed the hand of the Princess Royal, the eldest daughter of George II, who was married to William, Prince of Orange, and they had seen the young lady gossip had already marked out for the future George III: 'She is but eight years old but is one of the largest children I ever saw in my life. I fancy the Prince of Wales will hardly stay for her'.[2] At Hesse Cassel they were invited to dinner by the Landgrave, who was married to another of George II's daughters.

Dartmouth wrote: 'This is a mighty agreable Court, they use very little ceremony, both the Landgrave and his son are affable & easy, & every body is fond of the Princess [Mary]'. After the excitements of the journey Leipzig was rather dull, but they stayed there nearly nine months studying under the great constitutional expert Dr Johann Jakob Mascov, relieving the tedium with a trip to Dresden in February 1752, carnival time, 'where the whole business was nothing but Diversion from morning to night'.[3]

Before leaving Leipzig North received important news from home. On 8 April 1752 his father had been elevated to an earldom. When the Prince of Wales had appointed Guilford governor to his two eldest sons, with a salary of £1000 a year, it was also assumed, as Horace Walpole put it, that he had 'an earl's patent in his pocket'.[4] On the sudden death of the Prince, five months later, the King and his Whig ministers took the opportunity to bring the education of the new heir to the throne firmly under their own control. Guilford was replaced unceremoniously by Lord Harcourt, a man Walpole considered 'civil and sheepish',[5] who, presumably to Guilford's satisfaction, fell out with the Princess Dowager within a year.[6] Guilford had not only lost his salary but his hopes for an earldom were at risk as well. It appears the Prince of Wales had failed to tell George II of his promise to give Guilford this honour, probably because he was not entitled to make it in the first place. Given the King's dislike of his late son there was no certainty he would respect the undertaking but, after an anxious wait of a year, Guilford received his new dignity. As a result his son took the courtesy title of Lord North, the designation by which he is known to history, and without delay wrote to congratulate his father:

My Lord,
After having beg'd a thousand pardons for your two obliging letters ... I proceed to congratulate on your new increase in dignity. Indeed, my Lord, it gives me sincere pleasure merely for your Lordship's sake, exclusive of any advantage accruing to myself in particular, to see that His Majesty has confirm'd this favour, which the nation, at least the best part of it, had confer'd upon you a long while ago.

Your advancement, tho' it consists merely in a title, must be very agreeable to you on many accounts, as it takes off all appearance of your being in all ill-light with the court, as it is the fruit of merit and not of intrigue, and as the universal esteem and love you have gained will prevent its being either censured or envied.

I believe, my Lord, I may answer for your family that we are not ungrateful for the great care and trouble you have given yourself to render us happy and considerable. You have too good an opinion of me when you imagine me capable of adding a lustre to the dignity you have acquired. I am so far from thinking myself capable of adding a new lustre to it, that I have the greatest apprehension lest I should tarnish and diminish that which it has already. I hope that God will long preserve it where it is at present, that your Lordship may, by His grace, long enjoy an uninterrupted series of happiness, and continue as you are now – the support, defence, joy and ornament of your friends, your family, and your country.[7]

After Leipzig the travellers took in Hanover where they met the Duke of Newcastle, at the time one of the two Secretaries of State in the administration of his brother Henry Pelham. He was in attendance on George II, who was paying his biennial visit to the kingdom he much preferred to his British realm. Newcastle was a senior Whig politician. He enjoyed great powers of personal patronage as a major landowner in Nottinghamshire, Sussex and elsewhere, and had also established himself as the leading patronage broker of the age. It must be assumed to their satisfaction, he took North and Dartmouth under his wing, even addressing North as 'cousin'. (His father had been North's maternal great-grandfather's brother-in-law.)[8] When they resumed their travels North and Dartmouth kept up a regular correspondence with the Duke, who responded with overblown flattery:

> All your friends desire their compliments, and the whole Court, the King at the Head of it, never fail to do justice to you two. You are the favourites, & will continue so. I beg, dear Lord Dartmouth and you, will not think, that the Duchess of Newcastle, & I, shall ever look upon you Two as Tunbridge, or rather Hanover, Acquaintances, which pass off, *avec les eaux*. We shall long for the time, when you will come to us in England.[9]

Newcastle continued his campaign of praise when he got home. A year later Dartmouth's uncle Henry Legge asked him to stop, writing to Guilford: 'I wish between friends the D. of Newcastle would not celebrate them so much & I told him so the other day. It is a great disadvantage to any body to be over-commended before they appear, & nobody's Character ever answers to so great a degree of Expectation as is preparing for them'.[10] Nevertheless Newcastle was later able to assist North's career and gave him his first opportunity to shine on an important parliamentary occasion.

Berlin was the tourists' next stopping-place which, North wrote to Newcastle, 'was taken up in Festivals'. They went to balls several times a week and, as he told the Duke, 'the consequence of this was that we sat up late, & the consequence of sitting up late was that we lay long in bed in the morning, so that we divided the little stay we made in Berlin between hard exercise & sound sleep'.[11] They next moved on to Vienna, where they failed at first to meet the Empress Maria Theresa because, as Dartmouth wrote to Huddersford, she 'is not recovered from the fatigue she has lately been at in giving Birth to an Arch-Dutchess'. They were, however, present at the child's christening and commented favourably on the looks of the other nine members of the imperial family.[12] The summer was spent enjoying the social life of Vienna.

They appear to have been a popular couple wherever they went. Mr Golding informed Guilford that 'Mr North, by the ingenuity of his manners, add'd to the comelyness of his person gained himself an universal admiration'.[13] Comeliness is not a word that would later be associated with his appearance, though the portrait by Pompeo Batoni painted when he reached Rome shows a slim young man with an agreeable face. To the later surprise of his youngest daughter, Charlotte, he also acquired a reputation as a good dancer:

> I have been told that he danced the most graceful minuet of any young man of his day; this I must own surprised me, who remember him only with a corpulent heavy figure, the movements of which were rendered more awkward and were impeded by his extreme near-sightedness before he became totally blind. In his youth, however, his figure was slight and slim; his face was always plain, but agreeable, owing to its habitual expression of cheerfulness and good humour; though it gave no indication of the brightness of his understanding.[14]

After leaving Vienna North and Dartmouth travelled to Italy, calling at Venice, Verona and Milan before reaching Rome in December 1752. North complained to Newcastle that he found Italian society less friendly than German, but that this was more than offset by the number of things there were to see. They were dedicated sight-seers:

> Where we are at present there is an almost inexhaustible fund of entertainment. We have employed almost every morning since our arrival here (which was about two months ago) merely in seeing what deserves to be seen, & we shall be obliged to employ near a month more in the same business, before we shall have gone once over our task. The principal pleasure a Traveller has in Italy, consists, in the first place, in viewing the Antiquities of the country, & in the second in seeing the great perfection to which the Italians have pushed the arts of painting, sculpture & architecture.[15]

They left Rome after Easter and, following a visit to Naples, travelled homewards by way of Florence, Genoa, Turin and Switzerland; they arrived in Paris in October 1753, where they spent the winter.[16] Newcastle wrote one of his fulsome letters to his 'dear cousin' in February 1754, chiding him on his failure to send him news of Parisian life.[17] In the absence of any definite information it seems likely the time was spent by the step-brothers in the social round, though North also acquired his fluency in French. 'This acquirement', wrote his daughter Charlotte, 'together with the observations he had made upon the men and manners of the countries he had visited, gave him what Madame de Stael called *l'esprit européen*, and enabled him to be as agreeable a man in Paris, Naples and Vienna, as he was in London'.[18]

Agreeable is a term well justified in describing North. He returned from his Grand Tour a man of the world, cultivated, unobtrusively amusing and at ease in the best circles. Though not profound or given to original or abstract thought, he possessed a good clear mind that was frequently underrated by his opponents. His confidence in his social position never made him arrogant or quick to take offence and he remained throughout his life a very enjoyable companion. In 1775 the historian Edward Gibbon wrote to his step-mother: 'If they turned out Lord North tomorrow, they would still leave him one of the best companions in the Kingdom'.[19] In his autobiography Gibbon justifies his dedication of the third volume of *The Decline and Fall of the Roman Empire* to North while also providing a glimpse of him near the end of his life: 'The house in London which I frequented with the most pleasure was that of Lord North; after the loss of power and of sight, he was still happy in himself and his friends, and my public tribute of gratitude and esteem could no longer be suspected of any interested motive'.[20]

North's agreeableness was attractive but it could also be a potential handicap in a senior government Minister. It hid a dislike of confrontation and a distaste for unpleasant decisions. In essence there was a large part of him that yearned for a quiet life with his family and a few cultured or convivial friends; perhaps unsurprisingly he never managed to reconcile that daydream with his role as the leading politician of an eventful decade. It is not quite true to say that he became the King's First Minister despite himself, but rather that once he had achieved office he was never certain it was worth the sacrifices it demanded.

North and Dartmouth returned from their travels early in 1754. In little more than two years both had embarked on their political careers, one in the Commons and the other in the Lords, and both had married, North acting as Dartmouth's best man dressed in crimson velvet.[21] His election as an MP shortly after his return shaped the rest of his life, but it is probable that he regarded his own marriage as its happiest day. A year earlier the gossipy Mrs Delany had written to a friend: 'Lord North has proposed to Miss Speke. I don't know the answer'.[22] North's fancy had been caught by a young girl, Anne Speke, not yet sixteen, who was undoubtedly virtuous and warm-hearted but not very good-looking or as rich as supposed. They were married by the Bishop of London at St James's church, Westminster (now known as St James's, Piccadilly) on 20 May 1756.[23]

Neither North nor his family were famous for their good looks, a subject on which he used to joke in later life, but it is hard to believe that Lady Harcourt's cutting comments on Miss Speke made in a letter to her son were justified. After seeing North at a ball she wrote: 'I can by no means think him so very plain as many people do; I am sure he is beautiful in comparison of the Lady the world say he's to marry'.[24] In the portrait Ramsay painted of her a year or two after her marriage the young Lady North looks quiet and self-possessed and by no means unattractive. There is no difficulty in believing that North loved and cherished her for the thirty-six years they lived together. In this whole period there is only one story that reflects on North's sexual morals and it is probably a fabrication. In 1778 the *Town and Country Magazine* ran a series of satirical pieces under the general heading 'Histories of the Tête-à-Tête' and the March issue concerned 'The Pliant Premier and Miss Sp****', who were supposed to have regular assignations at Greenwich Observatory.[25] It is clear from the accompanying engraving showing a man wearing the Garter ribbon that the story refers to North, while Miss Sp**** was probably Charlotte Spencer, mistress to a series of rich or aristocratic patrons.[26] If North had been one of these the gossip would certainly have surfaced in the many unflattering cartoons published of him during his premiership, but none in the British Library in which he features involve sexual innuendo.[27]

Anne Speke was the only surviving child of a Somersetshire squire. On her father's death in 1753,[28] she inherited the estate of Dillington near Taunton where, when parliamentary and other duties permitted, she and North were regular visitors. According to contemporary gossip, Anne was an heiress, a figure of £4000 a year being mentioned more than once.[29] It is hard to reconcile that large figure with the constant money worries North suffered throughout his life. The subject of his personal finances will comes up throughout his life, almost as a leitmotiv to the story, but it is difficult to believe North (or his father) thought he was marrying money. Among the North Papers is an undated file note, possibly in Guilford's hand, headed 'Estimate of Miss Ann Speke's Personal Estate'.[30] It puts her landed property at £20,000, with a further £6000 for standing timber, lease renewals, furniture and plate. Set against these items is a figure of £7000 for outgoings due, leaving a nett amount of £19,000. As some of this wealth was in the form of possessions like plate which earned no revenue, the whole estate could hardly have produced much above £750 a year. Dillington was a nice property that provided a pleasant west country retreat and a modest income but it did not represent serious wealth.

It is possible the rumour-mongers were anticipating a quite different fortune. Through her mother Anne Speke was related to Sir William Pynsent, a rich, eccentric and childless Somersetshire landowner, and it was generally believed he intended to leave her his property, reckoned to be worth upwards of £2000 a year. Unfortunately in 1763 North bravely, or foolishly, supported the imposition of a tax on cider; this infuriated the west country gentlemen, Sir William among them, who is reputed to have burnt North in effigy.[31] When he died two years later it was discovered he had left everything to a man he had never met, the statesman William Pitt. North explained the matter phlegmatically to his father: 'Our neighbour Sir Wm Pynsent has left all his estate to Mr Pitt. It is reported, & from pretty good authority, that he left it all to me but alter'd his will in consequence of the Cider Tax'.[32]

Anne Speke may not have been a great catch but that is all the more reason for thinking she was North's own choice rather than his father's. After his own three marriages to rich and aristocratic ladies, Guilford may understandably have felt a little disappointed with his daughter-in-law, but if so for once he kept quiet. There is no hint in her many surviving letters that their relations were anything but warm. They all begin quite simply 'Dear Lord Guilford' rather than the more formal 'My Lord' or 'My Dear Lord' employed by North and Dartmouth, and they often end 'affectionately' as well as 'dutifully'. Guilford may have realised from the beginning that Anne's composed, uncomplicated nature was exactly what was needed to buttress his son's less resilient temperament and to counter his propensity for depression and self-doubt. Their youngest daughter, Lady Charlotte Lindsay, still remembered the warmth of their marriage when she was nearly seventy. Her mother, she wrote to Lord Brougham,

> was plain in her person, but had excellent good sense; and was blessed with singular mildness and placidity of temper. She was also not deficient in humour, and her conversational powers were by no means contemptible; but she, like the rest of the world, delighted in her husband's conversation, and being by nature shy and indolent, was contented to be a happy listener during his life, and after his death her spirits were too much broken down for her to care what she was. Whether they had been in love when they married I don't know, but I am sure that there never was a more happy union than theirs during the thirty-six years that it lasted. I never saw an unkind look, or heard an unkind word pass between them; his affectionate attachment to her was as unabated as her love and admiration of him.[33]

Whether they had been in love when they married may not be a very meaningful question in relation to a mid eighteenth-century couple of their position. North was not a romantic man and in the course of his career it is hard to find an occasion when his heart ruled his head. It is fair to believe his head was often doing duty for his conservative prejudices, for he conducted his life on sensible rather than emotional lines. Marrying Nance, as he called her, turned out to be a most sensible decision.[34]

3

Political Apprenticeship

Lord North was elected a Member of Parliament for the borough constituency of Banbury on 15 April 1754, when he was just twenty-two. His title was, of course, no impediment as it was purely a courtesy one, and he remained legally a commoner. Banbury was one of only five English constituencies, all boroughs, that returned a single member.[1] The use of the term elected is open to question. The total electorate, the corporation of Banbury, numbered eighteen and, as no one stood against North, none of them had to cast a vote. Before he moved to the Lords thirty-six years later he stood on a further ten occasions, half of them following appointment to government office (a requirement not dropped till 1919) and half after the dissolution of Parliament; he was never opposed. But like so much else in eighteenth-century politics appearance and reality do not always coincide, and North's acquisition and retention of his pocket borough seat was not the complete travesty of representative government that it now seems.

When his great-grandfather, the Lord Keeper Guilford, acquired the Wroxton tenancy through his marriage with Lady Frances Pope in 1672 he became the most important man in that part of Oxfordshire. He was a Tory who supported a high doctrine of crown prerogative and the full maintainance of the privileges of the established church. It was probably fortunate for him that he died three years before the Glorious Revolution and the arrival of William and Mary, as it is unlikely he could have reconciled himself to the new regime. His younger brother Roger, a successful lawyer and the biographer of the Norths,[2] became a Non-Juror and spent the rest of his long life on his Norfolk estate writing books (published posthumously) repudiating the propaganda of the usurpers.[3] The second Lord Guilford, son of the Lord Keeper, was also a strong Tory, but he was not a Jacobite and squared his conscience with accepting a job as a Commissioner of the Board of Trade and Plantations under Queen Anne. On the accession of George I in 1714 he lost it, but in 1725 he became reconciled to the Hanoverians and accepted a pension from the King; for the next four years, until his death in 1729, he supported the government in the House of Lords.[4]

His son, the future Prime Minister's father, was returned unopposed for Banbury in 1727, standing as an acknowledged Whig. When two years later he inherited his peerage his intended replacement, Lord Wallingford,[5] was defeated by one vote.[6] This unexpected reverse followed a critical letter Wallingford had received from Guilford telling him he should take the trouble to canvass for the votes of the corporation: 'Those I spoke to in particular ... were highly offended at your not thinking to ask for their votes and hoped that I would not endeavour to impose so unreasonable a thing upon the corporation as going begging to anybody that had so little regard for them as not to think their votes worth asking'.[7]

Guilford was no fool and knew the corporation should not be taken for granted. It is, of course, undeniable that the whole process was not, in modern terms, democratic (which was, anyway, a term of abuse in the eighteenth century), but Guilford's courtesies signify that the eighteen electors (who included some with Non-Juring sympathies) had a considerable sense of self-respect; a belief that their Member of Parliament was at least partially accountable to them, not simply in their private capacities but in their roles as senior citizens of Banbury.

In 1733 Lord Wallingford's victorious opponent died and both Guilford and the corporation clearly thought it was time for some fence-mending. Wallingford was again the nominee, and the letter Guilford wrote the electors on this occasion shows he considered they were citizens to be courted and not simply servants to be given their orders:

The obliging letter which I this day received from you on the occasion of Mr Chauncey's death deserves my earliest acknowledgements. I have with impatience desired a re-establishment of that friendship which used to subsist between my family and the corporation. As you have now restored it in so handsome a manner, you may depend on my continuing to cultivate it by taking every opportunity that shall be in my power of serving each of you in particular, as well as the corporation in general. Nothing can be more agreeable to me than the regard you are so good as to express on this occasion for my Lord Wallingford whom I heartily recommend to you, and think I may venture to answer (from my particular knowledge of him) that he will serve you in such a manner as shall leave you no occasion to repent of the favour you have shown him, or the confidence you have reposed in me.[8]

This time Wallingford was elected unopposed and represented Banbury until his death in 1740; thereafter Guilford had no problems securing the return of his nominee for the borough for the following fourteen years. Ironically the next election to cause him any anxieties was in 1754 when his son first stood for the seat. A comfortable arrangement had been concocted in Oxfordshire under which the county was allowed to return two unopposed Tories in exchange for a free run for the Whigs in the boroughs. In 1752 the Duke of Marlborough, the chief Whig magnate in Oxfordshire, decided to tear up this cosy agreement and to field two Whig candidates in the county at the next election. Guilford saw there was a real danger that the Tories would retaliate by running a candidate in Banbury. He must have been even more irritated that support for Marlborough's move had come from another important Oxfordshire Whig, Lord Harcourt, the man who had superseded him as governor of the royal children. Guilford managed to distance himself from the ensuing conflict in the county, which has been described as 'probably the most notorious county election of the century, [as] no expense or chicanery was spared by either side'.[9] Strenuous efforts were made to bribe the 4000 or so electors; the Tories spent over £20,000, while the expenses of the Whigs were partly defrayed by the King. Both sides claimed victory and both petitioned the House of Commons, but the Whig majority there made the result a foregone conclusion. Such unseemly goings-on were not to Guilford's taste at all. He had previously explained that he had 'many worthy neighbours who think differently from me in politicks, with whom I have a great deal of satisfaction in living upon good terms; if prudence would allow me to affect taking a leading part in this dispute, I should feel very little inclination for it'.[10] It must have been a relief to him that no Tory candidate appeared in Banbury. As it was the election went without a hitch, and Lord North took his seat in the House of Commons on the 29 May 1754. Over the many years he sat for the borough he never forgot to treat the eighteen electors with respect. In an oddly illogical way it gave strength to his conviction of the moral legitimacy of his presence in the House of Commons, and of a system which made him the properly chosen representative of Banbury.

The House of Commons to which Lord North had been elected, and which became the main focus of his life outside his family for the next thirty years, had a membership of 558. All the forty English county constituencies and nearly all the 203 cities and boroughs returned two Members each, while the Scottish and Welsh constituencies were single-Member. The size of the electorates varied from seven, in the well-known example of Old Sarum, to around 20,000 in the case of Yorkshire.[11] Voters were subject to a variety of property qualifications depending on the nature of the constituency, but as no poll was secret all were liable to pressure and bribery from their more powerful neighbours. Nevertheless it was beyond the resources of even the richest local magnate to buy all the votes where the electorate was large, or where there was a rival great man intent on the same course.

The system had evolved from medieval times when it was intended to provide representation for particular communities and interests, and when parity of numbers was not a major consideration.[12] Over the centuries shifts in population had distorted it and left it with little rational basis. Until the later years of the eighteenth century, however, pressure for reform was limited; whatever the logical shortcomings the arrangements seemed to work. At home British liberties were preserved within the rule of law, and abroad British honour was upheld. In common with most of his social equals, North denied the need for reform. After the upheavals of the previous century, the propertied classes generally opposed any changes that might threaten the stability of their own times.

The chamber in which the Commons sat was St Stephen's Chapel in the Palace of Westminster, divided by a screen into the debating-chamber itself and the lobby. It was described by a German traveller at the end of the eighteenth century as 'rather a mean-looking building'. As today, the benches for the government and its supporters were ranged along one side, and those for the Opposition on the other (with a few cross-benches on either side of the entrance), but Members might occasionally take a seat on the 'wrong' side when the House was crowded. The chamber measured only 57ft 6in by 32ft 10in (though not strictly comparable, dimensions for today's chamber are 103ft by 48ft), and there was seating capacity for 350 Members at most, with some additional space in the side-galleries.[13] The comparatively small, almost intimate size of the House probably favoured the informal, often witty style of speaking associated with North, rather than the more rhetorical mode adopted by Members such as Burke.

By the middle of the eighteenth century the parliamentary session usually lasted from November to May, with the Commons sitting on average for under a hundred days a year. There was an adjournment of four or five weeks at Christmas, and another of about ten days at Easter. Saturday sittings had been very rare since the time of Sir Robert Walpole, who liked to keep the day free for hunting.[14] Attendance figures are hard to assess accurately, but it known that in a series of important debates on Wilkes, in the spring of 1769, 458 Members voted – 100 less than the theoretical maximum. In practice 400 was considered a very full House, and the normal attendance even for important business was often less than 300.[15] The government, able to draw on its own facilities for organisation and communications, was usually more successful than the Opposition at securing the attendance of its supporters, but both were handicapped by the attachment of many Members to their country estates. This was not mere sentiment; landowning and farming was their major concern.

North's own attendance in the Commons for the fourteen years he was Leader of the House was a model of devotion to duty. Apart from periods of illness, it is hard to find evidence that he missed a single sitting. He undoubtedly found the poor lighting extremely trying to his bad eyesight, and the heat in the chamber when crowded (the result of the lowering of the ceiling by Wren),[16] must have been very uncomfortable to a man of his obesity clad in the full court dress he always wore on the front bench. Nevertheless, this chamber became the source of his authority and the stage on which he shone.

Lord North unofficially stood as a Whig but the term, together with the complementary one of Tory, has only limited usefulness in trying to unravel the complicated story of the politics of the second half of the eighteenth century. As Sir Lewis Namier put it: 'Whig and Tory were "denominations" – names and creeds – which covered enduring types moulded by ingrained differences in temperament and outlook'.[17] Used overconfidently as signposts, however, they often have a confusing tendency to point the wrong way. A hundred years before North's election men had fought as Royalists or Parliamentarians, and had died to worship as their consciences demanded, but as the eighteenth century wore on and the tide of Jacobitism receded (particularly after the failure of the 'Forty-Five'), the age of conviction politics gave way to the politics of position and patronage, of shifting alliances and unsavoury deals. In the sevententh century, and again in the nineteenth, there was no shortage of politicians who could articulate their principles, substantiate them rationally and explain where they were intended to lead. Such people were rare in the intervening century. That is, of course, an oversimplification and ignores men like Edmund Burke and the two Pitts, but the generality of politicians, including Lord North, were chiefly motivated by two conflicting considerations. The first was a sense of *noblesse oblige*, the belief that not only was it the right of a member of the upper classes to govern the country, but it was also his duty to do so. The second was the wish to use a political career to gain position, wealth and title. Within this framework the Whigs were marginally more favourable to Dissenters and to a moderate freedom of speech. As the party of the great landowners they did not want to see the Crown's powers increased at their own expense. The Tories, on the other hand, generally though not uniformly less wealthy than the Whigs, wished to

maintain the full authority and privileges of the established church, and
therefore opposed all moves towards greater toleration for those outside it.
They were also less interested in restricting the prerogatives of the Crown
if that merely added to the influence of the Whig magnates. Nevertheless,
the views of Guilford referred to earlier show how personal considerations
could be more important than convictions or party loyalties. Although a
Whig, he was not prepared to cooperate with a major Whig grandee, the
Duke of Marlborough, at the risk of damaging his good relations with his
'many worthy neighbours'.

Guilford's neighbours may well have believed their interests in Parliament were best represented neither by Whigs not Tories but by a third set
of Members, the Country Gentlemen, whose numbers fluctuated between
100 and 150. They valued their detachment from any faction or party.
Namier explained their position:

> Their watchword was independence: attachment to the Crown but no obligation
> to ministers. They entered the House with a sense of duty to the public; their
> ambition was primacy in their own 'country' attested by being chosen parliamen-
> tary representative for their county or some respectable borough (or else they sat
> for complete pocket boroughs of their own, preferrably without voters for whom
> favours might have to be obtained from Administration). Office, honours, or
> profits might have impaired their standing; the sovereign had therefore little
> occasion to disappoint them, or the minister to reward them; and they were
> treated with the respect due to the independent part they played.[18]

These were the men who, added to the core of Ministers and placemen on
whom every eighteenth-century government relied, were to be largely
responsible for sustaining Lord North's administration for twelve years.

For the sake of convention as well as parental approval North sailed
under the Whig flag, but in the words of his descendant, the eleventh Lord
North, his 'tendencies were Tory; he came from a Tory family and he had
never attached himself to the interests of any of the Whig houses',[19] a point
also made by Horace Walpole, who stated flatly that he was a Tory,
underlining the words for emphasis.[20] Although he naturally accepted help
from his important Whig friends and relations, he did not join any of their
factions or seek to form more than a loose coalition of his own supporters.
There was never an easily identifiable Northite party in Parliament as there
were Grenvillites or Rockinghamites. This detachment was a source of
strength to North as it encouraged the approval of the Country Gentlemen, and also made him a highly desirable First Minister to George III. The
King detested faction, as he believed it threatened the smooth functioning
of the constitution and his own place in it. North's lack of commitment to
any one part of the Whig system was a great attraction.

North was not, however, captain of a rudderless ship unable to steer a consistent course through lack of guiding principles. Although his tendencies were Tory the word conservative (with a small 'c') conveys his attitude better to modern ears. Whether the issue was starving peasants in Ireland or discontented colonists in America, North's responses were paternal; he hoped the misguided children would come to their senses and the risks of changing anything could be avoided. It was entirely in character that he once boasted in the House of Commons: 'I do not remember a single popular measure I ever voted for'.[21]

In the sentence that immediately followed the words just quoted North continued: 'I state this to prove that I am not an ambitious man. Men may be popular without being ambitious, but there is rarely an ambitious man who does not try to be popular'. On another occasion he told the House: 'I have never desired to sacrifice my duty to my ease'.[22] The question of North's ambition or lack of it has exercised everyone who has studied him. He became an MP in the first instance partly because his father wanted it, and partly because in reality there was very little else for him to do. Guilford kept the control of the family properties firmly in his own hands, and a career in commerce or one of the profesions was not open to a future Earl. In this respect, however, North was no different from plenty of other young men who became backbench MPs, except that history passed most of them by. What drove North on to become one of the best remembered if not one of the most renowned of British statesmen?

Money was clearly not the main object because, although North was always short of it, he took few steps to use his position to acquire more. His tendency to seek his father's approval at each career move, however, implies that a desire to please him may have played a part. Guilford himself had a high regard for outward success. His own career had, on its own terms, been satisfactory, but when he was sixty-nine he was delighted to accept the post of Treasurer to Queen Charlotte, much to Walpole's amusement, who described him as 'most harmless, half incapable and half superannuated'.[23] Guilford expected his eldest son to add lustre to the family name and North realised it; whether consciously or not, he was in part driven by the desire to stand well in his father's eyes. His rise was, however, also due to propitious circumstances, not least his attraction for George III when he needed to find a Premier to his taste; but in a competitive environment chance alone seldom propels a man to the top. It is probable that, despite his frequent and sometimes heart-rending appeals for release from his responsibilities, North became attached to power. The formation of the Fox-North coalition in 1783 will be examined later, but it is hard to believe that North's participation in it did not owe something to his fondness for office, or indeed to a streak of ambition lying deep within him. Otherwise it is almost impossible to make sense of his career.

When Lord North became a Member of Parliament in 1754 George II was on the throne with another six years of his reign still to run. The good impression North had made on the King when he paid his respects in Hanover was no handicap, but as a young backbench Member royal favour would not be of great significance. The King's First Minister at the time was the Duke of Newcastle, both one of the most important and the most ridiculed men to walk the eighteenth-century political stage. He had first attained high office in 1724 at the age of thirty-one, becoming Secretary of State (initially for the Southern Department) in Sir Robert Walpole's administration. He held this position, apart from a few brief intervals, for the next thirty years, for the last eleven of them in harness with his brother Henry Pelham at the Treasury. When Pelham died in the spring of 1754 Newcastle took over the premiership himself, reluctantly choosing the slightly disreputable Henry Fox to lead for the government in the Commons when he discovered, to his disappointment, that he could not successfully direct the Lower House from the Lords.[24] He appointed Dartmouth's uncle Henry Legge as Chancellor of the Exchequer, and North's uncle, his mother's brother Lord Halifax, as President of the Board of Trade. With these connexions and Newcastle's goodwill, North could expect a government post before too long; it was lack of suitable vacancies rather than scruples about nepotism that delayed any offer from the Duke for five years. Meanwhile North supported the administration and respected its leader without becoming his committed partisan.

Newcastle and North had much in common despite an age gap of nearly forty years. The older man was a conscientious churchman, and a devoted and faithful husband to his plain wife. Indeed the description by one of his biographers of a marriage that 'basked in the warmth of a mutual love that grew and matured over the years',[25] could equally well be applied to the Norths. In his public life the Duke took a minimalist view of the prime ministerial office, fearing responsibility and decision-taking in a way that was later mirrored in North's own career;[26] yet both men have in recent decades enjoyed sympathetic reappraisals of their reputations. The comparison must not, however, be pushed too far. Newcastle became an expert on foreign affairs, but in general his abilities were moderate. His position largely rested on ensuring the return of candidates favourable to himself in constituencies where his position as local magnate provided influence, and in developing a wider patronage network in the course of his long ministerial career. To many contemporaries, and to a number of later historians,

Newcastle was a faintly ridiculous figure. William Lecky, writing in the second half of the nineteenth century, referred to the Duke's 'confused, tangled, unconnected talk, his fulsome flattery ... his childish exhibitions of timidity, ignorance, fretfulness and perplexity ... ', while Trevelyan, in a memorable phrase, described him as 'the arch corruptionist'.[27]

In view of their evident mutual respect and the help Newcastle was to give North in getting his feet on the first rungs of the political ladder, it is tempting to make an ironic contrast between the two men, one venal and the other virtuous, but the antithesis would be false. The Duke was a supreme political operator, a man who knew the system inside-out and would be welcome in any age as a gifted party manager. Having inherited considerable powers of patronage he assiduously enlarged their scope, particularly in the sphere of ecclesiastical appointments.[28] (Promoting the right man to the Bench of Bishops added effortlessly to the administration's strength in the Lords.) North, on the other hand, inherited no electoral patronage. He himself represented the family seat of Banbury, and there is no sign in his correspondence with his father that Guilford could influence voting in other parts of the country where he owned property. Moreover, North was not a party man. He achieved office largely through his own abilities, and kept it so long as they were acknowledged by his fellow Members of the House of Commons. Like Newcastle, however, he never forgot that the whole political process operated more smoothly if oiled by the judicious distribution of favours. Once he became Prime Minister there were a large number of posts, both important and minor, that were in his gift, and the regular references to appointments in his correspondence with his father nowhere imply that North questioned the system. Within a few weeks of taking office he responded dutifully to requests Guilford had evidently made for various nominations:

> I have perused your Lordship's note, & will obey all your commands as fast as possible. Mr Gill is comptroller of the Pepper Office, an office of more profit, & much less labours than he had before. Mr Cluedom is a stamper in his room. Mr Wm Wyatt is a Tidewaiter on the Superior Fisk. I believe Mr Burgogne will be Comptroller of Chester, & I have Customer's place nearly of the same value to give to Mr Ashorn.[29]

Where his own family was concerned anecdotal evidence suggests that North regarded the exercise of patronage with a certain cheerful cynicism. When his half-brother Brownlow became Bishop of Lichfield at the age of thirty someone commented that he was rather young for the office; to which North retorted that, although that might be true, when he was older he might not have a Prime Minister for his brother.[30] The story may be apocryphal, but the sleight of hand he employed ten years later to secure from the King the rich see of Winchester for Brownlow is attested by Wraxall.[31] North first asked for his appointment to York, knowing perfectly well the King was bound to refuse as he had already promised it to someone else. He then suggested that Winchester, whose Bishop was believed to be dying, would assuage the disappointment of the earlier refusal. George III jumped at this easy way out of his dilemma and happily made Brownlow the new Bishop of Winchester, a position which provided him with a large income for the remaining twenty-nine years of his life.[32]

Lord North was never a man to change accepted methods and customs if they appeared to work satisfactorily, and it is unreasonable to condemn his use of patronage as corrupt. It was no less part of his job to encourage gratitude and reward support than it is in the interests of a modern administration to woo the electorate with tax cuts. The point is that both North and Newcastle were individually incorrupt in the important sense that neither was known to modify his decisions in response to monetary or other inducements. North accepted sinecures, and on one occasion financial help, from George III because he had little money of his own and he needed to live. He acknowledged his debt to the King, but it is extremely hard to demonstrate that his actions were thereafter any different from what they otherwise would have been. Straight bribery or delicately disguised *douceurs* were a normal feature of eighteenth-century public life, a reality recognised by North as well as by his friend Newcastle, but both men managed to pursue their careers without sacrificing personal integrity.

North's arrival in the Commons in 1754 anticipated by eighteen months the outbreak of the Seven Years War, when Britain and France battled for supremacy and trade in India and Canada, with Britain finally victorious thanks to Robert Clive in the East and James Woolfe in the New World. At first, however, nothing went right and it was soon obvious Newcastle was not a war leader. In 1756 he gave way to William Pitt the Elder, and North's hope of employment with a new administration rose. His aim was a seat on the Board of Trade; with support from Guilford he asked both Halifax and Legge to further his cause. Legge told Guilford he would like to help but added: ' ... I doubt if we shall be able to get him into the Board of Trade in the first Cargo since the vessel is small and the passengers many'.[33] His fears were justified and North had to wait for a suitable position for almost three more years.

The North's first child, George Augustus, was born on 11 September 1756. When the child was just over a year old North wrote to his father saying: 'He grows more stout, jolly and agreeable every day. He has a good deal of sense but is of a rather serious turn. His beauty is yet to come'.[34] His arrival, however, had added to the family's financial difficulties. Early the following year he was telling his father about their economical social life and his wife's lack of invitations to the season's balls, adding rather sadly: 'She endeavoured to make it up to herself by having a little accidental Hop the other night for some of her particular friends without a supper'.[35]

In January 1758 North was at Dillington and still worrying about money and considering how to liquidate his debts. He wrote to his father setting out various figures, estimating that his income never exceeded £2500 a year and that, after he had serviced an interest charge of £840, he was left with an annual deficit of £540. This interest charge is a recurring theme in his correspondence about his finances and appears to relate chiefly to funds he had had to raise for a settlement on his wife, though why Guilford allowed the young couple to embark on married life with this burden is unclear. The letter continued:

> Tho' this view of my estate is not agreeable I am neither greatly afflicted nor alarmed at it tho' I have very considerable book debts unpaid, yet I flatter myself by the sale of my timber to get myself pretty clear. However it will [be] impossible for me to go on with my eyes open without making some material alteration in my manner of living, I am ready and willing to make any retrenchment, & any alteration that shall be thought necessary, provided I can ensure myself the satisfaction of making two ends meet.[36]

Filed with this letter is a note in North's hand headed 'Estimate of Expenses' which puts his total outgoings at £2160 a year. Items under the heading of Housekeeping account for £620 of this figure, while the balance includes various sums for coachmakers, wheelwrights, saddlers and other tradesmen associated with the expensive business of eighteenth-century travel. There is, however, no separate figure for the rental of his London house. This modern residence on the south-east corner of Grosvenor Square had been bought by Guilford in 1736, but after he married Lady Rockingham they lived in her house in Henrietta Street and rented out his own.[37] By 1757 the lease had fallen in and it would appear that Guilford handed over the house to his son, though on what terms is uncertain. It was undoubtedly too large and grand for the hard-up Norths and for a year in 1765 they even had to let it and move in with Lady Drake, his wife's mother; but, apart from his time in Downing Street when he was Chancellor of the Exchequer and then Prime Minister, and another brief period of official residence near Horse Guards as Paymaster of the Forces, it remained their home for the rest of their lives.[38]

In July 1758 North again wrote at length to Guilford setting out a slightly impractical plan of retrenchment:

> I have endeavoured to form an estimate of what my family expences will probably be, if they are conducted with aeconomy [sic], & if I settle myself upon the plan of living eight months in the country and four in town, which by just riding up my self with one servant to London for two or three days at the opening of the Parliament I shall be able to do. I have enclosed the Estimate for your Lordship's perusal. If you think any alteration can be made in it to my advantage you will be so good as to let me know.
>
> This calculation is formed upon the supposition that I am to continue to live upon the footing I have begun, with the difference only of a shorter stay in London, and an absolute exclusion of every expence that can in the strictest sense be called superfluous. There are two reductions that may be made. One is Bryant's salary, of 30 guineas per an & the other's in stable expenses, in which, I certainly might save £50 a year by keeping my own Horses, but then I shall risk of being cheated.
>
> It is necessary to inform your Lordship that this calculation is greatly under my former expences, grounded upon the reformations I have already made, & upon the good opinion I have of our new cook who goes on upon a much more prudent & aeconomical footing than any of her predecessors.
>
> In the article of the wages I do not put the nurse upon the salary she receives now of £18 a year, but upon what she is to receive, which I state as £6 a year.
>
> I own that since the birth of George, I have felt a great inclination to take the Estates in Somersetshire. They are in themselves greatly improveable & they lie in such a manner, that with the certain reversion of Miss Speke's manor they will form by much the finest estate that will lie in possession of our family, & the most adapted to make them considerable.
>
> Your Lordship thinks one may live comfortably and conformably to the rank you would chuse to have us maintain in the world upon £900 a year. If you will send me the plan of life which will make that practical I promise beforehand to embrace it. All that I desire is to live decently within my income. To everything beyond that I am perfectly indifferent. Whatever you think superfluous in my manner of living, whatever circumstance of magnificence, vanity, pleasure, or even of conveniency you would advise me to forego, I do assure you that I am ready to part with it without the least regret.[39]

It is a pity that Guilford's letters to his son have not survived, as it would have been interesting to see how, if at all, he answered that last paragraph. It was one of the very rare occasions when a note of acerbity crept into North's correspondence with his father; it must have been intensely irritating to the young man to be lectured on his financial arrangements by someone whose family income was now several times what he was being instructed to live off.

Fortune never came North's way, at least not until he was too old and ill to enjoy it, but a few weeks before he wrote the earlier of those two letters to his father about money he took his first step on the road to fame. Pitt had found it hard to govern without Newcastle's skills as a political 'fixer', so in the spring of 1757 they formed a somewhat improbable alliance under which the Duke resumed the post of First Lord and Pitt became one of the two Secretaries of State. North was again disappointed of a government appointment, but his chance to shine came when Newcastle invited him to second the Address of Thanks in reply to the King's Speech at the opening of the parliamentary session on 1 December. He was a slightly surprising choice, as it seems his abilities as a speaker had not previously been put to the test. Lord Jersey, sending his congratulations to Guilford after the speech, referred to it as 'a maiden effort'.[40] Despite Horace Walpole's comments made three years earlier that 'I hear nothing but the parts and merit of Lord North',[41] there is no record of any previous speech on his part. Furthermore he was clearly not a 'natural' speaker. At a later date Wraxall wrote that 'his tongue being rather too large for his mouth, rendered his articulation somewhat thick, though not at all indistinct',[42] and Walpole commented on his 'deep untunable voice, which, instead of modulating, he enforced with unnecessary pomp'.[43] It was probably due to this style of delivery that he acquired the nickname Boreas, the Greek god of the north wind. His later mastery of the Commons was never dependent on great rhetoric.

There is no record of what North said in his speech but no doubt it followed the same fairly anodyne tone adopted by the proposer of the motion, Lord Royston, who regretted the recent failures of British arms at Quebec and Rochefort but otherwise steered clear of anything controversial.[44] It is, however, certain that North's debut was considered more than satisfactory on all sides. Dr Dampier wrote excitedly to Guilford from Eton, saying he had heard of his former pupil's success from an old Member of the House who had assured him he had never heard a young man do better.[45] North's cousin Charles Montagu, the Member for Northampton, also wrote to Guilford:

His performance is the subject of discourse in all companies. If anybody was sorry. I fancy it was the Secretary of State [Pitt] to have his work taken out of his hands and to see he had so dangerous a rival. I am not singular in this notion. He possessed himself perfectly well, his language was correct and not too flowery, no hesitation from beginning to end, his action decent and proper, his voice very clear and distinctly heard everywhere, never harsh, the present state of Europe finely represented, our misfortunes touched upon so as to give no offence to anybody: a most masterly performance it was indeed.[46]

It is hard to believe that William Pitt considered North a dangerous rival. The young man himself also took a sensibly modest view of his perform- ance, replying to his father's congratulations: 'I possessed myself and spoke I believe with a loud voice & a tolerable manner, & to that much more than to my matter, I owe my reputation'.[47]

Whatever Pitt's views on North, it was to him not Newcastle that he owed his first offer of a paid job (Members of Parliament were not paid, but ministerial posts usually carried a salary). Under the administrative arrange- ments then in force the two Secretaries of State shared responsibility for domestic affairs but divided foreign affairs between them on a north/south basis.[48] William Pitt was Secretary for the Southern Department; in that capacity he was responsible for relations with the Mediterranean states and the selection of diplomatic representatives accredited to them. The lega- tion at Turin, capital of the kingdom of Sardinia, was vacant and, after consulting Newcastle about a suitable candidate, Pitt wrote to his ally Lord Bute:

> I told the Duke ... that I should wish some young man of Quality, of Hopes for business, who might form in such a wise, able Court, where the good intentions of the Prince did not greatly need a surveillant, much versed in affairs, and such a young man I thought was Lord North. I mention him to your Lordship, as supposing Leicester House and Saville House wou'd approve such a nomination. I should be happy to know your Lordship's sentiments, as soon as convenient, till which I shall take no steps towards Lord North.[49]

North, however, refused the offer, though not before seeking Guilford's approval for his action:

> I return your Lordship a thousand thanks for your kind letter & advice. It not only confirms Ld H ... 's, and Mr L ... 's & my own opinion, but entirely coincides with my inclination. I am so well acquainted with your Lordship's tenderness & affection for me, and have always succeeded so well by following your counsels, that I was unwilling to give an absolute answer to Mr P..t without having first consulted you. Otherwise, the case appears to me so clear, that I might almost have ventured to have presumed your opinion, & have given an immediate refusal to the proposal as soon as it was made to me.
>
> Beside the strong reasons I sent in my letter the impossibility almost of getting with a wife & family to [our] place of destination in the present junction of affairs is a very material consideration. I have observed that most men who have passed their youth in foreign employment make no great figure in Parliament on their return.[50]

It is understandable that a son should wish to consult his father before turning down the first offer he had received of a paid job, particularly as only ten days later he had to write to him again about his money worries, but the letter makes uncomfortable reading. It is realistic in its assessment of what happens to a young man's career if he moves out of the limelight for too long (and incidentally lends strength to the view that North was not without ambition); yet even if allowance is made for the deferential style of eighteenth-century letter-writing, it suggests a need for parental support in the face of a difficult decision.

4

A Man with a Future

Lord North's rejection of the offer of foreign employment proved justified. A little over a year later, on the 24 May 1759, the Duke of Newcastle wrote to William Pitt: 'I this day recommended my Lord North to the King to succeed my Lord Bessborough in the Treasury. He is a near relation of mine, but I hope his appearance in Parliament will make the choice approved, and that he will be in time a very able and useful servant of the Crown'.[1]

A long footnote in Cobbett's *Parliamentary History*, published over forty years later, maintains that North was a compromise candidate for the post.[2] In this version Newcastle, on the recommendation of Lord Halifax, favoured the appointment of a Mr Oswald from the Board of Trade, while his rival Lord Bute was pushing his own man Mr Eliott from the Admiralty. Cobbett continues: 'The Duke of Newcastle, finding himself obstructed in his own nomination and resolving not to comply with that of Lord Bute, the dispute was settled by a third person, with the recommendation of Lord North', but this account seems on several grounds doubtful.[3] For once with the politics of the period the straightforward explanation is the most convincing. Guilford had been pestering Newcastle the previous month for positions for himself and North, writing to the Duke on the 21 April: 'Lord North being in Somersetshire, & myself too lame to wait upon Your Grace, I take the liberty of mentioning, in this manner, that I hope we shall not be out of Your Grace's memory, in case the changes occasion'd by the death of my Lord Leicester should furnish an opportunity of doing something for either of us'.[4] With that reminder fresh in his memory, with North's uncle Henry Legge already at the Exchequer and another uncle, Halifax, at the Board of Trade, it seems obvious the Duke wanted to promote a 'near relation' with useful family connexions, and at the same time secure the personal loyalty of a man who seemed to have a future. When he told Pitt of his hopes that North would be in time 'a very useful and able servant of the Crown' he probably meant it.[5] Newcastle may sometimes have seemed absurd but he had not been at the top in politics for so long without acquiring an eye for ability.

The position North was offered and accepted without delay was that of a junior Lord of the Treasury. Since 1714 the office of Lord High Treasurer had been 'in commission'; the responsibilities being held collectively by five Commissioners, usually known as the Lords of the Treasury.[6] The position of First Lord as chairman of the nation's finances was considered of sufficient importance that by the second quarter of the century it was always held by the King's First Minister. The Second Lord then became the Chancellor of the Exchequer, though when the Prime Minister was a Member of the Commons he normally combined both roles.[7] The three junior Lords were not passengers, though they performed few direct executive functions. They attended the twice-weekly meetings of the Board, shared responsibility for the decisions taken and had to be ready to explain and defend them in Parliament. In addition to this commitment North was evidently an inveterate joiner of committees, being reported to be a member of no fewer than forty-nine in the parliamentary session of 1758-59.[8]

With his political advance North also enjoyed a financial benefit, since the Lords of the Treasury, unlike MPs, were salaried. When the office of Lord High Treasurer had been put into commission the stipend of £8000 a year had simply been divided among the five new Commissioners, giving them a gross payment of £1600 each. (The First Lord's remuneration was later 'topped up' to £5000 from other sources.)[9] Allowing for various taxes and deductions, this left North richer by £1300 a year. According to his own estimates from a slightly later date, he was also drawing £1700 a year 'clear income from [his] estates' (chiefly Dillington), so he and his wife had £3000 a year to live off.[10] It is always risky to translate monetary values over 250 years, but by any calculation the Norths were not seriously hard up. From North's earlier letters to his father about his expenses, it would appear he was now in a position to get his finances onto a sensible footing, even taking account of the interest on the debt incurred at the time of his marriage. This proved not to be so. After three years at the Treasury he was still in difficulties, and in October 1762 he had to ask his father for help in raising a loan:

> It is impossible to express how much I feel myself obliged to your Lordship for your goodness to me, & for the very kind acceptance you have given my request. I am very sensible that my want of a constant attention to the management of my private affairs has been the principal cause of the streights [sic] in which I now

BOREAS.

I Promise to pay seventeen Millions in ten Years — if I am Minister.

Frontispiece to *New Foundling Hospital for Wit* (1772), alluding to North's budget speech on May 1 1772. *(British Museum)*

find myself; at the same time I must attribute some part of my difficulties to my having originally set out upon a positing beyond my fortune, & to the expenses incurred at my marriage ...

I do assure your Lordship that my delay in communicating my distress to you never proceeded from any doubts of your willingness to assist me, which your constant tenderness for me would never have permitted me to conceive, but from a very well-founded expectation of considerable fines from my estate, & from the reluctance I feel of proving in any respect a burden to you. I am not a bit the less concerned at the trouble I give you because I find your Lordship's affection for me makes you so ready to serve me, but I hope and really believe, that while I continue in office, my fortune will hereafter be so equal to me expences that I shall never have any occasion to trespass upon your goodness again.

I am, My Lord, your most dutiful Son, North.[11]

This letter evidently crossed with one from Guilford full of his usual good advice but with few positive offers of help, as two days later North wrote again, saying: 'I am much afraid that your good intentions will be fruitless as I scarce see any possibility of borrowing money upon bond'.[12] Sympathy for North's predicament is natural, but his remarks about his want of a constant attention to the management of his private affairs, and about his hope of better times ahead, catch the attention. Throughout this period there are references in his letters to the economical 'plan of life' he intends to adopt, but three years later, in July 1765, he is still putting it off. He has decided, he tells his father, to delay either parting with Ashsted (a country retreat he had taken in Hertfordshire) or letting his London house.[13]

Guilford was certainly tight-fisted and enjoyed the power over members of his family that his wealth (and their lack of it) gave him, but he perhaps suspected his eldest son was incompetent with money, and would always be in a financial muddle. Despite successive increases in salary together with substantial perks (including two free houses), by the mid 1770s North was heavily in debt. Why? He indulged in none of the pastimes by which aristocrats traditionally lost their fortunes. He kept neither racehorses nor mistresses, and his gambling was confined to a rubber of whist at White's on his way home in the evening.[14] Unlike his father, who spent considerable sums laying out the gardens and pleasure grounds at Wroxton, North's expenditure at the various houses he occupied was confined to minor alterations to his wife's home at Dillington. The inevitable conclusion is that the attention he gave to his personal affairs was spasmodic and ill-disciplined, a situation encouraged by the readiness of tradesman and others to give almost unlimited credit to a man with North's ultimate expectations. His easygoing approach to domestic matters was illustrated by his youngest daughter, who later wrote: 'To his servants he was a most kind and indulgent master', and tells the story of a 'drunken, stupid groom' who, despite his unique talent for putting her father 'in a passion', was always forgiven and died in his service.[15]

North's initial money problems probably stemmed from the financial arrangements made at the time of his marriage, which left him with a nett income barely sufficient for the style of living expected of a young noble-man and rising politician. Nevertheless, his subsequent failure to rectify the situation, even as his income grew with his career, can only be explained on the assumption that he was one of those people who, in their personal lives, never manage to regulate outgoings to match available resources.

In contrast to his handling of his own money, North rapidly acquired a reputation for his grasp and presentation of the national finances, and within two years of his appointment his name appears on the official Treasury lists immediately beneath that of the Chancellor.[16] It is possible this was partly due to his seniority of appointment over the other two junior Lords, but it seems that four successive Chancellors came to trust his judgement. His tenure at the Treasury Board lasted six years, surviving several changes of ministry, the first following (though not immediately) the death of George II on 25 October 1760 and the accession of his grandson George III at the age of twenty-two. Lord North and the new King, a man who was to play such a major role in his political fortunes, were alike not only in appearance but also to a considerable degree in character. Both were men of personal integrity and of irreproachable private lives. They shared a conservative cast of mind, seeking their models from the past rather than exploring the possibilities of the future, and both were influenced in their attitudes to parliamentary government by a common dislike of faction. The idea that democracy can be strengthened by well-disciplined parties alternating in the responsibilities and spoils of office is generally accepted today, but George III and North looked back to an ideal world where selfless men gathered round the King to carry on his government. There is an undated fragment in the Windsor Castle archives in the hand of George III in which he aspires 'to put an end to these unhappy distinctions of party called Whigs and Tory, by declaring that I would countenance every Man that supported my Administration and concurred in that form of Government which had been so widely established by the Revolution'.[17] North would have supported those sentiments. He never seriously tried to build his own faction or to join anyone else's, and he would have distrusted the party system that developed in the next century.[18] On the other hand, he was an altogether more easy-going man than the King. Like his father, North wanted to live on good terms with his neighbours and never pushed his political views too aggressively. It is no longer usual to dismiss George III as a bad King who tried (unsuccessfully) to subvert the constitution and enhance the royal power. He accepted, if sometimes reluctantly, that although he was entitled to choose his government his choice had to have the support of the House of Commons, and that if he tried to govern without it there would be a constitutional crisis. North also knew that that was the position, that it had been established since the Glorious Revolution and that it placed a definite limit on royal authority, but there were to be occasions when he allowed himself to be cajoled by the King into pursuing policies he no longer fully supported.

At George III's accession the ministry was headed by Newcastle and Pitt, but within two days a comparative newcomer to politics was introduced into the government. On the King's insistence John Stewart, third Earl of Bute, was appointed Groom of the Stole and made a member of both the Cabinet and the Privy Council. He was in every sense the 'King's Minister', the man on whom George III relied for advice and support to the virtual exclusion of anyone else, and was sometimes referred to as the 'Scotch Favourite'. Bute was a northern nobleman of no great wealth, with pretentions to learning and an interest in botany. In 1737 he had been elected by the Scottish peers to the House of Lords, as one of the northern kingdom's Representative Peers, but lost his seat four years later. It was another twenty years before he again sat in the Lords and his political experience was extremely limited.[19] He had, however, succeeded in attracting the attention of Frederick, Prince of Wales, and in 1750 he was appointed one of his Lords of the Bedchamber. When the Prince died six months later Bute (like Guilford) lost his employment, but he retained the friendship of the widowed Princess and by the second half of the decade had become her principal adviser and confidant. At the time it was assumed they were lovers and that this was the source of his hold over her, and through her over her son George, the future King. That theory is now discounted. The Princess was badly educated and easily impressed by Bute's parade of learning (not entirely spurious),[20] while his hold over her son is convincingly explained by John Brooke in his biography of the King: 'How shall we explain Bute's influence over King George III? It was simply that Bute was the first person to treat him with kindness and affection. He broke through the shell of loneliness with which the boy was surrounded. After such a life as the Prince had led, it was certain that the first person who did this would win his confidence'.[21]

The King's deep regard for Bute was maintained after his accession, and for the first year or two of his reign he continued in his letters to write to him as 'My Dearest Friend'.[22] At the election of March 1761 Bute was returned to the Lords as a Scottish Representative Peer. In selecting his new administration the King felt sufficiently confident to appoint his friend Secretary of State for the North, leaving the Duke of Newcastle at the Treasury and William Pitt as the other Principal Secretary. It seems unlikely the King expected, or even wanted, this ill-assorted trio to survive very long. Pitt was the first to go, resigning on 5 October 1761 because Newcastle, Bute and the rest of the Cabinet refused to sanction war with Spain, despite clear evidence that the Spanish were assisting France in the fight against Great Britain. Three months later it became obvious that Pitt had been right. In January 1762 Newcastle reluctantly declared war on Spain, asking Lord North to make the reply to the official announcement in the House of Commons.[23] His flattering request might have have been considered a poisoned chalice by its recipient. Not only was the King eagerly awaiting an opportunity to promote Bute and drop the Duke (achieved four months later) but North was being asked to perform that most difficult political act: a public volte-face. In the previous autumn the administration had lost Pitt because it refused to countenance war with Spain, now it was compelled to acknowledge he had been right. North, however, regarded Newcastle's invitation as a compliment and responded with alacrity. The letter dated 7 January missed him at Wroxton and was forwarded express by Guilford to Dillington, where it reached him on the 10th. North replied the same day:

> I esteem myself much honoured by yr Grace's commands & will obey them with great pleasure. There is no point of politics in the World in which I have so determined opinion as Aversion to a war with Spain, but, as I think, I have reason to imagine that yr Grace & the rest of his Majesty's servants are nearly in the same sentiments, and that you would never have engaged in this war if it could possibly have been avoided with honour & safety, I shall have no sort of objection to move an address of thanks to his Majesty & to say what little I can to persuade the House to come into the measure (since it is a measure of absolute necessity) with unanimity and resolution.[24]

His speech was well-received not least because he had the sense not to duck the reproach of inconsistency. James West, a supporter of Newcastle's in the Commons, reported the debate to the Duke:

> Lord North said that a question might be asked, why not declare war sooner, you might have taken the galleons? That it was not above six or seven weeks between the first proposal and the King's Declaration, that he believed the galleons were then arrived safe, but that if they had been in the Downs, he doubted whether the future would be so discernible as many thought & would before a Declaration of War have involved us in many difficulties ... The War is unavoidable. Therefore agree like men, with unanimity & harmony among yourselves & confidence in

your King, for candid observation, *out of this House*, has as bad an effect as open opposition.[25]

Horace Walpole wrote that in the course of this speech North had strongly attacked Pitt, 'calling him an abdicated minister, and violently taxing him with a fondness for new hostilities',[26] but this account is suspect. Vituperation was not North's style and there is no reference to such an attack either in West's report or in another that Lord Barrington sent Newcastle, which praised the moderate and conciliatory tone of the speaker subsequent to North, William Pitt himself.[27] This would seem most unlikely if he had just been savagely criticised. Probably the safest judgement on North's speech can be made from the outcome of the debate: the motion to support the war was carried without a division.[28]

By the end of May Newcastle had also handed in his resignation after objecting to the decision of his Cabinet colleagues, strongly encouraged by the King, to stop the payment of subsidies to Prussia, Britain's ally in the war with France. The King was delighted with the Duke's departure and at once offered the Treasury to Bute. To his consternation his Dearest Friend hesitated, uneasily conscious of his inadequacy for the job. George III brushed his fears aside:

> Nothing but the last lines of my Friend's note should have caused my troubling him again this evening, either the thought of his not accepting the Treasury, or of his retiring chill my blood; is this a moment for despondency? No for vigour and the day is ours; my Dearest Friend's sincerity when he talks of his own ignorance in business would be doubted by any man in the country but me. I know his worth, and therefore attribute it to the dejection arising from his fever.[29]

After Newcastle's resignation there was pressure in Parliament for an enquiry into the financial conduct of his administration. North was among those who remained loyal to the fallen Minister and opposed the proposals, for which the Duke was understandably grateful.[30] North acknowledged his thanks in a graceful letter, which also marked the end of a political association which had served him well:

> My Lord,
> I was at home yesterday when your Grace's very kind note was brought to my house. It is a great addition to all the former obligations for which I shall in all places & and at all times own myself indebted to yr Grace that you are so good as to take so much notice of the little matter I said in the House on Tuesday, which I owed to Truth & Justice as well as Gratitude. Your Grace's abilities and integrity in the execution of the office you held are allowed by every unprejudiced man in this Kingdom, & I was very happy in finding an opportunity of declaring how much my opinion in that respect co-incided with that of the publick. I beg leave to

assure your Grace that, tho we may sometimes differ upon questions of political expediency, I shall never fail in everything that relates personally to you, to shew the sense I have of the many and great favours I have received at your hands, I am My Lord, with the greatest Truth and Gratitude,
    Yr Grace's most obliged & faithful humble servant, North.[31]

From later comments made when faced with playing a major role in the affair of John Wilkes, North probably considered leaving office with Newcastle. Although no definite proof is available, he seems to have had little respect for Bute and even less for the bizarre incompetence of his new superior at the Exchequer, Sir Francis Dashwood.[32] He rejected, however, an attempt by Bute to lure him into a more prestigious job as Comptroller of the Royal Household. There would be no loss of income involved but by now North was clear he wished to remain at the heart of political affairs. He informed his father of his decision without seeking his views first: 'Last night after I wrote my letter to your Lordship, I had an offer of Comptroller of the Household made up of equal value with the Treasury. For general reasons, many of which will occur to your Lordship, I declined so I hope to hear no more of it'.[33]

Bute lasted less than a year as Prime Minister, resigning on 8 April 1763 after a turbulent debate on the cider tax, the measure which cost North so dear. Bute in fact carried the Bill but he had had enough: after a further brief period as the irresponsible power behind the throne his inglorious performance came to an end.[34] During the two and half years that saw the rise and fall of the King's 'Scotch Favourite', North had managed to keep a reasonably low profile as well as his post at the Treasury. This was an achievement, as Bute and the Norths were not in reality on very friendly terms, a situation that may have been exacerbated by the treatment Guilford had received from Bute.

After his accession George III was determined to marry without delay and lists of suitable German Protestant princesses were drawn up. The choice finally fell on a girl who was considered so unimportant that she had been placed bottom on the original schedule, Princes Charlotte of Mecklenburg Strelitz. She arrived in England in the company of Lord Harcourt on 7 September 1761, met the King for the first time the following afternoon, married him in the evening and embarked on a life of considerable happiness and many children. But a new Queen meant a new household and Lord Guilford pricked up his ears. Two months before Princess Charlotte's arrival he addressed a letter to Bute of which he kept a carefully corrected draft. Its combination of bluster, greed and obsequiousness shows his less attractive side:

Nobody could feel a more sincere joy upon his Majesties Declaration of his intended marriage & the prospect of an increase of his happiness than my self, & I beg leave to congratulate your Lordship on this occasion. I must confess I have heard with great concern that the Principal Employments about the intended Queen are already filled, & that there is no appearance of my protestations having been under consideration. They certainly stand before those of my Lord Harcourt, unless I have done something to render myself unworthy of receiving a mark of his Majesties favour. This is so notorious, that if I am now forget, the world must conclude the King has cast me off with displeasure, & contempt. By the uneasiness this would give me, your Lordship will easily believe I would think otherwise, if I could. At this crisis I desire the favour of your Lordship to ask for me of his Majesty the Office of Treasurer to the intended Queen dignified by the same salary as my Lord Bathurst enjoyed when Treasurer to the King as Prince of Wales, which I think I could accept with credit, notwithstanding the preference given to my Lord Harcourt, for whom I have a great personal regard.

If your Lordship will be so obliging as to lay my situation, & this request, before His Majesty, I shall have strong expectations from the goodness of his heart, which I know to be the best in the world. I beg pardon for giving your Lordship this trouble, which I may rather hope to obtain, as it is probably the last of the kind you will receive from, My Lord, Your etc etc.[35]

To this effusion Guilford received a five-line reply by return of post in which Bute said he had spoken to the King who commanded him 'to tell your Lordship that the Family of the Queen had been fixed for some time'.[36] There were no regrets, no attempts to soften the blow and by eighteenth-century (or most other) standards the letter was curt to say the least. It is clear Bute did not regard Guilford, or his son Lord North, as people he needed to cultivate.

When Lord Bute resigned he advised the King to send for George Grenville, younger brother of the affluent and arrogant Earl Temple and brother-in-law of William Pitt. Grenville was a far abler man than his predecessor but was greedy, self-righteous and verbose. The King complained: 'When he has wearied me for two hours he looks at his watch to see if he may not tire me for an hour more'.[37] George III rapidly developed a strong dislike for the man who had not only stepped into the shoes of his Dearest Friend, but had then also presumed to lecture him at tedious length. Grenville, however, was more intelligent than the King and, having initially accepted humiliating conditions which allowed Bute some continued powers of ministerial appointment, he had within six months compelled the King to sever all political communication with his former First Minister.[38]

One of the offices Bute was forced to relinquish at this time was the Keepership of the Privy Purse. Grenville, hoping to secure additional support for his administration in the Lords, had proposed Lord Guilford as his successor. The King, who had someone else in mind for the post, replied that 'it was not of sufficient rank for him', an argument which the well-informed Grenville quickly countered by reeling off all the peers who had held the position in previous reigns. The disagreement rumbled on for several days, Grenville even suggesting himself as a compromise candidate. Nevertheless, Grenville lost the dispute and Guilford again failed to achieve the dignified office he so longed to grace.[39] North resented this further rebuff to his father, so when a month later he was approached by his uncle Lord Halifax, one of the Secretaries of State in Grenville's administration, with a request to lead for the government in the case against John Wilkes, he was at first inclined to refuse: 'As the case stands at present, I have, personally, rather received civilities from Mr W[ilkes], and the marks of favour received from His Majesty by my father and myself are not such as to make the world expect that we should be the first in this declaration of duty'.[40]

When Grenville became Prime Minister he had also taken on the responsibilities of Chancellor of the Exchequer, retaining North at the Treasury Board. Grenville was an abler administrator than Sir Francis Dashwood. North found he was working with a man whose capacities he could respect,[41] but he never considered himself a committed Grenvillite and initially felt no particular reason to oblige when asked to play the leading role in the government's assault on Wilkes.

John Wilkes was born in 1725, the third son of a wealthy gin distiller whose children were the first generation of the family to be accepted into polite society. After a spell at Leyden University he married in 1747 an heiress ten years his senior and moved into her house in Aylesbury in Buckinghamshire. The marriage produced one daughter but was not otherwise a success. Ten years later it ended in a judicial separation that left Wilkes in possession of the house. In 1757 he was elected in the Whig interest as one of the two Members of Parliament for Aylesbury, not a particularly suitable seat for a man of moderate means as there were over 300 eligible electors hungry for bribes.[42] Wilkes had already acquired a reputation as a spendthift and a rake, a position he consolidated after his arrival at Westminster. He was a member of Sir Francis Dashwood's Monks of Medmenham and the rather more respectable but equally convivial Beefsteak Club. He had also at the age of twenty-four been elected a Fellow of the Royal Society, an honour which did not necessarily require great erudition but did imply an interest in scientific and philosophical enquiry.[43] Throughout the troubles he both caused and endured he was a hero to some and a villain to others, perhaps deserving neither term. He was a man of immense energy and considerable abilities and ambition, but he held no very certain vision of what he was trying to achieve. In 1762 the fastidious Edward Gibbon, a reluctant officer in the Hampshire Militia, found himself entertaining Colonel Wilkes of the Buckinghamshire Militia to dinner in the mess:

> I scarcely ever met with a better Companion; he has inexhaustible spirits, infinite wit, and humour, and a great deal of knowledge; but a thorough profligate in principle as in practice; his character is infamous, his life stained with every vice, and his conversation full of blasphemy and bawdy. These morals he glories in – for shame is a weakness he has long since surmounted. He told us himself, that in this time of public dissension he was resolved to make his fortune.[44]

A similar view was expressed (though more succinctly) by Edmund Burke, who considered Wilkes 'a lively agreable man, but of no prudence and no principle'.[45] A number of political contemporaries gave Wilkes their support, though often to further their own agendas, but his reputation as a libertine made it easier for many whose conservative instincts were affronted by his demagogy to seek his destruction. Wilkes was no political philosopher and, as he told Gibbon, 'was resolved to make his fortune', but his uncompromising insistence that the liberties of Englishmen were threatened in his person by a tyrannical executive not only stirred hearts but produced results.[46] Before he died in 1797, a respectable Tory and an ex-Lord Mayor of London, Parliament had formally renounced its earlier claim to reject a Member lawfully elected, and the freedom with which its proceedings could be reported in the press was greatly extended.[47] Wilkes, even if partly for his own ends and love of notoriety, was, unlike his opponents, working with the grain of history.

Wilkes published the first number of *The North Briton* in June 1762, a week after Lord Bute had become Prime Minister. As Chevenix Trench wrote in his biography of him, the paper represented something new in English journalism, 'for Wilkes realised more clearly than his contemporaries that the secret of propaganda is not reasoned argument, but the ceaseless repetition of a few simple ideas, preferably attacks on some person or cause already unpopular'.[48] *The North Briton* usually appeared weekly and was virulently anti-establishment in general and anti-Bute in particular, whose rise and influence the paper openly attributed to his position as the lover of the mother of the King. When Bute resigned Wilkes turned his guns on his successor George Grenville and, in the famous issue Number 45 published on 23 April 1763, suggested the Prime Minister had put lies into the King's mouth in the Speech from the Throne at the opening of Parliament:

The King's Speech has always been considered by the legislature, and by the public at large, as the speech of the minister ... I am in doubt whether the imposture is greater on the sovereign or the nation. Every friend of his country must lament that a prince of so many great and amiable qualities, whom England truly reveres, can be thought to give the sanction of his sacred name to the most odious measures, and to the most unjustifiable public declarations, from a throne ever renowned for truth, honour, and unsullied virtue.[49]

George III reacted with fury to the implication – that he was a well-meaning non-entity unable to stand up to his Ministers – and demanded Wilkes's prosecution. This faced Grenville and his ministerial colleagues with two problems. The first and more fundamental presents a paradox to all societies that place a high value on the freedom of the subject: how to defend freedom from unreasonable attack without at the same time compromising the liberties that are in need of protection. The number of people who defended Wilkes without necessarily approving his opinions or his behaviour shows that this point was taken seriously. An example was William Pitt, who in a debate in the Commons on 24 November 1763 said: 'No man could condemn *The North Briton* more than he did, but he would come at the author fairly, not by an open breach of the constitution, and a contempt of all restraint'.[50]

Grenville's other problem was that, although everyone knew Wilkes was responsible for *The North Briton* and its contents, his name appeared nowhere on it. To overcome this difficulty Lord Halifax the Secretary of State, acting with doubtful legality, issued a General Warrant for the arrest of the unnamed 'authors, printers and publishers'. After a good deal of confusion Wilkes ended up in the Tower, to which he was returned, after a preliminary hearing of his case in Westminster Hall, to the cries of 'Wilkes and Liberty' from the townsfolk along the route. At the next hearing the Lord Chief Justice, to the great embarrassment of the administration, ruled that as a Member of Parliament Wilkes was protected by privilege from arrest for anything other than treason, felony or breach of the peace, and that he must therefore be discharged.[51] The drama then moved to the House of Commons.

The letter from North to Halifax quoted above continued:

These reasons, added to the relation in which I have the honour to stand to your Lordship, and the kindness you have always showed me, will not fail to make everybody turn their eyes towards you when they see me take the lead in this affair: especially if it should happen, as it has sometimes, that when the question is moved and seconded, and spoken to by the Minister, the rest of the company should sit as quiet as if they had no tongues in their heads.

In this case, notwithstanding the majority, nobody would appear to have the business much at heart, but Mr Grenville and your humble servant. On all these accounts, I think my properer place will be to support the motion in the debate than to make it. At least, I think the several questions should be put into several hands, and not all given to me, so that Government may be certain of more members than one or two putting themselves forward in the cause.[52]

Without telling him, Halifax passed on North's letter to Grenville, expressing the belief that despite his apparent reluctance he could still be persuaded to play the part in the Wilkes debates they had fixed for him. Halifax knew his man. North longed to wriggle out of exposing himself in an unpopular cause but lacked the resolution to say no. Within a week he had accepted, writing unhappily to his father:

> Your Lordship will be in town at a very bustling time in both Houses, as I apprehend we shall invite the Peers to join with us in censuring the libel and determining the point of privilege. Nothing can go more against me than the business I am now upon, but while things stand in their present ticklish situation it is impossible to avoid it. You may be sure I will be very moderate in my expressions, but that will be no purpose. The part I take will be an unpardonable crime with the other side. I begin heartily to wish I had followed my own opinion in going out with the Duke of N.; I should have spared myself many an uncomfortable moment.[53]

It is clear from this letter North realised he would henceforth be branded as a reactionary, a Minister who favoured tyranny at the expense of liberty. The accusation was unfair but his fears were right; his reputation as an extreme conservative stemmed from the part he played in these Wilkes debates.

Grenville decided to place before the Commons three separate resolutions on three consecutive occasions: the first declaring the article in *The North Briton* a seditious libel; the second proposing that such an offence was not protected by parliamentary privilege; and the third intended to expel Wilkes from the House.[54] Despite his earlier pleas, North found he was expected to lead for the government on each occasion, but having now accepted the brief he played his part with vigour. In the opening debate on 15 November he roundly defeated an attempt by Pitt to give other business priority, and then proceeded to move that *The North Briton*, Number 45, was:

> a false, scandalous and seditious libel; containing expressions of the most un-exampled insolence and contumely towards his Majesty, the grossest aspersions upon both houses of parliament and the most audacious defiance of the authority of the whole legislature and most manifestly tending to alienate the affections of the people from his Majesty, to withdraw them from their obedience to the laws of the realm, and to excite them to a traitorous insurrection against his Majesty's Government.[55]

After a heated debate North's motion was carried by 273 votes to 111. On the 24 November 1763 he proposed that 'the Privilege of Parliament does not extend to the writing and publishing of seditious libels' with a speech that aimed to present Wilkes's critics as the true defenders of liberty and his abuse of privilege as a licence for wrongdoing. The motion was again carried by a large majority. There was then a pause in the proceedings. Wilkes was wounded in a duel and, before he was fully recovered, fled to France. On the 19 January North introduced his third motion and the following day Wilkes was, in his absence, expelled from the House of Commons without a division on the primary issue. North wrote to his father: 'It is a comfort to see the Administration conclude their campaign most reputably, notwithstanding the most numerous and violent opposition I ever remember'.[56] He must have trusted he had heard the last of Wilkes. Five years later he discovered he was wrong.

After the first Wilkes debate Horace Walpole wrote to a friend: 'Lord North ... took the prosecution upon him and did it very well',[57] and there is no doubt the opportunities provided by the debates confirmed his reputation as a first-class parliamentary performer. To explain or analyse his gifts as a speaker is as difficult, though not dissimilar, as understanding the magic of a long-dead actor. Particular skills and characteristics can be gleaned from contemporary accounts but the appeal of the total performance remains elusive. In North's case his strength as a debater did not apparently lie in great rhetoric. William Hazlitt, writing a generation after North's death, said: 'He spoke like a gentleman, like a man of sense and business, who had to explain himself on certain points of moment to the country, and who in doing this did not think that his first object was to show how well he could play the orator by the hour'.[58] He was, however, aided in his presentation of a case by a clear mind and an excellent memory which allowed him to refute his opponents' arguments extempore and without too much dependence on prepared notes. These valuable gifts were backed up by a wit and good temper to which his contemporaries of every political persuasion testified:

> Lord North was powerful, able and fluent in debate, sometimes repelling the charges made against him with solid argument, but still more frequently eluding or blunting the weapons of his antagonists by the force of wit and humour. Fox, conscious of the First Minister's superiority in exciting a laugh, and irritated at being often the object of his talent for ridicule, more than once tried to silence him by severity of animadversion.[59].

That comment by Wraxall is supported by another made in a letter from George Dempster, a senior contemporary of North's in the Commons, writing to his friend James Boswell in 1775: 'It is the fund of natural humour which Lord North possesses, that makes him so much a favourite of the house ... '[60] Another MP, the historian Edward Gibbon, made much the same point in his autobiography: 'The cause of government was ably vindicated by Lord North, a statesman of spotless integrity, a consummate master of debate, who could wield, with equal dexterity, the arms of reason and ridicule'.[61]

There was an additional factor that contributed to the establishment of North's increasing mastery of the Commons. His good humour and wit were powerful weapons in his armoury but they were underpinned by the patent seriousness with which he took his parliamentary duties, and the respect with which he always treated the House. In the course of a debate in October 1776 on the King's Speech an unimportant country Member, Sir Herbert Mackworth, was unwise enough to rebuke North, by then a Prime Minister of six years' standing, for a brief absence from the Chamber. This caught North on the raw and, after apologising to the House for troubling them over the matter, he explained that he rose:

> to meet the charge made against me by the right honourable gentleman who spoke last; lest, Sir, an absence of ten minutes, on a pressing call of business in the course of a debate, which, will probably continue fourteen hours, should be represented as a desertion of my post, in the moment of difficulty. I may, Sir, be deficient in many respects but of all wants I never imagined that a want of respect, diligence as a member, or attention to this House, would have swelled the long catalogue.[62]

In the weeks following the expulsion of Wilkes the Commons turned its attention to the important principles involved in the use of General Warrants. North appears to have spoken only once in these debates, probably because he considered he had already done more than enough to provide public support for an administration that was beginning to look frayed.[63] (The argument over the warrants was finally settled in 1766 when the Commons condemned them as illegal.)[64] On one of the divisions Grenville's majority fell to fourteen but he managed to stumble on for another year. In April 1765 the King, following his recovery a month or two earlier from his first attack of insanity, pressed for the introduction of a Regency Bill, under the provisions of which he could nominate the future Regent from a list of names attached to the legislation. Probably through distrust of her known friendship with Lord Bute, but with incredible folly, the Cabinet deliberately excluded the dowager Princess of Wales from the list. Although the omission was subsequently reversed by the House of Commons, George III reacted with understandable anger to the apparent insult Grenville and his Cabinet had offered to his mother.[65] The incident strengthened his determination to replace the government, and he asked his uncle the Duke of Cumberland to act as negotiator.

By July the King felt sufficiently confident to dismiss Grenville and most of his Ministers, including North's uncle, Lord Halifax, the Secretary of State. North also left the government, though his various biographers differ on whether he jumped or was pushed.[66] Probably he left of his own free will, though it is unlikely to have been as a gesture of solidarity with Grenville, who had a few months earlier turned down North's request to be granted the vacant Lord Lieutenancy of Somerset. Grenville had explained in a long, self-justifying letter that the previous incumbent, Lord Poulet, had taken so long to die that the King had had plenty of time to fill the post before hearing of North's interest in it.[67]

A further reason for believing North departed of his own accord is that he seems to have been considered for a place in the incoming administration under the Marquis of Rockingham. In at least three lists of possible new Ministers, prepared for the King's approval by the Duke of Cumberland, his name is down for the valuable and fairly important position of joint Paymaster General of the Forces, the post he was to hold a little later.[68] It is not very probable that the King would have dismissed him from the Treasury if he was then going to offer him promotion. If, however, North resigned and subsequently refused all offers from Rockingham, why did he do it? The loss of his salary was a serious matter and it was now that he was compelled to 'put off his town house' and move his family in with his mother-in-law.[69] If he consulted his father the letters have not survived. There is nothing else to suggest that in this instance he suffered from indecisiveness. Two possible explanations come to mind. First, the new administration was based on the great Whig families with whom North had few political affinities; and, secondly, it looked ramshackle and unlikely to prosper. North therefore judged that, despite the financial penalties, he would do better to move to the back benches and bide his time. Whatever the reasons he ended the year in an uncharacteristically complacent mood, writing to his father on Christmas Day 1765:

Notwithstanding the untoward political events of the last year, I never felt more perfectly easy, happy, and self-satisfied than I do at present; I think I have done what I ought, and what every reasonable and honest man will approve. I feel myself totally disencumbered from all connections, obligations, and engagements, and entirely free to choose the path that my conscience and opinion dictates. A very pleasant feel it is! I think I have done by all parties as handsomely as they could desire, and perhaps more than they could in justice demand. What is past gives me no regret. My present situation is comfortable and my future prospects by no means unpleasing. I may add that my pride, which was, I confess, a little mortified in the course of the year, has by the late offer been gratified to the utmost of its wish. Tho' in many of the questions that will arise in the course of this session I shall be forced, from fix'd opinion, to differ from the present Ministers, yet I shall do it without the least spleen or ill-will to their persons. I sincerely wish them success in their public labours, and hope that they will not in order to purchase a little momentary peace take any step that may lay the foundation of endless tumults for the future, and deprive this nation of any of its most valuable and essential rights.[70]

The 'late offer' almost certainly refers to an unsuccessful attempt by Rockingham in the latter part of November to use the good offices of Newcastle and Dartmouth to persuade North to join his administration. On 1 December Newcastle told Rockingham: 'Lord Dartmouth sent me word of Ld North's Refusal; I am very sorry for it . . . Lord North's Refusal, Barré's Refusal, & I think, plainly, Charles Townshend's Refusal, will have bad effects'.[71] It is interesting to note that Newcastle considered North's refusal on a par with those of two quite senior figures in its effects on the political situation.

5

Arrival

The new administration was the handiwork of the King's uncle, the Duke of Cumberland, who remained its most influential, if unofficial, member until his untimely (though not entirely unexpected) death at the age of forty-four on 31 October 1765. The administration was nominally in the care of the inexperienced, and somewhat reluctant, Marquess of Rockingham. It has been described by John Brooke as 'a constitutional anomaly ... It is the strangest cabinet in British history. It is the only one to be presided over by a Royal Duke. It is the only one formed round the principal members of the Jockey Club. Apart from Conway, who had served a few years as Secretary to the Lord Lieutenant of Ireland, none of the men who filled the principal departments of state had ever held political office.'[1] North would clearly add welcome ballast to such a government and at least one more attempt was made to lure him on board by offering him the Vice-Treasureship of Ireland in May 1766, a post that did not require him to leave England. He was tempted, partly because his step-brother Dartmouth had agreed to take the position of First Lord of Trade and Plantations (an office later to become Secretary for the Colonies),[2] but, in typical style, he managed to give the impression he had accepted the invitation while apparently intending to refuse it. Lord George Sackville said that he had twice agreed to serve and then changed his mind,[3] while Horace Walpole in his most acid vein wrote to North's cousin George Montagu:

> I know no news, but that the Duke of Richmond is Secretary of State, and that your cousin North has refused the Vice-Treasurer of Ireland. It cost him bitter pangs, not to preserve his virtue, but his vicious connections. He goggled his eyes, and groped in his money-pocket; more than half consented; nay, so much more, that when he got home he wrote an excuse to Lord Rockingham, which made it plain he thought he had accepted. As nobody was dipped deeper in the warrants and

prosecution of Wilkes, there is no condoling with ministers on missing so foul a bargain. They are only to be pitied, that they can purchase nothing but damaged goods.[4]

In his letter to Rockingham, North said: 'I beg pardon for all my difficulties which must have embarrassed you and my other friends, and particularly for this last change of opinion'.[5] He was uneasily poised between his wish for office, partly but not only for the financial benefits it would provide, and his hunch that to join such a rag-bag of Whig grandees would in the end do him no good.

While North was fussing about the offer of a post of only moderate importance he remained blind, like many others, to signs of far greater import from across the Atlantic, the first serious displays of American discontent. In the spring of 1764 the previous administration under Grenville had found itself in need of additional revenue. Rather than raise English taxes, it decided to extend to the colonies stamp duties on various legal and commercial documents long accepted at home. The Bill to put the proposal into effect was not brought before Parliament until March the following year, when Grenville dismissed warnings of colonial opposition by asking 'when will the time come when enforcing a tax will not give discontent ... ?'[6] North gave the Bill considered support, referring to 'the prudence of this tax' and to the caution of the House in delaying its introduction for a year.[7] The proposal met no opposition in the Lords, while in the Commons the vote was 245 to 49 in favour.[8]

The colonial response to the Stamp Act was unsurprisingly very hostile. It represented the first systematic attempt by the Westminister Parliament to raise a significant revenue from North America. Furthermore, the classes chiefly affected by the Act were precisely those which were the most articulate and influential: merchants, lawyers and printers. Reaction was immediate and uncompromising; non-cooperation escalated into violence, and by 1 November, when the Stamp Act was due to come into force, the imperial administration was largely reduced to impotence throughout the thirteen colonies. Further pressure was brought to bear on the home government towards the end of the year with the adoption of non-importation agreements by the key commercial cities of New York, Philadelphia and Boston, a move intended to damage British trading and manufacturing interests.

By the time news of the Stamp Act had reached America and news of the American response had travelled back to London, Grenville's administration – the originator of the whole affair – had been replaced by that of Cumberland and Rockingham. At first the new administration insisted that

An undated letter from North to his father, probably referring to the administration's defeat on the renewal of Grenville's Controverted Elections Act, 26 February 1774. *(Bodleian Library, North Add. C4, fol. 214)* the law must be enforced, and that troops already stationed in America should be used for this purpose. This proved unworkable as the military could only be employed with the express agreement of the civil authorities, namely the colonial Governors and their Councils, and the Councils somewhat naturally refused to sanction such action. Although not certain, it is probable that the Duke of Cumberland himself was the main proponent of repressive measures, and with his death one of the chief obstacles to a more conciliatory approach was removed. A few members and supporters of the Rockingham administration had always doubted the wisdom of the Stamp Act, and many more were happy to condemn actions, now seen to be flawed, taken by their predecessors in government. This growing readiness to accept modification, or even outright appeal, was reinforced by the almost universal belief that the British economy was suffering from the increase in costs and loss of trade associated with the Stamp Act, as well as from fears of the likely effects of the non-importation agreements. The downturn in commercial activity may in fact have been due to other causes, but the belief provided Rockingham and his Ministers with powerful arguments in favour of change.

The administration, however, was far from agreed on what form any change should take; whether the Act should be modified in response to specific American objections, or whether it should be totally repealed. National opinion was generally hostile to the rebellious colonists, and the King was unlikely to welcome any measures that threatened to dilute his government's authority over them. Rockingham's problem, therefore, was to devise a policy that a united Cabinet could present to a sceptical public and legislature. By early in the New Year a possible compromise had emerged. It was reflected in the King's Speech at the opening of the session on 14 January 1766, in which he expressed the hope that Parliament would arrive at 'such sound and prudent resolutions, as may tend to at once preserve those constitutional rights over the colonies, and to restore to them that harmony and tranquillity which have lately been interrupted by riots and disorders of the most dangerous kind'.[9]

To give effect to these sentiments the Rockingham administration brought forward two Bills simultaneously, the first providing for the unqualified repeal of the Stamp Act, while the second, which became known as the Declaratory Act, affirmed the right of Parliament to make laws binding the colonies 'in all cases whatsoever'.[10] What was given away with one hand was immediately taken back with the other. It was a compromise that settled nothing. As the events of ten years later were to demonstrate, the Stamp Act crisis allowed the colonists to discover their potential strength. Both Bills passed the Commons with comfortable majorities and, after clearing the Lords rather less easily, received the Royal Assent on 18 March 1766. North, following his conservative instincts, had spoken and voted with the minority against repeal and then joined the majority in favour of the Declaratory Act, [11] but, according to the agent for Connecticut in London, although he was 'against the Colonies in the affair of the Stamp Act he was not among the most violent'.[12]

For a brief honeymoon period the colonists were appeased by the withdrawal of the stamp duties, but they soon spotted that, with the Declaration, the English Parliament had reasserted its right to tax them, and their sense of resentment grew. Lord North was later to reap where he had helped to sow. It is tempting to excuse him on the grounds that he was only reflecting the mainstream of public opinion. George III, followed by the vast bulk of the governing class, believed that the sovereignty of Parliament over all his realms must be upheld. At least, however, the King was uneasily aware great events were stirring, writing at the end of 1765 to General Henry Conway, one of the Secretaries of State: 'I am more and more grieved at the accounts from America ... It is undoubtedly the most serious matter that ever came before Parliament'.[13] Unfortunately, George III possessed neither the imagination nor the generosity of spirit to understand the anger of his American subjects. Nevertheless, just as with the treatment of Wilkes, there were dissentient voices even in the upper reaches of the establishment, and a few people who feared for the future: Dartmouth, one of North's closest friends, was a strong opponent of the Stamp Act;[14] and in February 1766 in the Upper House Lord Camden, the respected Lord Chief Justice of the Common Pleas, said in a debate on the Declaratory Act:

> My position is this – I repeat it – I will maintain it to my last hour, – taxation and representation are inseparable; this position is founded on the laws of nature; it is more, it is an eternal law of nature; for whatever is a man's own, is absolutely his own; no man has a right to take it from him without his consent, either expressed by himself or representative.[15]

After the repeal of the Stamp Act the Rockingham ministry began to disintegrate. With Cumberland's death it had lost both its focal point and its main channel of communication with the King; there no longer seemed any valid reason for its existence. Staying in the country with friends in July, North wrote to his father: 'We are full of curiosity to know the outcome of the conference with Mr Pitt. Our last post brought us word that the King had sent for him'.[16] By the end of the month George III had persuaded William Pitt to form a government and Rockingham was dismissed. Pitt was given a free hand in choosing his ministers, though it was made clear the

King would not tolerate the return of George Grenville. The Duke of Grafton, a man more interested in his race horses, his hounds and his mistress (a tailor's daughter known as Mrs Horton) than in affairs of state, became First Lord of the Treasury, and the unreliable and untrustworthy Charles Townshend was appointed Chancellor of the Exchequer. Due to his growing ill-health Pitt took the non-executive office of Lord Privy Seal but, although Grafton was First Minister, there was never any doubt that it was Pitt's administration. Pitt weakened his position, however, by accepting a peerage only three weeks after taking office, a move that led North to express his misgivings to his father: 'Mr Pitt kissed hands yesterday on being appointed Earl of Chatham and Viscount Pynsent. I cannot say that upon first sight I should have advised this step. I should have thought the Administration more steady with him in the House of Commons'.[17]

North's concern with the administration's steadiness was understandable, as two days earlier he had been invited to join it. Pitt wrote to him, after listing the new senior appointments:

> Having now imparted to your lordship this outline, I have now the honour and pleasure to open to you by His Majesty's commands that the King would see with satisfaction Lord North return to his service. It is His Majesty's intention to make two joint Paymasters-General, and should your lordship (fortunately for the King's service) think it agreeable to you to be one of them, I should esteem myself happier in having writ this letter, which I now take the liberty to trouble you with, than in most where I have the King's commands to employ my pen.[18]

North lost no time in accepting, informing his father: 'The offer is very honourable, profitable and agreeable, and I see no reason on earth why I should refuse it'. His satisfaction, however, was tempered by 'a very unpleasant piece of news'. Dartmouth had turned down an invitation to stay at Plantations because, contrary to what he had been encouraged to believe, his department was not to be given independent status and its Minister made a third Secretary of State. Dartmouth's refusal was not due to hurt pride but to his conviction that American affairs needed the full attention of a politician of senior rank. As Lord Chesterfield wrote to him: 'If we have no Secretary of State with full and undisputed power for America, in a few years we might as well have no America'.[19] North regretfully found himself divided from his step-brother, 'opposed to one of the men in the world that I honour, love and esteem the most. These events damp all the pleasure of preferment'.[20]

With North's new job came an official residence near Horse Guards; he and his family moved there from his mother-in-law's house some time in the latter part of 1766.[21] It was another sixteen years before they were back in their own home in Grosvenor Square. They only lived in the Paymaster's residence for a year but North later looked back on it as a time of great content. Kitty (the daughter he described after her wedding as 'the best thing I ever gave away'),[22] later said that 'her father frequently would look towards this house from the windows of Downing Street and declare that he had never been happy since he had removed from the one to the other'.[23] North was now thirty-four and the father of five children, three boys and two girls.[24] It is clear from the letters which he and Anne wrote with conscientious regularity to Guilford that their family was of great importance in their lives, and that they saw more of their children than was often the case in an upper-class household. There are frequent references to their health, usually beginning 'thank God' and followed by an account of a recovery or the continuing absence of illness on the part of some member of the family. There are allusions to one or two miscarriages and the health of their third son Frederick is a recurring cause of anxiety – but he survived until seventy-one.[25] North himself was putting on weight, being described a few years later by Wraxall as 'middle size, heavy, large, and much inclined to corpulency'.[26]

The summer of 1766 had been good for the Norths. Temporarily without the responsibilities of office there was time for them to visit friends and to enjoy their children, though North was careful to assure his father that he was not spending money unnecessarily:

> Mount Edgcumbe, 15 July 1766
> Lady North and I leave the Brudenellls here & set out for Dillington tomorrow. We shall stop at Ashe & take up our children & carry them with us to Dillington. You need not be alarmed about the expense there. Hitherto there had been nothing done but what has been absolutely necessary to make the House habitable, & I hope to get all my workmen out of the House in a few days after I get there ... Lady N. has taken good care of herself tho' I do not believe that she has the same reason to be cautious that she had this time twelvemonth.[27]

North was still at Dillington a fortnight later when he received Pitt's invitation to join his administration. The office of joint Paymaster General of the Land Forces was a nice snug billet. The work was not overtaxing, and in addition to the house near Horse Guards it provided a salary of £3500 a year and ample opportunities for graft.[28] The Paymaster applied to the Treasury each year for the funds he considered were needed by the forces, then himself supervised their distribution to the various branches of the army, but as a contemporary booklet pointed out: 'the Treasury have no information in the office whereby they can judge of the sum necessary for the stated service, the same sum therefore is issued as is requested by the Paymaster'.[29] Venal Paymasters asked for more money than was immediately required, loaned out the balance and pocketed the interest. This was considered just acceptable, although William Pitt the Elder when he held the office refused to take advantage of the system.[30] There is no evidence that North behaved any differently; the recurring crises in his personal finances strongly suggests that he did not.

Why the King decided to make joint Paymasters General is not known, but it is quite possible the suggestion originated with Pitt himself as it provided him with an additional slot for one of his followers. George Cooke, North's colleague in the Pay Office, was an unimportant lawyer who had first entered Parliament twenty-four years before as a Tory, but later attached himself to Pitt as one of his most faithful supporters and was now being given his first government position.[31] North not only found Cooke an uncongenial colleague, particularly as he had supported the repeal of the Stamp Act and opposed the Declaratory Act, but (according to his son-in-law Lord Glenbervie) North was also 'much displeased when made Joint Paymaster at not having the whole office'. Glenbervie continued: 'Going up the stairs one day, followed by a messenger, and perceiving some filth on one of the steps, he said: "Take that away, and carry a half of it to Mr Cook".'[32] In practice it seems clear North was the senior partner. He not only occupied the official residence but in December 1766 he was made a Privy Councillor, an honour never achieved by Cooke.

In later years Lord North may have looked back on his tenure of the Paymastership as a time of contentment, but evidently it did not always seem like that to him then. Barely a month after North's appointment Thomas Whately, previously Secretary to the Treasury under Grenville, was writing to his former chief: 'It is now generally known that Lord North repents of accepting', and on 20 October he told Grenville 'I have a long letter from Lord North strongly marked with the uneasiness of his situation'.[33] North had good grounds for concern. Not only had Pitt escaped to the Lords but, after becoming ill, he retreated to Bath or one of his country houses. From the end of the year until his formal resignation, in October 1768, he played only an occasional and fitful part in the administration. This left the thirty-six-year-old Grafton in actual as well as nominal charge of the government. In the Commons the senior members of the Cabinet were Henry Seymour Conway, the Leader of the House, and Charles Townshend, the Chancellor of the Exchequer. Conway was irresolute and Townshend irresponsible, exuberant and unprincipled,[34] managing the Exchequer, as Valentine put it, 'as if it were his private gambling house'.[35] This was not the sort of company in which North felt comfortable. His father was also uneasy about the political scene and must have expressed his fears to North, who early in December wrote back: 'Your sentiments on public affairs are too just. The King's business, however, would go on well enough in the House of Commons if our Leaders there were looked upon to have a greater share of power'.[36]

There were problems outside Parliament as well. The weather had ruined the harvest, corn prices had risen and there were riots and demonstrations in various parts of the country.[37] North wrote to his father from Dillington in the spring of the following year: 'The Load of the Poor upon us, in these hard times, is unconceivable, but we hope they are relieved & we know they are quiet, & therefore we submit to it without much reluctance'.[38] His muted response to the needs of the poor strikes an uncomfortable note, but he was a man of his times and position – the upper classes did not discover they had a social conscience until the next century.

North also had family troubles. He must have been wrong about his wife's condition when he wrote to his father in July as she had a miscarriage in the autumn, something which depressed his spirits and added to his worries.[39] Then in late December he became alarmed on learning that two eminent doctors, Sir Clifford Winteringham and Mr Bromfield, had been summoned to Waldershare to attend his step-mother.

He wrote to his father: 'We wait with great impatience & anxiety for the return of your physician & surgeon, that we may learn how they left Lady Guilford ... we partake very sincerely in your distress'.[40] She died on Christmas Day and, as she was childless, the London gossips started to speculate on the contents of her will.[41] She had inherited the estate of Waldershare and a large fortune from her brother, who had died at nineteen, but there were two half-sisters whose children might reasonably have expected to benefit at the Countess's death. Nevertheless it is hard to believe Guilford was surprised when the will was read and he found he was the chief beneficiary, inheriting property and investments that were said to be worth £6000 a year.[42] The collective tribute he paid to his three wives on their monument in Wroxton church is to the point: 'They raised their Husband to a Degree of Happiness far beyond what Man ought to expect in this mortal State, & added Proofs at their Death of Sincere Affection and Esteem'. Guilford was now a very rich man, but there is little to suggest that he adjusted his attitude to his son's financial problems, or indeed to those of anyone else.

Three weeks after his wife's death Guilford drew up a list of debts left by his own father on his death thirty-seven years before. They amounted to some £1100 and were still unpaid. On the list, addressed to his executors,

Guilford acknowledged 'having [recently] received an accession to my personal estate' but, far from settling the debts as a result of this windfall, he left instructions that they should be paid only after his own death. If that in fact happened, the creditors would have waited a minimum of sixty-one years for their money.[43]

In January 1767 Charles Townshend presented his first budget, which included a provision for land tax at the not unprecedented rate of four shillings in the pound. On 27 February, to the administration's embarrassment, an Opposition amendment to reduce the tax to three shillings was passed by eighteen votes, involving a potential loss of revenue of £500,000.[44] At an earlier stage Townshend had referred to his intention of raising revenue from America, though apparently without consulting his Cabinet colleagues, and subsequent accounts have sometimes implied that the land tax vote was directly linked to the Chancellor's public declaration on colonial taxation.[45] In reality Townshend had been examining the question of taxing America for some weeks prior to the budget, and his insistence on the benefits of such a move occasioned no great surprise or hostility. By the end of June a Bill to levy duties on American imports of glass, lead, paper, painting materials and tea (by far the most important of the commodities) had passed both Houses with minimal opposition, receiving the Royal Assent on 29 June. At the same time the Chancellor reorganised the customs service in America to enforce efficient collection of the new taxes.

The recognition of American grievances and the policy reversal represented by the repeal of the Stamp Act had occurred little more than twelve months earlier, yet the new, unsympathetic mood that allowed the easy passage of the Townshend duties altered little in the years that followed. It was still the predominant attitude when Lord North became responsible for trying to reconcile the conflicting demands of Britain and her American colonies. Underlying this point of view was the growing conviction that parliamentary legislation (reflecting parliamentary supremacy), rather than the exercise of the Royal Prerogative, was the appropriate instrument of imperial control. Seen from this standpoint, the repeal of the Stamp Act had been a regrettable but essentially tactical concession, whereas the important matter of principle had been upheld in the Declaratory Act. A further (though largely irrelevant) argument put forward in favour of the Townshend duties was to make a distinction between external and internal taxation, the former raised primarily on British goods entering the colonies, and therefore the legitimate concern of the mother country, while the latter was deemed the proper sphere for colonial decision. This distinction was clearly contrary to the spirit of the Declaratory Act, and was only used by Townshend for presentational purposes; he thought it might temper colonial opposition to his measures.

There was one other aspect of the Townshend duties that Americans came to find particularly objectionable. When the duties were first mooted in Parliament in January they were presented as a contribution to the costs of maintaining the British army in America. As, however, Lord Barrington, the Secretary at War, estimated the annual figure at over £400,000 (later increased to £570,000), Townshend's expectation of raising some £40,000 from his duties would not have gone very far to ease the burden on the British Exchequer. Nevertheless, the principle that the colonists should make some payment towards their own defence was not unreasonable. But by May Townshend had changed his mind: he informed the Commons that the revenue from the new duties was to be used for the salaries of certain colonial Governors and judicial officials currently a charge on local assemblies. In practical terms the impact of this decision was limited. In a few cases permanent funds were already available for colonial civil lists, and some salaries were supplemented from London.[46] Moreover, the move only brought about a change in the method rather than in the ultimate source of any stipends locally funded, representing little nett gain to the British Treasury. The motives behind Townshend's manoeuvres were political not financial: to reduce the dependence of royal officials on local assemblies; and to emphasise the authority of the imperial Parliament. When the rationale behind his actions was perceived in America one more brick was added to the edifice of colonial resentment. In later years North always denied that he had given any support to these unwise proposals, and there seems no reason to doubt him.[47] As a member of the government, however, it was difficult for him to oppose them publicly.

Such considerations of collective responsibility were unimportant to Townshend. When he openly dissented from the administration's policy of establishing an enquiry into the affairs of the East India Company, Chatham roused himself from his depressive inertia and arrived back in London, on 2 March 1767, after an absence of more than two months.[48] He immediately set about finding a replacement for Townshend, writing to the Duke of Grafton that 'the writer hereof and the Chancellor of the Exchequer aforesaid cannot remain in office together'.[49] It is not known if anyone else was approached first, but by 4 March he had, with the King's approval, asked Grafton to dismiss Townshend and appoint North in his place. The Duke may have been inexperienced but he was not naive and, before obeying the first part of the instruction, he decided he must seek North's agreement to the latter part. He failed, and it is clear from the timing of the correspondence that North had no hesitation in refusing the offer. At 9 a.m. on the 5 March, less then three full days after Chatham's arrival in London, the Duke wrote to the King:

> The Duke of Grafton presumes to acquaint his Majesty that he saw Lord North last night, who with every Testimony of Zeal for the King's Service & support to his Administration saw the Business too much involved for him to undertake so difficult a Post. The Letter inclosed which he received this morning speaks more strongly his mind that the D. of Grafton can attempt to deliver it: and he humbly submits to his Majesty whether it would not be more prudent that this offer should not be made publick by that Lord waiting on his Majesty at the Queen's house.
>
> The Duke of Grafton, if his Majesty thinks proper, can easily send to stop Lord North, particularly as the Suggestion came originally from himself.[50]

The King replied by return:

> On returning from riding I have received your letter enclosing that of Lord North; I am much pleased at the Zeal he testifies to my Service, but am sorry he cannot bring his mind to accept the Office of Chancellor of the Exchequer; I am thoroughly of [the] opinion he ought not to come to Me this Morning as this refusal cannot be kept too private; I desire that You will before You come to Court call at Lord Chatham's & advise with him who may with most propriety be thought of for Chancellor of the Exchequer.[51]

All concerned wished to keep the proposal secret, presumably because there was no point in offending Townshend before his successor had been found. North had an understandable reluctance to leave the untroubled waters of the Pay Office, but fear of Townshend's enmity must also have influenced his decision. Immediately after his refusal he wrote to Grafton: 'As I returned from your Grace's this evening a reflection suggested itself to me, which I think I ought to communicate to you. What has passed this evening between your Grace and me need not be known to any, but His Majesty and ourselves'.[52] Shortly afterwards Chatham's mental and physical health deteriorated and the attempt to find a new Chancellor was abandoned. Nature then played another trick. Sometime that summer Townshend is reputed to have said to a companion on seeing North approaching: 'See that great, heavy, booby-looking seeming changeling. You may believe me when I assure you as a fact, that if anything should happen to me, he would succeed to my place, and very shortly after come to be First Commissioner of the Treasury'.[53] On the 4 September Charles Townshend unexpectedly died.

With the king's full support, Grafton at once invited North to become the new Chancellor. North hesitated, as he was at Wroxton where his father was seriously ill, possibly dying.[54] He replied to Grafton's letter on the 6 September:

I have just received your Grace's letter, and am much shocked at the news it brings. I am greatly honoured by the proposition your Grace makes to me, but it is too important a subject for me to be able to give an immediate answer to it. That, you will be so good as to permit me to defer, till I have the honour of seeing your Grace in London, which I hope to have, at the time appointed in your letter.[55]

After quoting this letter Grafton's memoirs continue: 'Lord North came up to London according to his intention, had a very gracious audience with his Majesty, was afterwards with me to state his reasons for declining the office, and set out directly to rejoin his father at Wroxton'.[56] North's love for his dominating father is sometimes difficult to comprehend but it cannot be doubted. It seems probable he declined the offer partly because his mind was on the sick-room at Wroxton, and he wanted no outside distractions. Moreover, if his father died he would no longer need his official salary, and his subsequent move to the Lords would rule him out for the post he had been offered. This interpretation of North's initial refusal is supported by the letter he wrote to Grafton on 10 September immediately after his return to Wroxton:

> I am just arrived here, full of the warmest sense of gratitude to His Majesty, and your Grace, but very uneasy for fear that my refusal of the honorable offer lately made to me, should have given offence, or appeared to proceed from want of zeal to His Majesty, or regard for his present ministers ... Upon my return here, I find Lord Guilford astonishingly recovered, the cause of his illness removed, and the whole family in spirits. Mine are so much raised by it, that, if you continue to find any real difficulty in disposing of the seals, I shall be ready to obey any call from His Majesty, or your Grace, tho' I own, I am better pleased to serve on in my present office.[57]

Grafton had meanwhile made other arrangements for the Chancellorship through a Cabinet reshuffle, and had then felt free to set off for a break at Euston, his estate in Norfolk. North's letter caught up with him on the road. He immediately drove to the house of a nearby acquaintance, and wrote letters for the waiting messenger to take back unscrambling the arrangements he had just made and confirming North as Chancellor of the Exchequer.[58] Grafton had no wish to allow him to escape a second time. After hearing the good news George III wrote an interesting comment to Grafton: 'it appears strongly to me as if Lord Halifax has caught at what I said regarding Lord North's friends & has been the means of obtaining Lord Guilford's consent, for I know no one has so much weight with him'.[59] Guilford's recovery not only removed a possible impediment to North's acceptance of the post, it also gave the old man a chance to reinforce his son's faltering ambitions.

North's appointment was generally welcomed and the report sent home by the agent for Connecticut probably represented what most non-partisan observers thought:

> Lord North has taken the place of Chancellor of the Exchequer, and is esteemed a man of good abilities, though by no means of such brilliant talents as his predecessor. It is said, he understands the business of the finances very well, and it is thought will be inclined to frugality, and economy in the conduct of the revenue. He was with the Ministry in all the measures of last winter, but did not speak very often in the house; when he did, he was well heard, and has a dignity in his manner that gives weight to his sentiments, which were generally sensible, cool, and temperate.[60]

North himself, however, had lost none of his diffidence and sense of inadequacy. Less than five weeks after accepting the important post he was to occupy for the next fifteen years, he wrote to his father: 'I am afraid it will soon be found how unequal my abilities are to the task in which I am engaged, but if His Majesty and his ministers have made an insufficient Chancellor of the Exchequer they may thank themselves for it, for I can truly say I never obtruded myself upon them, and do not desire to continue in my place an hour after it shall be found prejudicial to the public'.[61]

On his appointment as Chancellor, North and his family left the Pay Office and moved into Downing Street, to a house then unnumbered but later to become famous as Number Ten. Sir Robert Walpole had accepted it from George II on condition it should remain as the official residence of the First Lord of the Treasury or his nominee. In fact during the eighteenth century it was more often occupied by Chancellors of the Exchequer than by Prime Ministers, many of whom had fine town houses they had no wish to exchange for the comparatively cramped quarters in Downing Street. North, however, was only too happy to avail himself of free accommodation and to continue letting his own house off Grosvenor Square. At the same time his promotion boosted his social desirability. Two weeks after his appointment the Honourable Mrs Osborn (a sister of the unfortunate Admiral Byng) wrote to her grandson, a diplomat serving in Venice: 'Lord and Lady North dind [sic] with me the day they went out of town, as he would be a great man soon, I began my solicitations before he was so, and put in my Claim with regard to you'.[62]

Shortly after he became Chancellor North wrote to his father indicating another aspect of his growing importance:

> The Duke of Grafton did not come to town time enough on Wednesday to be at the Cabinet himself, and so I was not summoned. But I have seen him since, and he has assured me that he understood it to be the King's intention that I should

always be summoned and considered as a member of the Cabinet. I have not the vanity to imagine that my advice can be of any consequence in the planning of Government, but this I am certain of, that it will be very difficult for me to act in concert with the Cabinet and promote their plans in Parliament unless I am present at the meetings at which they are formed.[63]

North's predecessor Townshend had been the first Chancellor of the Exchequer to attend meetings of the Cabinet by virtue of his office but, as this quotation makes clear, North's presence was required because he was now regarded as the government's chief spokesman in the Commons.[64] This position was formally recognised the following January when he succeeded Seymour Conway as Leader of the House. As Grafton was indolent and Chatham incommunicado North had, at the age of thirty-six, become a key member of the administration. He had arrived at this situation with several considerable advantages.

Despite his earlier regard for Newcastle, he had never attached himself to any parliamentary faction and the Country Gentlemen could without undue licence regard him as one of themselves. He had risen to his present eminence through his own abilities and had incurred remarkably few political obligations in the process.

Another advantage enjoyed by North was his recognised ability and probity in financial matters. Horace Walpole referred to the City's increased confidence following his appointment,[65] and in his memoirs Grafton said of him: 'At the Treasury, his talents for business in finance were eminently superior to any thing we had seen in Mr Townshend'.[66] The Duke took full advantage of this happy state of affairs and according to Grenville neglected his duties at the Treasury Board, leaving 'the business almost entirely in Lord North's hands . . . trusting him much more than he did Charles Townshend'.[67] The Opposition was faced with the difficult task of attacking someone who was clearly the right man for the job.[68]

Lord North had a third great asset in his new, high-profile position. His good humour made him generally liked and he was extremely slow to anger. As Wraxall remarked: 'An unalterable suavity and equality of temper, which was natural to Lord North, enabled him to sustain unmoved the bitter sarcasms and severe accusations levelled at him from the Opposition benches. They always seemed to sink into him like a cannonball into a wool sack'.[69] Years later George III referred to 'that easy natural flow of genuine good-natured wit, which distinguished Lord North and forced a smile from those against whom it was exercised'.[70] North enhanced this general air of relaxed good temper by sometimes sitting on the Treasury bench with his eyes closed or with a handkerchief draped over his face. Almost certainly this was not affectation and stemmed from a wish to spare his weak sight, but it was hard for his opponents to be effectively unpleasant to a man who appeared to be quietly asleep a few yards away. On one occasion Edmund Burke used a Latin quotation in the abuse he was hurling at North, who woke sufficiently to correct Burke's pronunciation and then returned contentedly to his slumbers.[71]

Lord North's rise to prominence coincided with a time of social unrest. The price of food had risen following the poor harvest of the previous year and in May 1768 sailors at several British ports struck for higher wages (which made the situation worse), and the coal-heavers, deprived of their livelihood by the strike, attacked the sailors. The weavers of Spitalfields rioted against the introduction of new labour-saving machinery, and hatters, tailors and glass-grinders downed tools and joined in.[72] Horace Walpole tells the extraordinary story of an alehouse keeper called Green who when attacked by coal-heavers he had antagonised shot eighteen of them dead while defending his house. He was acquitted of murder so his sister threw a party to celebrate during which the infuriated coal-heavers dragged her out into the street and murdered her. As Walpole explained, what appalled him was not simply the brutality but the apparent impunity it enjoyed:

> I should scarce have ventured this narrative, had not all the circumstances been proved in a court of justice. Yet how many reflections must the whole story create in minds not conversant in a vast capital – free, ungoverned, unpoliced, and indifferent to everything but its pleasures and factions! Who will believe that such a scene of outrage could happen in the residence of Government? – that the siege lasted nine hours, and that no Guards were sent to the relief of the besieged till five in the morning?[73]

Given the already existing threat of social unrest, North's heart must have sunk when he heard of the return of John Wilkes from France in February 1768. In his absence he had been outlawed and convicted of blasphemy and libel but, as he had run out of money and was sinking into the obscurity he feared more than anything else, he had decided to return and face the consequences.[74] These proved more satisfactory than he could ever have hoped. On 11 March Parliament was dissolved and at the general election Wilkes stood for the City of London. He came bottom of the poll, but immediately offered himself for Middlesex (not all contests took place on the same day) where to everyone's astonishment he won by a handsome margin. He then surrendered to the judicial authorities and was sentenced to twenty-two months in the King's Bench prison in Southwark and fined £1000. Riots in favour of Wilkes at once added to the government's other problems in the capital.

North is standing astride the river of corruption flowing from Westminster Hall; he is distributing bribes with his right hand, and grasping the torch of American liberty in his left. The figures on the right are Britannia and John Wilkes. *London Magazine,* November 1774. *(British Museum)*

Part of the administration's difficulties arose from an inability to antici-
pate events. Ministers found it hard to take Wilkes seriously or to regard
him as more than an impudent trouble-maker. In his memoirs Grafton
wrote: 'On the first consultation in Cabinet on the management in Parliament Mr Wilkes being chosen Member for Middlesex, there did not appear
to the Lord Chancellor, or to any of us, the difficulties, which after arose'.[75]
These difficulties were compounded by differences of opinion on the best
way to handle the situation. The Lord Chancellor referred to was Lord
Camden, who a year later was writing to Grafton: 'As the Times are, I had
rather pardon W. than punish him. This is a political opinion independent
of the merits of the case'.[76] There was a school of thought that the best way
to deal with Wilkes was to ignore him and it is possible North's political
instincts initially inclined him to that point of view,[77] but it was certainly not
the opinion of George III. Before Parliament met North decided that in his
capacity as Leader of the House he should call together a meeting of senior
ministerial supporters on 25 April to try and hammer out an agreed policy.
The King was evidently uncertain of North's strength of purpose and
immediately before the meeting wrote to him seeking to stiffen his resolve:

> Tho entirely confiding in Your Attachment to my Person, as well as in Your hatred
> of every Lawless Proceeding yet I think it highly proper to apprize You that the
> Expulsion of Mr Wilkes appears to be very essential & must be effected; & that I
> make no doubt when you lay this affair with Your usual precision before the
> meeting of the Gentlemen of the House of Commons this Evening, it will meet
> with the required Unanimity & vigour.[78]

Neither this meeting nor a subsequent one on 11 May, also chaired by
North, produced any firm conclusions and it is probable that if Wilkes had
been prepared to keep out of the public eye he would, despite the King's
opposition, have been quietly allowed to take his seat in the Commons at
the end of his sentence. Descent into shabby obscurity was, however, the
last thing he wanted. In May a mob tried to release him from prison and in
the subsequent brawl several people were shot dead by soldiers from the
regiment of Guards called in by a magistrate.[79] There is no reason to think
Wilkes encouraged the mob, but he made no attempt to disown its activities
and the incident did no harm to his popularity with working-class Lon-
doners. His crucial move, however, was to announce in the autumn his
intention of presenting Parliament with a petition for the redress of his
grievances, which he followed with the rejection of Grafton's conciliatory
suggestion that if he withdrew the petition the proceedings against him in
Parliament would be dropped.[80] Opinion hardened against Wilkes, as

North explained to his father: 'The Administration were well inclined to do nothing upon the subject of Mr Wilkes, but he has resolved to force his cause upon them & upon the house by presenting a petition ... We shall probably have much tumult, noise & clamour in the course of this business but I do not see how it can end without his expulsion. He has brought it on himself & must answer for the consequences'.[81]

It is not entirely clear from this letter whether North regretted the necessity of a course of action forced on the administration by Wilkes's behaviour or whether he was glad there were now sure grounds for moving against him but, whatever reservations he may have had earlier, he now took firm control of the campaign. Six years before he had been a slightly reluctant lieutenant, now he was the general in charge and his handling of the proceedings established him once and for all as a confident master of parliamentary tactics.

On the 27 January 1769 Wilkes's petition came up for debate in the Commons. North argued that consideration should be restricted to two specific points that Wilkes had raised against senior law officers.[82] He won the vote by 278 to 131 and the next day received the congratulations of the King: 'Nothing could afford Me greater pleasure than Your account of the great majority the last night, I attribute this principally to the ability shewn by You in planning the Measure & in the Execution of it'.[83] The petition itself was then disposed of and on 3 February the question of Wilkes's expulsion came before the House. Speaking for the motion North said: 'After what has taken place, I consider his expulsion to be necessary for the honour of the House, and the tranquillity of the kingdom'.[84] He had the satisfaction of seeing it carried by 219 votes to 137.

Two weeks later, again to the cry of 'Wilkes and Liberty', the voters of Middlesex reelected him unopposed, and the following day the Commons expelled him for the second time by an even larger majority. When the third round of this pantomime took place in March, North achieved his objective without even the formality of a division, but in the course of the debate he commented: 'If ever this question should again come before us, I shall deem that man the true member for the county of Middlesex, who shall have a majority of legal votes'.[85] North had acted properly when he had argued that a convicted outlaw could not be permitted to sit in Parliament, but he possibly overstepped the bounds of constitutional propriety when he sought to impose on the electors of Middlesex a man not of their choosing. This is what now happened. An existing MP, Colonel Henry Luttrell, resigned his seat and in April stood for Middlesex against Wilkes. He was defeated by 1143 votes to 296 but, after a heated debate, the Commons decided to reject Wilkes and to seat Luttrell. The government majority was much smaller than after the earlier debates on Wilkes, betraying doubts among many Members on the legality, or at least the wisdom, of the proceedings, but for the time being the matter was closed. George III wrote another letter to North, expressing his satisfaction at the behaviour of the House of Commons: 'but whilst I commend this, I cannot omit expressing my thorough conviction that this was chiefly owing to the Spirit and good conduct you have Shewn during the whole of this unpleasant business'.[86] North's second involvement with John Wilkes not only confirmed his reputation as a conservative, it also strengthened the King's view of him as a man who was sound, someone he could trust with the affairs of the nation, and possibly someone he could sway.

In addition to his problems over Wilkes, North had other difficulties facing him in the Commons in 1769. In February the King asked for funds to pay off accumulated Civil List debts of more than £500,000, but the Opposition demanded detailed accounts showing how the money had been spent before voting to supply it. North readily agreed to the request for accounts but subsequently pointed out the figures would take a little time to prepare, and that it was the usual procedure to consider such a royal message without delay. 'Is it honourable, is it just, to leave his Majesty under this difficulty?' he asked. 'Even if the accounts were of a nature that we could produce them in twenty-four hours, that is not a reason why this question should wait even for three hours'. The Opposition complained North was being less than candid but he won the vote by 248 to 135.[87]

North's attention was also demanded by the East India Company, something that was to continue with increasing urgency for the next few years. It has been reckoned that between 1768 and 1774 he spoke no less than 164 times in the Commons on the subject.[88] As a result of British successses in the Seven Years War the Company, with its three Residencies of Bengal, Bombay and Madras, had become the predominant European power on the subcontinent, and its influence and potential revenues had been further enhanced by its own efforts.[89] At this juncture the ostensible point at issue was how the Crown as well as the Company could benefit financially from the growing British presence in India, but underlying it was the constitutional and legal position of the Company itself.

When the matter had been considered two years earlier Chatham favoured a deal whereby the Crown took over the territories and then paid the Company to administer them, an arrangement supported by North. With Chatham's decline, however, a weaker scheme was negotiated by which the Company's dividend was limited to 10 per cent and it paid £400,000 a year to the Treasury. These terms were revised in 1769 when the dividend limit was raised to 12 per cent and the settlement was guaranteed for five years. North secured the agreement of the House of Commons for this arrangement without difficulty. He made it clear that he still supported 'the clear right and claim of the Crown to those acquisitions' but said that in this instance he preferred 'the method of bargain and amicable agreement to a Parliamentary inquiry and legislative decision'.[90]

In April North presented his second budget. In it he developed a theme which would recur throughout his stewardship of the nation's finances: the repayment of government debt. He defended lotteries as a respectable method of achieving this aim, arguing 'that a lottery being a tax on the willing only, though many might object to it, as an encouragement of gaming, yet he thought the public would be right to avail themselves of the folly of mankind ... ' Later in his speech he said:

> From the improving state of the sinking fund, he hoped the nation would be able to discharge at least a million and a half of debt every year: when the people in the Alley saw the ministry go on from year to year, without borrowing money, the little money they then would be enabled to pay with, would naturally turn their minds to the old stocks, and consequently would raise them to perhaps what they had been in the last peace, and restore public credit to its pristine state.[91]

Speakers from the Opposition benches questioned whether North was underfunding the armed forces at the expense of national security but the promise of prudent house-keeping was music to the ears of the Country Gentlemen. He had no difficulty carrying his proposals,[92] and the next day an MP called Richard Rigby wrote to his patron, the Duke of Bedford: 'Yesterday Lord North opened his budget in the Committee of Ways and Means; and in the four-and-twenty years that I have sat in Parliament, in very few of which I have missed that famous day of the Sessions, I verily think I have never known any of his predecessors acquit themselves so much to the satisfaction of the House'.[93]

The really threatening cloud on the administration's horizon, however, was America, even if to most Ministers the cloud still seemed the size of a man's hand. On looking back the progress of the British government towards catastrophe in America seems like the march of the deaf and the blind, but to North and many of his political associates the colonists were wayward children whose return to the family home was best ensured by firmness, though not by undue severity. In a debate in April 1769 he said: 'Let America look to Great Britain as a kind of parent and friend',[94] and a year later Lord Chatham insisted: 'They [the Americans] must be subordinate. In all laws relating to trade and navigation especially, this is the mother country, they are the children; they must obey, and we prescribe'.[95] It may now seem odd that intelligent politicians should fail to understand the resentment of Americans over taxation by a body in which they had no voice, but the British believed that the principle of parliamentary sovereignty over the colonies was the main issue at stake. North supported this view, and at the same time shared the common (though not universal) misapprehension about the depth of colonial feeling. When Grafton asked his Cabinet on 1 May to support the repeal of all the duties imposed by Townshend, North voted with the five to four majority in favour of retaining that on tea, having declared in the debate a fortnight before: 'I see nothing uncommercial in making the Americans pay a duty upon tea'.[96] If he had decided the other way history, and his part in it, might have been very different.

In the course of 1768 the extent of the colonists' hostility to Townshend's unwise duties had become clear, together with the inability of the British government to enforce them. It is perhaps a convenient oversimplification to say that Grafton's administration was split down the middle over how to handle the developing American confrontation, but it contained doves and hawks and the doves were weakened when the ailing Chatham resigned in October 1768, a departure that was immediately followed by that of the Secretary of State for the South, Lord Shelburne, a leading conciliator. Grafton was now actually as well as formally the leader of a far from united administration, a situation he found disconcerting.

North was by temperament a dove, a man who hated strife, but in the gradual escalation of the American crisis he evolved, with every encouragement from George III, into a rather unconvincing hawk. In his dealings with the colonies he was stubborn; he had become convinced that any concessions by the mother country would be interpreted as cowardice rather than generosity. In a debate on American discontent in December 1768 he declared: 'I think no line can be drawn; you must possess the whole of your authority, or no part of it'.[97] Later that day he resisted any suggestion that American taxes should be reduced just because they had encountered strong opposition: 'The extraordinary appearance this would have in America; the encouragement it would give our enemies, and the discouragement it would give our friends; the impossibility of acting with authority, if our authority received another wound, all bind us not to take that question into our consideration again'.[98]

A month earlier, again on the subject of American taxation, North was said to have announced in the Commons: 'that he would never think of repealing it *until he saw America prostrate at his feet*'.[99] The quotation comes from a letter written home by the same agent for Connecticut who a little over a year before had expressed his belief that North was 'not among the most violent' against the colonies, and his use of emphasis in this later letter suggests a degree of surprise. He was not, however, misreporting North's words, as during another debate on America in the following January they were flung back at him by Colonel Isaac Barré, an intemperate radical who championed the cause of American liberty: 'On a former occasion, the noble lord told us, that he never would repeal this law, until he saw America at his feet. I, Sir, never desire to see America at our feet. Instead of laying upon the ground and licking the dust, I wish to see her raising her head, firmly asking for her privileges, pleading her services, and conscious of her merit'.[100]

There is little doubt that from George III downwards most people in England thought the colonies would benefit from the smack of firm government. North was later subject to bitter criticism not because he had opposed American independence but because he had failed to do so successfully. Nevertheless, in following the story and North's part in it, it is important to remember that from the very beginning there was a minority of men both in Parliament and outside it who were uneasy at the hard-line policies pursued by successive administrations.

One of the very few contemporary cartoons that alludes to the alleged blood relationship between North and George III. They sit side-by-side, both wearing the Garter ribbon, posed to emphasise their likeness. Other members of the ministry sit round the table; the King is blindfolded, unable to see his Ministers pursuing their own interests at the expense of his. Published 22 December 1773. *(British Museum)*

6

The King's First Minister

During the summer of 1769 the Grafton administration looked increasingly unstable. Not only were the differences within the government over both America and Wilkes public knowledge, they were exacerbated by Chatham's partial return to health and active politics. He made no secret of his present hostility to the policies of the administration he had himself created, which made the position of his remaining adherents in the Cabinet awkward. North had the difficult role of defending this disunited body and its actions in the Commons, a task he performed with confidence and skill. He had become a master of procedural sleight of hand and of deflecting questions he did not wish to answer. As a previous biographer put it: 'North rarely debated any opposition motion in the form in which it was first proposed. His habit of amending the sense out of opposition motions was so much his trademark that when he did not try to do so, they would start looking for the joker'.[1] Despite the pressures, however, he remained buoyant. In May, on the way back from seeing his father, he found time to visit his son George at Eton and told Guilford he 'found all the company in health and spirits. The boys were very merry and noisey as usual ... I have had the satisfaction today of finding my family in London full as well, full as merry, and almost as noisey as the boys at Eton'.[2] North seldom allowed politics to interfere with the intense pleasure he derived from his family life.

On the afternoon of 20 December 1769 North received a note from the King which read: 'Lord North – I wish to see you about eight this Evening'.[3] The inference has been drawn that at this meeting George III asked North whether he was prepared to become his First Lord of the Treasury if Grafton decided to step down.[4] There is no certain evidence to support this conjecture but, given the political situation and the later course of events, it seems a reasonable assumption.

Taking account of North's character and his subsequent hesitations it also seems probable he gave the King a non-committal reply. This may not have worried the King much because he knew North well and no doubt reckoned that, provided he did not give a definite refusal, pressure could if necessary be applied at a later date to win acceptance. The King's main concern and his constitutional duty was to find a First Minister who was acceptable to Parliament. He was not therefore acting improperly in talking to North 'off the record' (if he did) as soon as he believed Grafton's departure was imminent. Above all he dearly wanted a Minister acceptable to himself, one who was not Grenville, Rockingham, Chatham or any other faction leader.

The New Year opened with a flood of petitions to Parliament from all parts of the country calling for political and economical reform. To a considerable extent these had been orchestrated by the Opposition Rockingham Whigs but they reflected a high level of public discontent. Most of them shared a common condemnation of Parliament's refusal to seat Wilkes. In the debate on the Address after the opening of Parliament on 9 January North spoke at some length on the subject. Despite a reference in the *London Magazine* to his 'poor defence of the ministry', he appears from the full report of his speech in Cobbett to have made a confident attack on the petitioners.[5] He ridiculed them as people of no importance and little understanding, who were 'not proof against the sophistry, influence, the promises, and the threats of a jealous and restless faction'. 'It is well known', he said, that by such activity 'men have been induced to set their hands to petitions which they have never read, and give countenance to complaints which they have never heard'. Having established, at least to his own satisfaction, the generally low social and intellectual standing of the signatories to the petitions, he rounded off his argument by explaining why it was therefore legitimate to disregard their views: 'I have as high a sense of the rights of Englishmen, as any gentleman of this House, yet I can never acquiesce in the absurd opinion that all men are equal, nor ever pretend to level all distinction, and reduce the various classes into which the polity of civil life has divided the individuals of this Kingdom, to a state of nature, for the sake of flattering my own vanity by a little popular applause'.[6]

North's speech is an interesting example of his tactical skill in deflecting attention to a subsidiary object. The real issue was the grievances raised in the petitions, in particular the state of the country and the treatment of Wilkes, but North made it appear that it was the petitioners themselves and their credentials that were under scrutiny.

At the end of the debate the government won by the apparently easy margin of 254 votes to 158, but it was an illusory victory.[7] In the course of the debate in the Commons the Commander-in-Chief, Lord Granby, had spoken of his regrets at the support he had previously given the administration over Wilkes; and in the Lords the Lord Chancellor, Lord Camden, had felt free to join Chatham in an attack on the government of which he was a senior member.[8] Two Cabinet Ministers backing a motion of censure on their own ministry was unprecedented. After the debate Camden was dismissed, probably on the insistence of the King,[9] and Granby resigned, to be followed by a number of middle-rank Ministers, including the Duke of Manchester and the Earl of Coventry, both of whom were Lords of the Bedchamber, and the Duke of Beaufort, the Master of the Horse.[10] Grafton had trouble filling the vacancies, particularly the most important of them, the Lord Chancellorship. George III intervened and, with a mixture of threats and bribes, persuaded Charles Yorke, a previous Attorney General and a respected lawyer, to ignore the advice of his Rockinghamite brother, Lord Hardwicke, and accept the Great Seal.[11] Yorke agreed on 17 January, but was immediately overcome with remorse at deserting his friends for the sake of his ambition, then took to his bed and died on the 20th. At the time suicide was suspected but he was already a sick man who for the past few days had been under considerable strain; it is far more probable that he died a natural death, possibly from a burst blood vessel.[12]

Grafton had briefly hoped that with the appointment of a new Lord Chancellor his administration could take on a fresh lease of life but Yorke's death, which he was personally convinced was suicide, broke his nerve.[13] The next day Grafton offered his resignation to the King, which he says in his autobiography was accepted with earnest expressions of regret.[14] It was not made public immediately to allow the King time to find his successor. Although Grafton served twice more in ministerial office as Privy Seal he was never again a contender for serious political power. Walpole ascribed his resignation to lack of spirit in the face of adversity,[15] but his decision, which was unexpected in political circles,[16] may have been influenced by a change for the better in his domestic life. In the course of the previous year he had divorced his wife by Act of Parliament, dismissed his mistress Mrs Horton (paid off, North told his father, with £500 a year 'while she behaves well'),[17] and made a very happy second marriage with the daughter of the Dean of Windsor. Until his death forty-one years later he lived a virtuous life, devoting much of his time to Unitarian theology and accepting the presidency of the Vice Society.[18]

On 22 January 1770 the King sent another one-line summons to North for a meeting that evening.[19] There is no doubt that on this occasion George III offered him the premiership, though offered is possibly the wrong word, implying a prize eagerly sought. It is clear North hesitated and came under considerable pressure to brush his hesitations aside and accept the office, but both he and the King were playing for high stakes. If North refused, or alternatively accepted and then failed to secure the support of the Commons, the King would be compelled to fall back on the detested Whig faction leaders to form a government. North, for his part, would find himself in the political wilderness. George III's determination to overcome his Minister's lack of enthusiasm for high office is apparent from a letter he wrote to North after their interview:

> After seeing you last night I saw Lord Weymouth [Secretary of State] who by My Direction will wait on You with Lord Gower [Lord President] this morning to press You in the strongest Manner to accept the Office of first Commissioner of the Treasury. My own mind is more and more strengthened with the rightness of the measure that would prevent every other desertion. You must easily see that if You do not accept I have no Peer at present in my Service that I could consent to place in the Duke of Grafton's employment, what ever You may think do not take any decision unless it is the one of instantly accepting without a further conversation with Me. And as to the other arrangements You may hear what others think but keep Your opinion till I have seen You.[20]

Two days after this letter, before North had given the King a definite answer, and with Grafton still officially in office, the Opposition tabled a motion of censure on the unending topic of the Middlesex election. North defended the government vigorously and on the evening of 25 January the Opposition was defeated by forty-four votes, not an enormous margin but evidently sufficient to persuade him to accede to the King's wishes. It was a brave decision. He was taking over a weakened administration without the benefit of either a personal following in the Commons or the authority and prestige of Grafton's ducal title. Success was not inevitable.

At some point over the next two days North informed the King of his favourable decision but it was agreed not to announce it or Grafton's resignation before the 30 January, to give the new First Lord time to rally potential supporters.[21] On the 31st, with the appointment now public knowledge, North met the House of Commons. The Opposition had presented yet another censure motion, once more officially on the subject of Wilkes, but with the covert motive of destroying both North and his administration before he could find his feet. He faced the House with remarkable sang-froid. Walpole says that 'with great frankness and spirit, [he] laid open his own situation, which, he said, he had not sought, but would not refuse; nor would he timidly shrink from his post'. When rudely attacked by Colonel Barré, who spoke of him as a man of no consequence, he replied 'not only with spirit but good humour, and evidently had the advantage, though it was obvious how much weight the personal presence of a First Minister in the House of Commons carried with it'.[22] Despite everything the Opposition could fling at him, North ended the debate with a majority of forty.

The North administration was in business and remained so for the next twelve years. The next day the King wrote to him: 'I am greatly rejoiced at the conclusion of the Debate a Majority of 40, at this particular crisis considering it is upon the old ground that had been at least ten times before the House is a very favorable auspice on Your taking the lead in Administration. Believe Me a little spirit will soon restore a degree of order in my Service'.[23] The King's injunction to his Prime Minister to have confidence in 'a little spirit' echoes the similar exhortation he gave him two years earlier when urging the expulsion of Wilkes. It suggests that George III was still not totally confident of North's steadiness under fire.

Why did George III choose Lord North and why did North accept a post for which he was far from sure he was suited? The first question is a good deal easier to answer than the second. From the King's point of view North was the obvious, almost the only choice. On the negative side, he was not associated with any of the factions and he shared George III's preference for a ministry not too dependent on any of the great Whig magnates. If North could not be persuaded to take the Treasury it would fall almost inevitably into their hands, because other than him there was no one outside the factions of sufficient stature and ability whom the King could summon to his aid. Some contemporary letters sound a note of surprise or caution at North's appointment, and the *London Chronicle* reported he was considered by some 'a mere *Locum Tenens*', but there was little suggestion he was not of the necessary calibre.[24] Comparing him to his predecessor, Walpole wrote to his friend Horace Mann in Florence: 'In the meantime Lord North is First Minister. He is much more able, more active, more assiduous, more resolute, and more fitted to deal with mankind'.[25] Such praise would one day ring hollow but at the time he was recognised as a skilful manager of the House of Commons and an able and conscientious Minister of Finance. The King may have had some reservations over North's toughness but his choice was neither surprising nor irresponsible. In one sense, at least, it was justified by the outcome: a ministry of twelve years' duration.

It is harder to understand why the rather irresolute North, albeit under pressure, agreed to serve as First Lord. Ambition must have played a part if, as suggested earlier, a streak of it lay buried within him. He had been a hard-working politician for sixteen years and it is hard to believe that he was uninterested in the supreme prize when it became available.

Nevertheless, North's doubts about his fitness for office were partly genuine; they were more than a reflection of eighteenth-century good manners, a becoming reluctance (which no one took too seriously) to admit to worthiness for preferment. Only a few weeks before he accepted the King's commission to form a government he wrote a poignant letter to his father. The letter is dated from Downing Street, 1 December. There is no year, but references in it to the Bunbury Separation case, and to the recent death 'in vastly opulent circumstances' of Lady Frances Arundel, leave no doubt the letter was written in December 1769.[26] In part the letter reads:

> This day has been so charming, that I envied you and Brownlow at Waldershare. Indeed, my situation is such, that I envy everybody; I always hated my part, but this aversion increases daily. It is very hard, that when a man has no favour to ask but his own dismission, he is not able to attain it in two years. I can not bear to lead this life any longer.[27]

It is impossible to be certain what moved the man who wrote that letter to accept heavy additional burdens before two months were out, but it is possible that the wish to earn his father's approval may have played a part in the decision North finally took. There is no surviving record of a request for advice but that would hardly have been necessary. North would have known that with Guilford's own hopes of preferment through a court appointment still unfulfilled, he would very much have appreciated the reflected honour due to a Prime Minister's father. After every allowance is made for the exaggerated expression of sentiment in much eighteenth-century correspondence, his letters to his father often betray a need for parental approval. Part of the letter in which North doubted his adequacy for the position of Chancellor of the Exchequer has been quoted above; the opening lines of the same letter show whose encouragement he would most welcome:

> The departure of the post prevented me ... from thanking you as I ought for your very kind & affectionate letter of the 8th of this month. Tho' your Lordship's good opinion of me had probably a great mixture of partiality in it, it makes me inexpressibly happy, & I am confident that nothing can more powerfully recommend me to those with whom I am to act for the future than the mark of your approbation; I flatter myself that I shall never forfeit it through want of duty to your Lordship, or of gratitude for your unceasing goodness toward me, or by a deviation from that fidelity and integrity which ought to guide all my actions in the execution of my office.[28]

Although superficially tempting, it is unprofitable to try and see North's relationship with George III as a reflection of that with his father. He respected the King, revered his office and liked the man, but there is little sign of the emotional intensity that characterised his relations with Guilford. The one common factor in North's dealings with both men was his highly developed respect for the authority each represented. He was seldom able to say no to either of them, so when the King urged him to accept the premiership he would have found refusal hard to contemplate.

When Lord North became Prime Minister he retained the posts of Chancellor of the Exchequer and Leader of the House of Commons. In the absence of a fully developed prime ministerial function, an administration was very dependent on the political and administrative skills of these two officers, and it was perfectly acceptable that either or both positions should be filled by the First Lord himself. In North's case the arguments in favour of this arrangement were particularly strong. He was an acknowledged expert on fiscal matters, and management of the Commons was essential to his administration's well-being. Furthermore, as he was the only member of the Cabinet he inherited who sat in the Lower House, he had little choice in the matter. The drawback of this triple responsibility was that North was overworked, or at least provided with more work than he could easily handle. He was seldom absent from the Chamber when the Commons was sitting, and took a leading role in most of the debates, rising to speak or intervene some 800 times in his first five sessions as Prime Minister.[29] The Cabinet and the Treasury Board met twice weekly and his presence was expected at both. He had extensive patronage reponsibilities and was bombarded with requests for employment. He also had to be available whenever he was required by the King. As he explained at a later date to George III:

> Lord North thinks it his duty to represent to his Majesty that to perform the duties of the Treasury, to attend the House of Commons at the rate of three long days a week, to see the numbers of people who have daily business with the First Lord of the Treasury, and to give all thought to the principal measures of government . . . is enough to employ the greatest man of business . . . and is infinitely more than Lord North can undertake . . . [30]

The burden that North was to carry for so long probably contributed to his increasingly frequent attacks of ill-health,[31] and certainly to his periods of depression and to his inertia in the face of difficult decisions, yet it is hard to believe that overwork was the sole cause of his distress. When Parliament was sitting he undoubtedly kept long hours but that was normally only for five or six months in the year. When the House was in recess he found time to pay visits to his father at Wroxton or Waldershare and occasionally to his wife's property in Somerset.[32] He also had a relaxing country retreat at Bushy on the north bank of the Thames near Hampton Court. In 1771 George III offered North the Rangership of Bushy Park, an office which entailed no duties and provided the amenity of a pleasant, medium-sized country mansion, which North asked to be put in his wife's name to give her security of tenure in the event of his death. It became his favourite residence, a place where he often entertained official visitors and political colleagues, though Saturdays and Sundays, according to his daughter Charlotte, were reserved for his family and one or two intimate friends.[33]

North's problems did not stem simply from overwork or from lack of opportunities for relaxation, but from his temperament and the way it led him to conduct affairs. In the Treasury and in the House of Commons where he felt on top of the responsibilities he was undoubtedly efficient, but in other fields he was disorganised and vacillating, weaknesses which inevitably increased the hours he needed to devote to public business. These failings were compounded by a tendency to concentrate on the trees at the expense of the wood or, as a contemporary civil servant put it, a 'preoccupation with too much business of detail, which prevented him finding time for great superintending duties'.[34] An often quoted instance of his inability to confront complex and controversial issues was his handling of Irish matters in 1779. At the request of the administration, the Lord Lieutenant of Ireland, Lord Buckinghamshire, had prepared a full set of papers on the current rebellious state of the country which landed on North's desk in the middle of July. He had not read them by the end of the year but soon after their arrival his assistant, John Robinson, Senior Secretary of the Treasury, wrote to the King's adviser Charles Jenkinson about North's neglect of the documents: 'He [North] had no time, he was kept so employed in Treasury Matters which might be done by other Lords, but that he had no Lord to sit with him, or for him, and in short that no one would do anything and then [he] fell into one of his distressing Fits'.[35]

Another reflection on North's methods comes from the diary of Thomas Hutchinson, the loyalist Governor of Massachusetts, who had been forced to retire to England in 1774. Writing a year later he said a colleague attributed 'the delays which attend business of all sorts, to Lord North's consulting so many persons, who are of different opinions; and from this difference he remains undecided himself for some time, is apt to change. Others charge him with aversion to business in general, tho' when forced to engage, he shows himself exceeding capable'.[36] Few questioned North's capacities when he chose to apply himself; it was his sometimes haphazard methods, and his tendency to concentrate on detail rather than the overall picture, that could cause frustration to those who had to deal with him.

On Grafton's departure most of his Ministers still in office agreed to serve with North and there was no major reshuffle. The Lord Chancellorship still proved difficult to fill, being put into commission until it was accepted a year later by Henry Bathurst, an undistinguished lawyer created Lord Apsley for the purpose.[37] Lord Rochford and Lord Weymouth continued as Secretaries of State for the Northern and Southern Departments respectively, Lord Gower remained as President of the Council and the elderly Sir Edward Hawke, a famous naval hero, stayed at the Admiralty.[38] The only newcomer to the Cabinet was North's uncle Lord Halifax who, with the King's approval, was appointed Privy Seal despite a growing fondness for the bottle.[39] Weymouth resigned the following December, after failing to persuade his colleagues to adopt a more robust attitude to the ambitions of Spain over the Falkland Islands dispute, when North replaced him with the able and experienced fourth Earl of Sandwich. After only three weeks as Secretary for the North (Rochford having taken the opportunity of transferring to the more prestigious South), Sandwich became First Lord of the Admiralty early in 1771 – Hawke, who was too old and too infirm for such an important responsibility, having been eased into retirement with the aid of a peerage.[40] Sandwich had held the position twice before. He was a knowledgeable and committed naval administrator and he remained at the Admiralty as one of North's principal lieutenants throughout his premiership.

Sandwich's place as Secretary of State was taken by Halifax, who had become an ageing man of fifty-five years and declining health. The King commented to North 'had I been in his Situation and of his Age I should have preferred his Motto'.[41] It read *Otium cum dignitate* (leisure with dignity). Halifax's place as Privy Seal went to the Earl of Suffolk, an important Grenvillite, who on Halifax's death in June 1771 followed him as Secretary for the North. His uncle's death brought North two bonuses. First his predecessor, Grafton, agreed to return as Privy Seal and, although he declined a seat in the Cabinet, his presence in the administration encouraged others to support it. North's second bonus has already been mentioned. Halifax had been Ranger of Bushy Park. While he was still on his death-bed, George III wrote North a warm letter promising him the succession to the sinecure:

> The sincere regard I have for You makes me though much hurt at the certain loss of so amiable man as Lord Halifax, yet with pleasure acquaint You that whenever

I shall receive the account of his death, I shall immediately appoint You Ranger of Bushy Park as I am resolved to make out none of these Grants but during pleasure, and have done so in the cases of my Brothers. I am certain You will very willingly accept it on that footing which from the conduct You uniformly hold must be a tenure of a permanent kind. I cannot conclude without assuring You that every opportunity of shewing You the sincere regard I have for you is giving Me the greatest pleasure.[42]

Only two days later the King gave further evidence of his sincere regard by promising North the Garter as soon as the next vacancy occurred, stressing his particular satisfaction at conferring an honour that North had never sought: 'I mean to bequeath this Order on You, which I shall do with the greater pleasure as I never have had any intimation from You that it is an honour you are in the least ambitious of'.[43] He received it a year later, the first commoner to do so since Sir Robert Walpole and, according to the *Gentleman's Magazine,* celebrated the occasion with 'a splendid entertainment at his house in Downing Street'.[44] Thereafter he was known in the House of Commons as the 'Noble Lord in the Blue Ribbon'.

North's only serious disappointment during his first year of office was the refusal of Dartmouth to join the government. In the rearrangement of posts that occurred in January 1771 he was offered a Secretaryship of State. It is not entirely clear why he declined to join his step-brother's administration at this juncture, as he had held office before and would hold it again. Possibly his previous association with the Rockinghamites was responsible, but it may have been his own preference for a private life that tipped the scales on this occasion.[45] In any event North told the King he would prefer to explain the reasons in person 'as he cannot do justice to Lord Dartmouth's sentiments in the compass of a note'.[46] It was this refusal on Dartmouth's part that produced the petulant response from Guilford alluded to earlier: 'The more I reflect upon your refusal yesterday the more I am vex'd. To have you appear to the world wanting in Duty & regard to the King, Love to your country, friendship to Lord North, & affection to me, is what I thought I should never live to see. I am much too hurt to talk upon the subject, & hope we shall never name it, as I cannot help being, Your affectionate G.'[47] In correspondence over the next few days Guilford climbed off his high horse in response to Dartmouth's cancellation of a planned visit. He ended by saying: 'A pretty good night has calmed my spirits, so pray let us neither talk, nor think, any more of this disagreeable affair. I have satisfied my mind, that if you had seen things in the light I did, you would not have taken the step; & if I had seen them only in the light they appeared to you, I should not have taken it so unkindly. God bless you all'.[48] The incident does not appear to have disturbed the close friendship between the step-brothers, and within little more than a year Dartmouth had joined the government.

Despite his temporary failure with Dartmouth, the new First Lord presided over a Cabinet which included men of experience and ability. At no stage in his career, however, did North manage to wield his Cabinet into a body where the collective authority was greater than the individual strengths of its members. There were two reasons for this. The first was contemporary constitutional theory under which the focus of authority was the King and the role of the Cabinet was to serve as his council. Ministers held their appointments from him and were responsible to him for the way they ran their departments. They met together in Cabinet to offer considered advice to the King and to coordinate their response to political challenge, but the notion of collective responsibility was still to be fully developed. It is true that Camden and Granby had had to go after opposing the government of which they were members, but the essential point is that they had spoken against a government the King supported, and it was probably the King rather than his fellow Ministers who had insisted on Camden's dismissal. The weakness of this system in wartime was plain to see but it could, nevertheless, be overcome under those conditions by leaders of the strength and vision of either Pitt. North had neither the temperament nor the inclination to play such a role.

North's own character was the other and principal reason his Cabinets never achieved their full potential as cooperative entities. His youngest daughter wrote: 'He never would allow us to call him Prime Minister, saying there was no such thing in the British Constitution',[49] and in his day that was a tenable if over-fastidious understanding of the position of the First Lord of the Treasury. On this interpretation he was little more than *primus inter pares*, the man who for the sake of convenience took the chair at Cabinet meetings and usually acted as the channel of communication with the King. This attitude was already becoming dated, as is shown by a comment on North's ministry made by Sir Nathanial Wraxall who was elected to Parliament in 1780, and was therefore barely a generation his junior: 'They [the Cabinet] were, in fact, rather his co-equals than his subordinates, as they ought to have been, and the public service suffered, as I well know, from their want of union, or from their clashing interests and private animosities'.[50]

Towards the end of his ministry North made a public denial in the Commons of any prime ministerial aspirations:

> He desired in the meantime that it might be recollected, he never had pretended to be Prime Minister; he had only acted as one member of the Cabinet; not that he

said this by way of evasion, he meant to evade nothing but the charge of presumption of his being Prime Minister, a presumption he had never assumed and which therefore he ought not to be charged with; at the same time that he said this, he held himself answerable to his country for every part of his conduct.[51]

He was later uneasy about the detached approach he had taken to collective Cabinet decision-taking. Four years after making those comments, at a time when he was out of office, he is reported to have said: 'If you mean there should not be a government by department, I agree with you: I think it is a very bad system. There should be one man, or a Cabinet, to govern the whole, and direct every measure. Government by department was not brought in by me. I found it so, and had not the vigour and resolution to put an end to it'.[52]

7

A Confident Start

At first North's position as the new First Lord looked insecure. In a debate on 7 February 1770 Thomas Townshend, who had briefly held North's previous job as joint Paymaster General, [1] first praised his abilities and then added: 'But there he sits, without a friend, without an acquaintance'.[2] Two weeks later Edward Gibbon was rather more sanguine, writing to his step-mother: 'However, the general opinion is that the next fortnight must decide the fate of the Ministry. If Lord North (whose spirit & abilities are certainly great) holds out till then, the Minority will probably divide desert & run away'.[3] North more than held out. His majority of forty on 31 January rose to seventy-five on 12 February on an Opposition Bill to disenfranchise certain government employees.[4] At the end of the month he achieved a majority of 133 when George Grenville demanded details of expenditure incurred under the Civil List, a move intended to infer corruption in high places.[5] North had replied to the debate in his most self-confident vein:

> It is exceedingly pleasant to find Gentlemen, who have themselves benefited by the munificence of the Crown, and who are themselves hourly pocketing the public money, making so strict an examination into the disbursements of the Civil List, and weeping so tenderly over the oppressions of their poor country. However, as I would at all times rather reason then rail, and as I am desirous of leaving the liberal field of invective wholly open to the enemies of administration, I shall proceed at once to the reasons which induce me to oppose the present question.[6]

On the day Grenville's motion was defeated George III sent North a note: 'The seeing that the Majority constantly increases gives me great pleasure'.[7]

The Opposition attacks continued through March but North consolidated his position by defeating the most serious, in particular one from the Chathamites in uneasy alliance with the radicals of the City of London, still resentful over Wilkes. The City, led by Alderman William Beckford MP, the Lord Mayor, presented George III with a Remonstrance which in insulting terms denounced the ministry and by implication the King himself. It ended:

> Since therefore the misdeeds of your Majesty's ministers, in violating the freedom of election, and depraving the noble constitution of parliaments, are notorious, as well as subversive of the fundamental laws and liberties of the realm ... We your Majesty's remonstrants, assure ourselves, that your Majesty will restore the constitutional government and quiet your people, by dissolving parliament, and removing those evil ministers for ever from your councils.[8]

The King's reply adopted a tone of regret rather than anger: 'I shall always be ready to receive the request and to listen to the complaints of my subjects; but it gives me great concern to find, that any of them should have been so far misled as to offer me an Address and Remonstrance, the contents of which I cannot but consider as disrespectful to me, injurious to my Parliament, and irreconcilable to the principles of the constitution'.[9] The next day, when the Commons debated the Remonstrance, North took his tone from the King and resisted the temptation to seek the punishment of those responsible for it. He had no wish to make martyrs and treated his opponents with courtesy: 'These gentlemen will at least do justice to the patience and lenity of the House that has permitted them to declare their sentiments ... '[10] His emollience was vindicated as he won the main vote by the large majority of 163. The next day he received yet another approving note from George III: 'Nothing can be more respectful to Me nor more honourable for themselves than the conduct of the Majority yesterday of which I will say more when I see you this day'.[11]

With one or two minor exceptions North had won all the divisions since he took office, usually with increasing majorities. Opinion was firmly moving his way. On 24 April Lord Barrington, the Secretary at War, could write to a friend: 'Lord North bids fairer for making an able and good minister than any man we have had a great while ... I think that heats are subsiding, and that men are coming to their senses'.[12] A few days earlier North had told his father: 'Thank God, we draw to a conclusion of the Session, & then, I flatter myself, we shall have done'.[13] On 19 May Parliament went into recess for the summer and few people any longer doubted that, in choosing Lord North, George III had effected a major change in the political landscape. There was now an administration that commanded wide support in the House of Commons.

In building a majority an eighteenth-century administration could usually rely on the votes of the placemen and pensioners, Members who held some paid position or sinecure at the pleasure of the government or who sat for a Treasury borough, but they were an uncertain quantity. Some were difficult to remove and were therefore impervious to pressure, some could afford to ignore a potential loss of salary, and others, where matters of principle were involved, would follow their consciences even if this led them to vote with the Opposition.[14] Their numbers are hard to estimate, but were certainly not as high as the figure of 192 suggested by one biographer of North.[15] As they were mostly interested in a quiet life and an absence of upheaval, they would have been inclined to support the new administration as a continuation of Grafton's.

A far more important group of Members in relation to North's early success were the Country Gentlemen. According to Lord Feilding, speaking later in North's premiership, these independent-minded men were 'neither to be frowned into servility nor hussaed into faction', and it was by their support 'did the present minister stand'.[16] They appreciated his financial prudence and his detachment from faction politics, and during the first few weeks they gave him the benefit of the doubt. Their significance must not be given too much weight: 'To have become a force in politics they would have needed a leader and a degree of organisation – to have become in other words a political party – which was clearly impossible for independent country gentlemen'.[17] On the American war, however, the most contentious issue of North's ministry, they gave him consistent support which was only withdrawn when the defeat of British policy was seen to be inevitable.

It is as difficult to put a confident figure on the numbers of the Country Gentlemen as it is with the placemen, but perhaps together they comprised something over half the Commons membership of 558.[18]. Even on the unlikely assumption that all these Members ever voted as a body, they would not on their own have been able to ensure the longevity of North's administration. That was due to an important additional factor in the political situation, the failure of the Whig Opposition to present a united front.

Nevertheless, North confronted a formidable array on the Opposition benches in both Houses, including Chatham and Rockingham in the Lords and Burke and Barré in the Commons. The followers of George Grenville were unsympathetic to the new administration, and those of the Duke of Bedford, while rather more friendly, could not be relied on to support it. Yet the ministry survived and flourished. Chatham was not a natural peacetime politician. He was haughty and difficult and he was viewed with suspicion by the other faction leaders. By the end of 1770 he had quarrelled with Rockingham.[19] On Grenville's death in November the

Grenvillites also deserted Chatham and made their peace with North. Moreover, the Opposition groups were unable to agree among themselves on some of the main issues of the day, such as the correct procedure for prosecuting press libels (a by-product of the Wilkes affair), or the best way of handling the fractious American colonies,[20] while the Rockinghamites had an aristocratic disdain for Chatham's radical middle-class allies in the City.[21]

North's first three months as Prime Minister were not solely occupied with repelling attacks on his government over home affairs. There were three overseas territories, two of them British and one quasi-British, that demanded the attention of the administration. The last, India, was officially the responsibility of the East India Company. North managed to postpone parliamentary consideration of the unsatisfactory state of affairs that had developed there until the following year.[22] The other two territories were America and Ireland. They forced their way onto the immediate political agenda, despite North's apparent belief that the threat each presented was exaggerated. Both countries suffered from the general English assumption that the purpose of their existence was to enhance the prosperity of England or, if that is putting it too crudely, that their commercial activities should not incommode those of the mother country. Trade with third parties was therefore largely forbidden to protect English exports, even when the depressed state of the Irish economy was causing hardship.

Due to its colonial status, the constitutional situation of America was very different from that of Ireland. It was directly subject to the Westminster government whereas Ireland was an independent kingdom with its own Parliament. The practical effect of Ireland's nominal independence was, however, extremely limited. Poynings' Law, passed in 1494, laid down that no measure of the Irish Parliament could come into force without the consent of the English Privy Council, while the Declaratory Act of 1719 made Ireland subject to legislation passed at Westminster. In addition Ireland's Protestant governing class had close family and political links with the English establishment and, unlike America, the island was close enough for the successful exercise of imperial power if required. The similarity in the American and Irish situations in the 1770s must not be overstressed, but in two respects North and many of his contemporaries approached their imperial responsibilities with the same attitudes to both countries. First, and to their credit, they believed they must uphold the primacy of Parliament under the settlement of 1689 as the guarantee of liberty for all the King's subjects wherever they lived.[23] It was chiefly for this reason North insisted that the thirteen colonies must accept the principle of taxation by Westminster, and only secondly for the contribution any revenue would make towards American expenditure.

A less admirable strand in North's handling of Ireland and America was insensitivity. Like many people brought up in a secure and privileged environment, he never found it easy to imagine himself in another person's shoes. Due to recent changes in policy the English-appointed Lord Lieutenant of Ireland now resided in Dublin not London, and exercised his powers directly rather than through the local magnates known as Undertakers. Unsurprisingly these vested interests resented their loss of power and patronage. In November 1769 they tried to emphasise the independent authority of the Irish Parliament by persuading it formally to reject a finance measure received from London and then, having made their point, to accept it. The Lord Lieutenant, Lord Townshend, thereupon prorogued the Irish Parliament before it could cause any more trouble.[24] In May 1770 this action was challenged in the House of Commons. The motion was proposed by an Opposition Member with Irish family connexions, Boyle Wallsingham, who drew a parallel between Ireland and America, pointing out that the Irish had seen the Americans, 'a people much younger, and more obliged' disobey British Acts of Parliament 'with the greatest success'.[25] This brought forth from North a response which was lamentably inappropriate to the current state of the Irish economy:

> The distresses of the Irish nation, Sir, have been painted in most melancholy colours, by the honourable gentleman who made the first motion, and they would really deserve our serious consideration, if it were not for one unfortunate circumstance, which is, that his picture is totally a child of the imagination. To prove this, let us only enquire into the present state of Ireland: is its trade upon the decline, is the landed property decreasing in value, or are the people becoming poor? Alas, Sir, nothing like it. The trade of our sister nation never flourished so much; the value of landed property is hourly increasing; and so far are the people from being impoverished, that, if we except some places very remote from the metropolis, where laziness is attended with its never-failing companion, wretchedness, all is a continual scene of abundance and festivity.[26]

The first time America came up for debate during North's premiership was on 5 March 1770. The repeal of all the Townshend duties except tea, narrowly agreed by the Grafton Cabinet nearly a year before, had not yet been put into effect but, when merchants from the City of London petitioned for repeal on commercial grounds, North thought his position was sufficiently established to seek the necessary parliamentary approval. The petitioners wanted all the duties abolished including that on tea, but North was not prepared to agree. He argued in favour of removing the duties 'which bear upon the manufactures of this country; such as the duties upon glass, red lead etc'. As far as tea was concerned, 'it is an object of luxury; of all commodities, it is the properest for taxation; the duty upon it is light, and such as it can very well bear'.[27] North's hand was strengthened by the composition of his Cabinet. The four members who had supported total repeal the previous May had all departed, whereas the five hard-liners still remained. This made it easier for him to ignore the warnings of a number of colonial Governors that partial repeal would not set American fears at rest.[28]

North was in an uncomfortable position, as he wanted to maintain Parliament's right to tax the colonies without increasing his difficulties with the colonists. 'I wish for harmony; but I see no prospect of obtaining it. If I thought I could appease that factious and disobedient temper which prevails, I should be glad to do it.' But there was a limit to his tolerance: 'And yet, to these people, who ought to be our subjects, we are to make concessions, because they have the hardihood to set us at defiance! Sir, no authority was ever confirmed by the concession of any point of honour or point of right'. Towards the end of his speech he affirmed what he undoubtedly believed to be true: 'I wish to be thought, what I really am, to the best of my conviction – a friend to trade, a friend to America'.[29]

North wanted to stand on the middle ground but, like others in that position, found himself attacked from both sides. From the Opposition benches Thomas Pownall, who had been Governor successively of Massachusetts and South Carolina, and therefore spoke from first-hand knowledge, warned North that his partial acknowledgement of American grievances would not serve its purpose: 'You have done things which call in question whether they have courts or not – whether they have a Bill of Rights or not – whether the Habeas Corpus Act extends to that country or does not. Though the people of America have not come here with these questions, they lie rankling in their bosoms'.[30]

Other Opposition speakers, including the Chathamite Colonel Barré, also called for total repeal, but from his own benches North was criticised for giving away too much.[31] Welbore Ellis, harking back to the repeal of the Stamp Act, said: 'We have tried what rescinding would do, and it has only made the malady worse', and Lord Barrington proclaimed: 'Whether right or not, the laws must be obeyed ... the law extends to all America'.[32] At the end of the debate the amendment to include tea in the repeal provisions was lost by sixty-two votes, a considerably smaller margin than North had been enjoying in divisions on home affairs.

The administration's American policy was again under attack early in May 1770 following a critical motion moved by Edmund Burke, but on this occasion North achieved the comfortable majority of 120 and America was not again considered by Parliament until 1773.[33] The interval was not, however, used by North to develop an overall strategy for reaching a *modus vivendi* with the discontented American colonists. Some comments he made during the debate on the repeal of the Townshend duties show that he regarded such an endeavour with little enthusiasm or hope:

> The want of a strong government [in America] is obvious; but to effect that, it requires great abilities, great experience, great knowledge. Gentlemen within doors having been calling out for a plan these five years; but neither within doors nor without has any been proposed, that would place America and this country upon a proper footing. I will not say that the object is too great to be ever attained. I will use my endeavours; but I tell the House, how arduous I consider the attempt.[34]

While Parliament was in recess during the summer of 1770 an international crisis that had been simmering for some years finally blew up; North handled it with a skill that reinforced his recent successes over the Opposition.

It is a matter for debate who first discovered the uninhabited Falkland Islands in the South Atlantic,[35] but in 1690 Captain John Strong, to whom the British Admiralty had granted a privateer's commission to seize French shipping, became the first Englishman to set foot on the islands. He named the sheltered channel where he dropped anchor Falkland Sound, in honour of the third Viscount Falkland, then a Commissioner of the Admiralty, but his visit had no particular significance in terms of a territorial claim. Sixty years later Admiral Lord Anson, as First Lord of the Admiralty, became interested in the Falklands for their potential as a naval base strategically placed in relation to the Cape Horn and Magellan Straits passages, but little was done about it.

Among the few visitors to the Falklands during the first half of the eighteenth century were fisherman from St-Malo in Brittany, who named the islands Les Malouines after their home port, a name subsequently changed by the Spanish to Las Malvinas. In 1763 the French Foreign Minister, the Duc de Choiseul, authorised Antoine Louis de Bougainville, a young officer who had served with distinction under Montcalm at Quebec, to equip two ships at the expense of himself and his family, and to establish a French settlement on the Falklands. The expedition set sail from St-Malo on 15 September and made land on the West Falklands on the following 31 January. In search of a better anchorage Bougainville sailed eastwards; at the head of what is now Berkeley Sound in the East Falklands he found conditions suitable for a settlement, which he named

Port Louis, and on 5 April 1764 took formal possession of the islands in the name of Louis XV. Within two years the new colony had grown to some 150 settlers.

News of the new settlement reached the Spanish government in the course of 1764, causing consternation. Whether Spain had any legal claim to the Falklands – either under the famous papal bull of 1493 dividing the western hemisphere between the two Iberian powers, or on grounds of proximity to its existing territories – was debatable, but it clearly had a strong practical interest in the control of islands so close to its southern colonies and its main trade routes from the Pacific. After a good deal of diplomatic activity, Choiseul reluctantly agreed to cede the new colony to Spain in return for a generous payment to Bougainville. At a ceremony at Port Louis on 1 April 1767 Bougainville personally handed over the territory to the Spanish, who placed it under the authority of the Captain General of Buenos Aires, Don Francisco Bucareli.

Meanwhile British strategic interest in the Falklands had revived, and in June 1764 the government despatched two ships under Commodore John Byron (the grandfather of the poet) to survey the islands with a view to settlement. Due to faulty charts and bad weather it was January 1765 before Byron reached his destination, where he dropped anchor in the subsequently named Byron Sound on the north-western side of the West Falklands, and called his base Port Egmont after the First Lord of the Admiralty. At some unknown date that January he formally took possession of all the islands in the name of George III. Having completed a survey of the West Falklands he briefly moved eastwards, but failed to discover the French colony at Port Louis. With the aid of a homeward-bound ship he encountered at Puerto Descado on the mainland, his despatches reached London in June. Ignoring rumours of French settlement the British government now sent out a military expedition under Captain John McBride, which reached the islands on 8 January 1766 and made Port Egmont its base. It was eleven months before McBride discovered the location of the French settlement. He then delivered a withdrawal demand to the Governor, which was ignored, returned to Port Egmont, and thence back to Britain.

The British settlement was at first unaffected by the transfer of Port Louis to Spain, but the Spaniards were in no doubt that its existence posed a threat to their security in South America. On 17 May 1770 Bucareli despatched a force of five ships and some 1400 troops from Montevideo to demand the departure of the British from Port Egmont, and to reassert the rights of the Spanish Crown. His instructions from Madrid had been couched in terms that allowed for subsequent repudiation of his actions if that should prove necessary. For the British garrison there was no alternative to capitulation; their humiliation was increased by the temporary removal by the Spaniards of the rudder from the British guardship to delay its departure for home. The news of the Spanish capture was thus delayed and did not reach London till late September.[36]

Lord Weymouth, the Southern Secretary, at once fired off a belligerent note to Madrid,[37] but when North arrived back in London from Wroxton, where he had been staying with his father, he instituted a rather more cautious line. His wish to avoid war with Spain, if it was possible to do so without national disgrace, was supported by George III, who later in the crisis wrote to him that 'for every feeling of humanity as well as the knowledge of the distress War must occasion makes me desirous of preventing it'.[38] North was well aware that honour (on both sides) was the stumbling-block rather than rights. He regarded the Falklands as a 'barren and useless rock', not worth the risk of war, and said in one of the parliamentary debates on the dispute: 'From the beginning, the principle on which we have treated has not been one of right, but of honour'.[39] Charles III, the Bourbon King of Spain, was notoriously touchy on the subject of his honour and refused to entertain any solution to the crisis that seemed to reflect on it unfavourably,[40] while George III was nearly as sensitive on the subject. In his Address at the opening of the parliamentary session on 13 November, he referred to Bucareli's seizure of his possesions as deeply affecting 'the honour of my Crown'.[41]

Quite apart from his distaste for extreme solutions, there were two particular considerations North had to bear in mind when facing the possibility of hostilities. The first was the likelihood that the two Bourbon powers of Spain and France would act in concert. The French Foreign Minister, the Duc de Choiseul, was suspected of exploiting the situation to seek revenge for the reverses inflicted on his country by Britain in the Seven Years War, and British agents reported the mobilisation of the French Atlantic fleet.[42]

North's other worry was the state of the British fleet. The reluctance of the House of Commons to vote money for defence in time of peace was nothing new, but on 29 November it belatedly agreed to a rise of a shilling on the land tax to pay for an increase in naval strength from 16,000 to 40,000.[43] Unfortunately the problem of past neglect was compounded in the critical months of 1770 by the failing grasp of Sir Edward Hawke at the Admiralty, at a time when energetic direction of naval affairs was badly needed. On the 27 July the dockyards at Portsmouth, the largest in the country, were devastated by fire. 'All stores and furniture of 25 capital ships, including every mast, yard, sail, cable and cordage for them was destroyed.'[44] If war had come early in 1771 the combined fleets of France and Spain would have easily outnumbered that of Great Britain.

When, therefore, North intervened in the negotiations he held a weak hand, but he may have sensed that despite warlike noises none of the three countries involved really thought the incident worth an international war. The fact that the conflict could not be localised strengthened the position of the peacemakers. As well as support from the King, North was able to rely on the backing of his Cabinet colleagues who, with one notable exception, hoped for a diplomatic solution. The exception was Lord Weymouth, who believed that the affront to national honour demanded an armed response, and by his own uncompromising tone in his communications with the Spanish court did his best to bring it about.[45] Even by the standards of the day Weymouth was an extraordinary man to hold a position of such importance. Horace Walpole commented:

> His extreme indolence and drunkenness made it impossible that he should exercise the duties of his office in time of war. He seldom went to bed till five or six in the morning, nor rose till twelve or one. His parts must have been great, for in that besotted state he was still able to express himself in the House of Lords with elegance, quickness, and some knowledge, in a few short sentences; not indeed deserving all the applause bestowed on them by his faction.[46]

By the beginning of December Weymouth was in a Cabinet minority of one. When he demanded the withdrawal of the British Ambassador from Madrid the other members refused to agree and he resigned. To emphasise he departed the administration with no ill-will he asked that in the subsequent reshuffle of jobs his brother, Henry Thynne, should be made Postmaster General, a request North was happy to oblige.[47]

During the early weeks of the crisis Parliament was in recess and the government's handling of it was not therefore subject to public scrutiny but, as the Connecticut agent William Johnson wrote home in October, that would soon change, though not necessarily with untoward results:

> Parliament is summoned to meet for the despatch of business so early as the 13th of next month, when they will be obliged to open at least a part of their designs, and we shall be able to judge with more certainty what we have to expect. However it terminates, it is certain the spirited conduct of Lord North has given him a great reputation, and tends strongly to secure him in his present situation; indeed, everything at this moment seems to promise permanency to the present Administration.[48]

Johnson's cheerful optimism was not entirely shared by North. On the day Parliament met his wife wrote to Guilford that 'Ld North has had a head cold and been a little low-spirited with the thought of the approaching

Parliament, but his cold is much better, and I dare say his spirits will soon mend . . . '[49] North had a considerable capacity for meeting trouble half-way and for worrying about problems that might never arise, but once he was in the thick of things on his feet in the House of Commons his courage, good humour and panache seldom deserted him. This was true of his part in the various debates on the Falkland Islands crisis that took place over the next three months.

The Opposition attacked the administration for its apparently faint-hearted response to the insult offered by Spain and for not defending British rights more vigorously. North advised caution, pointing out (possibly tongue-in-cheek) that the Governor of Buenos Aires may have acted on his own initiative and without proper authority: 'That the King of Spain gave any directions for the seizure there is no evidence; and unless we had such evidence, it would have been highly improper to lay it at the door of his Catholic majesty, when the only overt act was that of the Governor'.[50] North may not have believed that but (unlike Weymouth) he considered it necessary to provide Charles III in Madrid with an escape route that did not involve loss of face. North's strategy was essentially to downgrade the importance of the whole affair.

In his quest for peace North was quite prepared to use France, the traditional enemy of Britain, as an intermediary. He rightly calculated that Spain was unlikely to go to war without French support, so much of his diplomatic activity was directed at Versailles. Fortunately for the British government Louis XV also had no appetite for war, and just before Christmas he privately made this clear to the Spanish King. At the same time he dismissed Choiseul.[51] Meanwhile North, without consulting his fellow Ministers, had asked the French Ambassador in London to convey to Madrid a secret verbal assurance that if Spain withdrew its garrison from the Falkland Islands Britain would, after a decent interval, do the same, an offer subsequently endorsed by the Cabinet.[52] It allowed Charles III to order his Governor in Buenos Aires to evacuate the islands without admitting defeat; three years later the British followed suit.

After the Napoleonic wars the islands were reoccupied by the newly independent Argentine Republic. In autumn 1832, after a series of squabbles over fishing rights, Lord Palmerston sent two warships to reassume possession of the Falklands, and on 3 January 1833 the British flag was raised at Port Louis and the Argentine officials were expelled.

When the settlement North had reached was debated in Parliament on the 4 February 1771 and again on the 13th, the Opposition tried to make political capital from his failure to have secured unqualified recognition of British claims by Spain. There were mutterings about a 'Secret Article' in the terms of the settlement which had not been disclosed to the House, a charge which was perfectly true but which North ignored.[53] He was also closely questioned on the role France had played in reaching the agreement with Spain but refused to give a direct answer. Colonel Isaac Barré told him: 'It is the public opinion of all Europe, that the whole transaction is by France alone. There is not a man, not a woman, upon the continent, who does not know it. It has been contrived for the disgrace of this country'. North countered by demanding: 'Let him bring forward his women; let him bring forward his men; let us have something besides common rumour . . . '[54] North's replies were not entirely convincing but he brazened it out and, as he had negotiated a settlement that left no one dishonoured and avoided the risk of a major war, there was not too much uneasiness over how it had been achieved. On the division of the 4 February his majority was 116 and on the 13th in a more crowded House it was 118. North had ended his first year in office with a solid achievement to his credit and his reputation still rising.

Before leaving the Falkland Islands affair there is an odd story to report which may shed some light on North's character and habits. The French ambassador in London, M. Francés, attributed the successful outcome of the negotiations not only to skilled diplomacy but also to the effects of a convivial dinner-party. In a confidential letter to Choiseul, dated 22 December 1770, he explained that he had, by request, called on North at nine o'clock in the evening and found him and his Cabinet colleagues very much the worse for drink. Francés nevertheless engaged the First Lord in discussion on the crisis, and discovered to his surprise that North when drunk expressed precisely the same views in precisely the same way as he had previously done when sober. Francés concluded that he must be repeating opinions already well-entrenched in his mind, and was therefore saying what he really believed. When this evidence of North's sincerity was passed to Paris it persuaded the French government to take his peace proposals seriously, which led to the satisfactory resolution of the crisis.[55]

The story sounds implausible. Heavy drinking among British statesmen was not unknown, but it is hard to believe North would organise a meeting with the key foreign representative in the Falklands negotiations and then allow himself to drink too much beforehand. Either Francés exaggerated the degree of inebriation, or he had misunderstood the nature of the invitation and found himself involved in a social occasion in which the conversation by chance turned to current affairs. That interpretation still leaves open the possibility that North had drunk too much, though managing to retain a capacity for lucid expression. His corpulency and comparatively early death, probably from dropsy,[56] suggest overindulgence

– a note that appeared in the *Morning Herald* in August 1782 listing the amusements of various Men of Fashion proposed the Festive Board for North. (His pious step-brother Dartmouth was said to prefer the pleasures of The Tabernacle.)[57] Nevertheless, no other contemporary memoirs or letters refer to a lack of sobriety on his part; food rather than drink seems to have been his weakness.

The Whitehall Pump.

Westminster Mag. Ap. 1774

Lord North pumps water on Britannia and America, the latter in the form of a Red Indian. The figures on the left include Lord Apsley (the Lord Chancellor) and Lord Sandwich; the pump bears the head of George III. *Westminster Magazine*, April 1774. *(British Museum)*

8

The East India Company

In 1769 Lord North thought he had reached a reasonable compromise with the East India Company, despite his belief that the Crown had 'the clear right and claim' to any territories it acquired. He had, however, only addressed the immediate financial problems, and his hopes of evolutionary, self-induced reform within the company were optimistic.[1] A year earlier the *Annual Register* had commented: 'The affairs of the East India Company were now become as much an object of annual consideration as the raising of supplies'.[2]

For more than 150 years the East India Company had been a relatively straightforward trading enterprise, competing for markets and goods with other European companies, and living off the profits it made from these commercial activities. To protect its operations armed forces and fortified centres were necessary, but they existed primarily to serve the Company's role as a trader, not for territorial expansion. During and after the Seven Years War this situation changed radically. At the battle of Buxar, in October 1764, the Company defeated a hostile army led by an alliance of Indian rulers and won effective control of Bengal. A year later it secured from the Mughal Emperor in Delhi the right to collect the tax revenues in Bengal, Bihar and Orissa in return for an annual tribute.[3] Many of these new responsibilities were necessarily exercised through local Indian officials,[4] but almost accidentally the Company in India had evolved into the imperial agent for the British Crown. Its trading activities were now supplemented by its functions as administrator and tax collector; the object became to maximise local surplus revenue for transmission to London. Partly through economic decline in Bengal in the 1760s, and partly through higher than expected collection costs, these territorial revenues were never as great as forecast, but in the peak year of 1766–67 they amounted to more than £2,500,000.[5]

The Company's independence was nevertheless circumscribed by political realities. It relied on the British fleet for naval protection against the French, it needed government financial support from time to time, and in the final analysis its prosperity was dependent on the monopoly enshrined in its charter which required periodic renewal by Parliament.[6] Looked at the other way round, no British administration could ignore the health of an organisation that effectively ruled a large part of what was then the British Empire. In a debate on the situation in America in the Commons, on 5 December 1768, North expressed himself 'unwilling to be thought not desirous of bringing to a settlement those two great national questions, the state of the East India Company, and the affairs of America'. He acknowledged that 'in point of revenue and navigation, it [the East] cannot be put into competition with America', but by coupling the two questions together he was reflecting the importance already attached to the management of the East India Company and its territories.[7]

The Company's managing body was the twenty-four strong Court of Directors, but ultimate authority lay with the Court of Proprietors, or General Court, which elected them annually. There were about 2000 proprietors, each of whom held a qualifying minimum of £500 East India stock,[8] and they included a number of peers and Members of Parliament. Throughout much of North's early years as a Minister the Company suffered from bitter internal feuding, but effective intervention by the government was hindered by the presence of directors and stockholders both within its own ranks and on the Opposition benches.[9] Despite their differences on other matters, most stockholders agreed that the occasional necessity for financial help from the government did not justify its interference in the operations of the Company.

Apart from receiving dividends on the stock there were two ways money could be made from the East India Company. The most direct was to be sent to India as a servant of the Company. Private trading was condoned (a practice the Company found it hard to control), and many men who left home poor returned a few years later wealthy 'nabobs'.[10] This had the unintended effect of drawing the attention of the British public to the dubious aspects of Company rule in India,[11] but naturally those who gained from such misrule (together with their relations) had no wish to see reform introduced under pressure from a British administration. The other and more indirect way in which fortunes were made (and lost) was by speculation in the Company's stock, particularly following the tax collecting privileges arranged with the Mughal Emperor, and reorganisation of the Company's local administration by Robert Clive after his return to Bengal in 1765. On the receipt of his first optimistic despatches in April 1766, in

Fig. 1 Lord North by Pompeo Batoni, 1752/53. This portrait was painted in Rome while North was on the Grand Tour with his step-brother Lord Dartmouth. *(Earl of Guilford and National Portrait Gallery; photograph Courtauld Institute of Art)*

Fig. 2 Francis North, seventh Lord North and first Earl of Guilford, father of the Prime Minister, by Sir Thomas Gainsborough. *(Earl of Guilford; photograph Courtauld Institute of Art)*

Fig. 3 Lady Lucy Montagu, the Prime Minister's mother, by Alan Ramsay. She married his father, Lord Guilford, in 1728, and died six years later. She was the daughter of George Montagu, first Earl of Halifax. *(Arthur Ackermann and Peter Johnson Limited)*

Fig. 4 Elizabeth, Viscountess Lewisham, attributed to Elizabeth Bardwell. She married the Prime Minister's father as his second wife in 1736. Her son by her previous marriage became the second Earl of Dartmouth, North's American Secretary from 1772 to 1775. *(Earl of Guilford)*

Fig. 5 Katherine, Countess of Rockingham, by J. Vanderbank. She married the Prime Minister's father as his third wife in 1751, adding considerably to the wealth of the Norths. *(Earl of Guilford; photograph Courtauld Institute of Art)*

Fig. 6 Lord North by Sir Joshua Reynolds, probably painted at the time of his marriage. *(Bruce C. Bossom; photograph Courtauld Institute of Art)*

Fig. 7 Anne Speke, the Prime Minister's wife, by Alan Ramsay. She married Lord North in 1756, when she was sixteen. This portrait was probably painted a year or two later. *(Earl of Guilford; photograph Courtauld Institute of Art)*

Fig. 8 William Legge, Viscount Lewisham (later Earl of Dartmouth), his half-brother Brownlow North (later Bishop of Winchester) and his step-brother Frederick North (later Prime Minister), by Enoch Seeman. *(Private collection; photograph Courtauld Institute of Art)*

Fig. 9 Brownlow North, the Prime Minister's half-brother, by H. Howard. He was successively Bishop of Lichfield, Worcester, and Winchester. He is shown in the robes of Prelate of the Order of the Garter. *(Earl of Guilford; photograph Courtauld Institute of Art)*

Fig. 10 Wroxton Abbey (Oxfordshire), the principal North family seat from the end of the seventeenth century, from a drawing by S. H. Grimm. It was held on lease from Trinity College, Oxford. Under the terms of the property's transfer to the college by Sir William Pope after the Dissolution of the Monasteries, the right of life tenancy was retained in favour of his heirs, one of whom, Lady Francis Pope, married the first Lord Guilford, the Prime Minister's great grandfather. (*Bodleian Library, Gough Maps 26, fol. 69*)

Fig. 11 Dillington House (Somerset), inherited by Anne Speke three years before her marriage to Lord North in 1756. It became a regular holiday home for North and his family; the illustration shows the house as it was in their time. (From *The Mynster of the Isle* by James Street, Taunton, 1904)

Fig. 12 Waldershare Park (Kent), the south front in the late eighteenth century, from a print by J. Barlow. The property came into the North family through the marriage of the Prime Minister's father to the Countess of Rockingham.

Fig. 13 Bushy Park (Middlesex), The Ranger's House. In 1771, on the death of Lord North's uncle, Lord Halifax, the Rangership of Bushy Park, a sinecure office in the gift of the crown, became vacant. George III offered it to North, who asked that it should be put in the name of his wife. It became his regular country retreat, especially at weekends or when business compelled him to remain near London. *(Borough of Richmond upon Thames, Local Studies)*

Fig. 14 Thomas Pelham-Holles, first Duke of Newcastle, by William Hoare. As Secretary of State and then, more briefly, as First Lord, he held almost unbroken office for thirty-eight years. *(The House of Commons; photograph National Portrait Gallery)*

Fig. 15 King George III by Sir William Beechey. *(National Portrait Gallery)*

Fig. 16 Lord George Germain, from a mezzotint after Sir Joshua Reynolds. He was North's American Secretary from 1775 to 1782. *(National Portrait Gallery)*

Fig. 17 William Legge, second Earl of Dartmouth, by Sir Thomas Gainsborough. Dartmouth served in his step-brother's Cabinet as American Secretary from 1772 to 1775, and subsequently as Privy Seal. *(Earl of Dartmouth)*

Fig. 18 John Montagu, fourth Earl of Sandwich, from a mezzotint after Johann Zoffany. He served three terms as First Lord of the Admiralty, the last time in North's administration from 1771 to 1782. (*Board of Trustees, Victoria and Albert Museum*)

Fig. 19 Charles James Fox after Sir Joshua Reynolds. Fox and North briefly held joint office in the notorious coalition of 1783. (*Duke of Grafton; photograph Courtauld Institute of Art*)

Fig. 20 The House of Commons, addressed by William Pitt the Younger, 1793, by Carl Anton Hickel. (*National Portrait Gallery*)

Fig. 21 Lord North, in the robes of Chancellor of the University of Oxford, by Nathaniel Dance. *(Earl of Guilford; photograph Courtauld Institute of Art)*

which he forecast revenues that 'cannot fall far short of four millions per annum',[12] the stock stood at 164; in the course of the next year it rose at one point to 273. The stock gained a new and unsavoury reputation and, according to one historian of the Company, 'there can be no doubt that from 1776 onwards it became the chief subject of speculative dealings in the world markets'.[13] Speculators dislike regulation and favour rising dividends, so the directors were under pressure to resist government interference and to maintain or increase dividends even when profits failed to justify such action.

In his first eighteen months as First Lord North made no attempt to bring the affairs of the East India Company before Parliament, despite increasing disquiet about its position. He clearly hoped it was a problem that if ignored would go away. By the middle of 1771, however, the Company's financial position was going rapidly downhill. Its military expenditure had increased, for fear of French attack or local insurrection, and revenue was reduced by trade depression and famine in Bengal.[14] Despite these unfavourable circumstances the Company raised its dividend for 1771 to $12\frac{1}{2}$ per cent, the maximum allowed under the 1769 agreement. The following year a serious credit crisis developed in the City of London and several important banking houses closed their doors. As a result the Company's cash flow from its twice-yearly London auctions dropped, while pressure for settlement from its creditors increased. Due to the financial crisis the Bank of England's ability to help the Company with its liquidity problems was curtailed.[15]

Government interest in the affairs of the Company was finally forced on a reluctant North, not only by the possibility of its financial collapse but also by public opinion. Stories of gross misrule in India were circulating widely, leading Horace Walpole later to comment:

> The oppressions of India, and even of the English settled there, under the rapine and cruelties of the servants of the Company had now reached England, and created clamour here. Some books had been published, particularly by one Bolts and Mr Dow, the first a man of bad character, the latter of a very fair one, which carried the accusations home to Lord Clive; and the former represented him as a monster in assassination, usurpation and extortion, with heavy accusations of his monopolising in open defiance of the orders of the Company – the latter charge being confirmed by letters under his own hand. To such monopolies were imputed the late famine in Bengal and the loss of three millions of its inhabitants. A tithe of these crimes was sufficient to inspire horror.[16]

By October 1771 North realised not only that India required his attention but also that he needed knowledgeable advice and support in his dealings with the Company; he therefore sought the services of Lord Clive.

Clive was in many ways fitted to act as North's mentor, but his usefulness
was limited by his reputation for corruption and the visible evidence of the
vast wealth he had accumulated in India. At the end of the month North
approached him through Alexander Wedderburn, the Solicitor General, a
political associate of Clive's.[17] He rather discouragingly told Clive: 'From
the tenor of the conversation [with North] it appeared to me that no idea
had as yet presented itself that could be the foundation of a plan'. At the
same time Wedderburn forwarded North's own letter to Clive, which
read:

> The Solicitor General having inform'd me, that it is his intention to write to your
> Lordship by this post, I have desired him to enclose this note to you; The very
> intricate & dangerous situation of our possessions in India will, probably, make it
> necessary to bring them under the consideration of Parliament during the next
> Session. The Question is in itself most arduous, & I confess, that I stand in need of
> much information on this subject; your Lordship, from your extensive knowledge
> of it, can be of great service to me, & I have no doubt, but that your public spirit
> will incline you to give me every assistance in your power; I shall be much obliged
> to you, if you will do me the honour of calling upon me, when you return from
> Bath; your time shall be mine ... [18]

North and Clive evidently met a few times to discuss India but no plan of
action was developed.

Despite North's apparent belief that East Indian affairs must be brought
before Parliament, the King's speech at the opening of the session on 21
January 1772 included only an oblique reference to the subject: 'The
concerns of this country are so various and extensive as to require the most
vigilant and active attention, and some of them, as well as from remoteness
of place as from other circumstances, are so peculiarly liable to abuse and
exposed to danger, that the interposition of the legislature for their
protection may become necessary'.[19] In seconding the Address of Thanks
the Hon. Frederick Vane, a government supporter, made a direct attack on
'the malversation of the East India Company's servants' and suggested that
'at present the Company had not that power over their servants, to compel
their orders to be obeyed'.[20] He was, however, the only speaker to raise the
subject and he was simply asking for the Company authorities to be given
greater powers of control over their employees, not for that control to be
vested in the British government.

While Lord North hesitated, the Company decided it must make a show
of putting its own house in order and started to draft a reform measure,
known as the Judicature Bill, to lay before Parliament. Its provisions were
moderate but sound, and included an overhaul of the judicial system in
Bengal and the establishment of greater powers of control over the

Company's servants.[21] Unfortunately internal arguments delayed the drafting process and it was not until 30 March 1772 that Laurence Sullivan, one of the Company's most influential directors, moved for leave to bring in the Bill.[22] Leave was granted but by then opinion was moving strongly against India House. The Bill was read a first time on 13 April but, in a Commons speech on the same day, General John Burgoyne made a vehement attack on the Company in which he said both the interest and the honour of the nation were at risk: 'To the interest of it, inasmuch as the influx of wealth from India makes a vital part of our existence; to the honour of it, inasmuch as the most atrocious abuses that ever stained the name of civil government called for redress'.[23]

Burgoyne's demand for the appointment of a Select Committee to examine the running of the Company received widespread support, including that of the Prime Minister. This was surprising as North had appeared to favour the Company's attempt to reform itself, and he must have realised that there would be little point in proceeding with the Judicature Bill if there was a committee examining precisely the abuses it was intended to remedy. He had not spoken in either of the debates directly concerning the Bill, but he now made a brief intervention on Burgoyne's motion:

> He was glad to find the affairs of the East Indies taken up by a gentleman unconnected with administration; that a Bill had been brought in by one of the directors, which he thought was much more proper, than if brought in by administration; but that he certainly should be for making the enquiry by a select committee, and should have been for it the first day of the session, as he always thought it the most proper mode.[24]

The Select Committee was appointed. Although the Judicature Bill received its second reading on 4 May, interest in it waned and it was allowed to lapse with the end of the session in June.[25] It is not certain the Bill would ever have passed the House, at least in a form likely to achieve significant change in India, but the first serious attempt at Company inspired reform would have had a good deal more chance if it had received consistent support from North. He presumably went off on his summer holidays believing the appointment of the committee had relieved him of the worst of his worries over India. In reality the crisis was still to come.

During the summer the Company's financial situation deteriorated, and on 7 August it informed the Treasury that it might be compelled to default on its obligations by the end of September. North was relaxing at Bushy Park, where he remained for most of the month, but it is clear from his surviving letters that he kept in close touch with government business.[26] He paid at least one visit to London,[27] and it was during his stay at Bushy that he made one of his most important ministerial appointments by persuading his step-brother Dartmouth to accept the post of Secretary for the Colonies, made vacant by the resignation of Lord Hillsborough, and since 1768 upgraded to the status of Secretary of State.[28] It is therefore likely that North was kept well-informed of the developments at India House. Burke later wrote that 'while Lord N. was in the Country his correspondence with the Company was amicable, and in the style of mutual accommodation'.[29] There is, however, no evidence that at this stage he tried positive intervention, nor did he feel it necessary to remain close to London for the whole summer.

On 24 August North apologised to the King for not waiting upon him at St James's, explaining that he was 'just stepping into the post chaise' to join his family in Oxfordshire.[30] By 18 September, when he wrote to Wedderburn concerning the appointment of Lord Clive to the Lord Lieutenancy of Shropshire, he was at Dillington in Somerset.[31] In that letter North said he would be back in town 'in a little more than a fortnight's time', so when he returned (via Wroxton) on 2 October he was not hurrying back in response to a fresh crisis but following his prearranged plan.[32]

On 23 September the Company's Court of Proprietors had been told by the directors that a decision on a dividend would have to be postponed, pending negotiations for financial assistance from the government.[33] On his return to London, North's attitude seems to have hardened and within three days he had reluctantly decided that the matter must be brought before Parliament. On 5 October he wrote to his father: 'We have other political matters under consideration which are very unpleasant & I fear that we must be obliged to call the Parliament together before Christmas. In short, there are vexations enough in my office to make me melancholy amidst all the honours I receive'.[34]

Negotiations between the Treasury and India House proceeded slowly while North tried to formulate a policy that was acceptable both to the diehards in the Company and to the radical elements in the Commons. At some point after his return to London he received a visit from Clive,[35] who subsequently wrote to Henry Strachey (who had been his private secretary in India): 'Lord North, when I saw him, seemed industriously to avoid entering upon the subject of Indian affairs; and I do verily believe, from sheer indolence of temper, he wishes to leave everything to Providence and the Directors; and that he means nothing more by the meeting of Parliament, than to enable the Company to find money to discharge the demands that are at present made upon them'.[36]

It is possible Clive misinterpreted North's reluctance to discuss Indian affairs, and that it was fear of provoking premature opposition that made him reticent rather than indolence or indecision. He was at last trying to square up to the problem. By the time Parliament met on 26 November his administration had evolved a reasonably coherent policy based on two considerations. First, the British government had no wish to take over the responsibility of ruling the Company's territories, particularly in the face of strong opposition from India House. Secondly, no financial help would be offered to the Company until it had put in hand a radical overhaul of its organisation and of the way it exercised its powers in India. This resolute line received firm encouragement from the King, who never completely trusted his First Minister's courage. In a letter to North the day before Parliament opened he referred to some alterations to his forthcoming speech, and then told him:

> Though the Speech is softened I have no objection to that as I know I may depend on Your remaining stiff in treating with the Company; till now the conduct You have shown towards the Directors is much to Your honour, but any wavering now would be disgraceful to you and destructive to the Public, but I know You too well to harbour such a thought.[37]

The King's Speech referred explicitly to the difficulties confronting the East India Company,[38] and both the mover and seconder of the Address of Thanks in the Commons were forthrightly critical of its conduct. The seconder, Dr William Burrell, even posed the radical question of whether a charter 'is so sacred a thing',[39] indirectly an attack on property rights which North for one was reluctant to contemplate. His own proposals, however, were also fairly bold. He told the House he wished to establish another committee of enquiry but (in the words of Walpole) 'he meant it should be a Committee of Secrecy, as there were secrets in their books not fit to be made public'.[40] North does not appear to have implied that the Company had anything disreputable to hide but that the committee should not be impeded in its work by the normal requirements of commercial confidentiality. It would have access to 'the Company's affairs in general, as well as their secret and confidential transactions', and the membership would be kept small to minimise the dangers of leaks.[41] North also ensured the committee had an efficient secretariat. General Burgoyne unsurprisingly objected to the establishment of the new body, as he considered it was a slur on the competence of the Select Committee of which he was chairman, but North brushed these complaints aside. He was perfectly agreeable that Burgoyne's committee should continue to probe past misdeeds, but the Committee of Secrecy was intended to shape the future.

His proposal was accepted without a division.[42] As the time for the recess approached, Edward Gibbon wrote to his friend John Holroyd: 'The Parliament is gone to sleep to wake again after Christmas safely folded in Lord North's arms'.[43]

Despite this early success, opposition to any form of regulation of the Company by government hardened, particularly among the proprietors. The directors recognised the advisability of cooperation with North and his Committee of Secrecy but they were powerless to act without the approval of the General Court. Much of the antagonism stemmed from unenlight-ened self-interest, and the belief that more regulation would mean fewer opportunities for making money, but there was also a more principled strand in the objections. In October 1772 the Marquis of Rockingham had written to Edmund Burke: 'All thinking men must already acknowledge that the influence of the Crown and the means of corruption are become very dangerous to the Constitution and yet the enormous addition of power which Government are aiming at by subjecting the East India Company to their control does not strike and alarm as much as it ought'.[44]

Those were sentiments North would have respected and may well even have shared. He had no wish to see the power of the state increased at the expense of private interests, which would account for the hesitancy with which he approached the East India crisis. As late as April 1773, at a time when he had clearly resolved to impose firm conditions on any government assistance to the Company, there is still an element of ambivalence in his thinking. In a debate in the Commons he set out his views on the Company's Indian territories:

> I think, Sir, they ought to be left for ever in the Company; I am fully and clearly of that opinion; if not from right, at least from policy. But, Sir, this depends upon their conduct; if they, in future, govern them no better than they have hitherto done, my opinion will be very different. Nay, I shall then think it advisable, notwithstanding the terms mentioned in the motion, to reject their having the possession at the end of two, three, or four years.[45]

The Committee of Secrecy got to work with speed and produced their first report on 7 December 1772 followed by another in February, both with proposals for the tighter regulation of Company affairs. Simultaneously the directors at India House were pressing the administration for a loan of £1,500,000 at 4 per cent and for duty concessions on tea exports. North's written response was firm:

> As it is very improbable that Parliament will think fit to direct that an application be made for the relief of the Company without making at the same time some

effectual provision for preventing the repetition of the same errors and abuses as have brought the Company into their present difficulties, and as it seems equally natural to expect that some further propositions should be made to Parliament by the Company respecting the possession of the territorial acquisitions and revenues in India, the agreement concerning which will expire in 1774, Lord North recommends it to the consideration of the directors whether it can answer any good purpose to proceed in settling a plan of the kind proposed by them to be offered to Parliament unless they do also prepare such other propositions to be laid at the same time before Parliament as they shall judge best calculated for securing in future the better Government of the Company's affairs as well at home as in India.[46]

Throughout the discussions on the future of the Company North was given advice and support by George III. Immediately after opening Parliament on 26 November 1772 the King wrote to him urging the preparation of a plan against the probability that India House would fail to come forward with an acceptable plan of their own, commenting 'if you form it Yourself it will be just, and there are men of ability in Parliament will certainly support it well in the House'.[47] Only ten days later the King returned to the subject with a further admonition to his First Minister: 'I trust that if you proceed with the same assiduity and temper this business though arduous will turn out to the security of the Company, the Advantage of the Public, and Your personal honour'.[48] The King continued to take a close interest in the affairs of the Company. In March 1773 he wrote to North about 'the ill conduct of its Directors and rapine of its servants';[49] two months later he commended him on achieving the introduction of the East India Bill without a division;[50] and on 18 May gave him some brisk encouragement: 'I was in hopes the East India Bill would have been read the first time this day, the longer it is delayed the more people will be trying to move vexatious questions to postpone the business; but I trust Your candour will not let them carry this too far; and where intentions are so just as Yours, with Spirit and perseverance the end will be obtained'.[51]

It might be unfair to North to suggest that his determination to push Company reform through Parliament might have been less resolute without the support of George III, but he must have found it very welcome. Despite considerable opposition from both India House and parliamentary faction he succeeded in seeing three separate East India Bills onto the statute book. The first, the Tea Act, abolished the export duty on tea, and gave the East India Company a monopoly in the trade with the American colonies. The Company had built up large stocks of unsold tea in London which it needed to liquidate; undercutting the tea smuggled into America from Holland was one way of doing it. Unfortunately, North flatly refused to cancel the Townshend import duty at the same time, partly on principle and partly because he believed the expected increase in trade would lead to greater colonial tax revenues.[52] This misjudgement led indirectly to the Boston Tea Party the following December, but the passing of the Tea Act, a measure so evidently advantageous to the Company, helped North to force his other proposals through Parliament.

The terms of the Loan Act were bitterly opposed by the proprietors but North was firm. In a debate on 25 May he said he would be sorry if the resolutions were 'understood as the least in the style of menace to the Company' but his speech left India House in no doubt that the settlement of outstanding debts must be the first charge on profits, and that unless these conditions were accepted harsher terms would be imposed.[53] North subsequently retreated a little on government claims to a share in certain Company revenues but, in its essentials, the Loan Act finally passed on 29 June 1773 was the one he wanted.

The Tea Act and the Loan Act were primarily devised to alleviate the present troubles of the East India Company but the third measure, the Regulating Act, looked to the future. The aim was to improve the quality and probity of Company administration without destroying its independence. Senior officials in India would still be Company servants, but nominees for the newly established Governor-Generalship and his advisory Council would require Crown or parliamentary approval, and appointments to the Supreme Court in Bengal would be vested in the Crown.[54] Rules were also introduced regulating private trading by Company servants in India. At home the voting qualification for proprietors was raised from a stockholding of £500 to one of £1000 and directors were to be elected for four years not one. The Bill passed the Commons by 110 votes in a thin House on 10 June, was approved by the Lords after what was described as 'a warm debate' and became law on 21 June.[55]

North's efforts to get his three East India Bills through Parliament were not helped by the deliberations of the Select Committee still actively at work under General Burgoyne. It had produced reports highly critical of various Company servants but the main target was the greatest nabob of them all, Lord Clive. North was in a difficult position. Both he and the King disliked greed and the acquisition of riches by extortion. It is true that the borderline between gifts and bribes was hazy in the eighteenth century but both privately believed that Clive had crossed it. He was, however, a Member of the Commons (an Irish peerage was no disqualification) and in general he was a supporter of North's attempts to remedy the ills of the East India Company. To add to his problems North presided over an administration that was split on whether Clive should or should not be prosecuted.

North's solution to these difficulties was to argue that the accusations against Clive were not a ministerial matter at all and should therefore be left to the private judgement of individual Members. He distanced himself from the proceedings as far as he could and only intervened on a technical point in the debates on 19 and 21 May when Clive was under fierce attack.[56] Walpole said North 'changed his own opinion, at least his conduct, in the course of the debate, had consulted no members previously at a meeting, and with his usual indifference slept during some of the most interesting parts of the discussion'.[57] North's tactics worked. He voted for censure at the end of the debate but was probably relieved that he was on the losing side and that the result exonerated Clive by a majority of sixty.[58] The next day he received a characteristic letter of commendation from George III:

> The Vote carried this Morning is a very strong proof of the propriety of Your leaving to private Gentlemen the punishing the Servants of the East India Company, and by that wise conduct You as an individual have been in a minority that with every Man of honour must do You Credit at the same time that the Minister had nothing to do with it; but I owne I am amazed that private interest could make so many forget what they owe to their country, and come to a resolution that seems to approve Lord Clive's rapine, no one thinks his services greater than I do but that can never be a reason to commend him in what certainly opened the door to the fortunes we see daily made in that Country. I cannot conclude without adding Your conduct has given the greatest satisfaction.[59]

Lord North's efforts to breathe new life into an East India Company still allowed its independence were not entirely successful. The government now recognised its responsibilities in relation to Company activities, but the machinery for exercising them was inadequate. By the late 1770s the Indian territories were in a state of disarray, due in part to personal animosities between Warren Hastings, the new Governor-General, and his Council colleagues, and in part to the hostile activities of Hyder Ali and other Indian rulers.[60] At home the Company's financial position was threatened by trading difficulties arising from the American war. When the charter, together with the Regulatory Act, came up for renewal in 1780 North's attention was wholly focused on America and only minor changes were made to the measures. A further attempt at regulation in 1783 led indirectly to his final departure from office. It was left to the succeeding administration of William Pitt to achieve effective reform.

North's role in the struggle for Company reform was not inglorious. In his book on the Company H. V. Bowen wrote: 'Unlike his predecessors [he] made a very real attempt to come to terms with the responsibilities that went hand in hand with the extension of the Company's commercial and political responsibilities'.[61] Against his own instincts and strong opposition, North managed to introduce an element of government control into the affairs of a private corporation because he became convinced justice and good order demanded it. Wholesale expropriation of the Company was never a political or practical option, but the limited degree of official supervision introduced by North provided the breach through which later reformers advanced. It also provided civil servants with the chance to become familiar with East Indian administration.[62] North emerges from the story as an honourable man, but he might have been surprised if he had known that Laurence Sullivan, the East India director, described him in a letter to Warren Hastings as 'the boldest minister this realm has been blest with since the days of Oliver Cromwell'.[63]

9

The Good Years

By the early summer of 1772 the Falklands crisis had been successfully defused, the problems of the East India Company temporarily deflected on to General Burgoyne's Select Committee, and awkward colonists across the Atlantic seemed little more threatening than rebellious children. In May North wrote a four-page letter to his father which in part read:

> I ought a long while ago to have returned my thanks for your most kind and affectionate letter, and to have repaid your congratulations in kind; but your letter found me in the midst of the distress and agitation of an approaching Budget, and in a state of mind which made me consider my situation and my office with less comfort, if possible, than I do at other times. If I have once in my life been so happy as to be able to serve my King and my country from the accidental situation in which I stood, it must always be my wish to be released from a station which is too great for my abilities before I have entirely forfeited the little reputation I may have gained, and done more mischief to the Public by my want of knowledge, activity and talents, than I did good to it by preventing the whole frame of administration from falling to pieces in a moment of trouble and danger. These reflexions, which are always the uppermost in my thoughts, are certainly more troublesome and uneasy to me in hours of perplexity such as those in which I received your letter. I have since deliver'd of my Budget, and having now more leisure and ease of mind, I cannot employ myself better than in acknowledging the repeated marks of your Lordship's goodness and affection towards me. I most cordially join with your family, relations & friends in rejoicing at the good accounts we receive of your health from Bath, & in wishing you many happy returns of your Birthday, & a long continuance of a life which has always been dedicated to advancement of our happiness.[1]

North's self-confidence was always an uncertain quantity, yet both the tone and the timing of that letter seem odd. He was still under forty, his health had not yet started to deteriorate, and to the world he appeared well on top of his job. Two years later Chatham wrote to Lord Shelburne: 'I have long held one opinion, as to the solidity of Lord North's situation; he serves the Crown more successfully and more sufficiently, upon the whole, than any other man now to be found could do. This tenure seems a pretty good one. Who, by the way, my dear Lord, ever had a better?'[2] The five years leading up to the American war were North's high noon but an undertow of anxiety was often there.

Particularly striking in that letter to his father is North's comment about 'the distress & agitation of an approaching Budget' because foes as well as friends acknowledged both his presentational skills and his underlying grasp of the national finances. By North's time Budget Day had become an important parliamentary occasion.[3] Rigby's praise of his 1769 budget speech has been quoted earlier, and it can be matched by the judgement of Sir Nathaniel Wraxall, who heard North in his last two years as Chancellor: 'In opening the Budget, he was esteemed peculiarly lucid, clear and able. On that Account it constituted a Day of Triumph to his friends and supporters'.[4]

At the Exchequer North pursued one clear and consistent policy, the husbanding of national finances through the reduction of the National Debt. In 1775 he was able to tell the Commons that over the previous twelve years (for eight of which he had been Chancellor) the National Debt had fallen by £10,000,000 (or over 7 per cent) and that the interest burden had been lowered by £470,000 a year.[5] After 1775 this progress was inevitably halted by the financial demands of the American war, but it had not been solely due to the prudent use of occasional budget surpluses; it also owed much to North's intelligent development of annual national lotteries. Originally linked to the issue of new government bonds as an attractive if speculative bait for potential purchasers, all the proceeds from the lottery were returned as prize money and there was no nett gain to the Treasury. In 1769 North introduced his first revenue lottery unconnected with any government loan, and by restricting the prize money made a clear profit of £180,000 and avoided the necessity that year of raising any new taxes. He also employed lotteries to achieve the redemption of existing government stock. In 1772 he wanted to use surplus revenue to redeem £1,300,000 of government debt but, if it was paid off at par of £100 when the current market price was around £87, an unjustified windfall would be given to holders of the stock selected for redemption, leaving himself as Chancellor open to criticism. So he devised a scheme whereby stockholders would be offered only £90 but allowed to buy four lottery tickets at £12 10s. for every £100 of stock surrendered. The lottery made a small profit and the Treasury saved on the costs of redemption. After 1775 lotteries reverted to their original purpose of attracting applicants for new loans but North's

Loaves and Fishes. North's stilts are supported by Lords Mansfield and Bute; papers hanging from his pocket are inscribed Titles, Pensions. The figure escaping in despair is John Wilkes. *Town and Country Magazine*, 9 May 1772. *(Kenneth Baker)*

use of them during his early years at the Exchequer showed imagination and confidence.

North was also anxious to ensure that applications for lottery tickets, which could usually be passed on at a premium, were handled by the Treasury on an even-handed basis. When his father asked in April 1770 for preferential treatment for a friend he replied: 'My lottery will, I believe, be on a footing which will not permit me to oblige my friends as they & I should desire'.[6] Some two years later Guilford tried again and North considered it expedient to explain in some detail how the system operated:

> More, infinitely more than the whole Lottery was bespoken & agreed for, before I opened the proposition in Parliament. The persons who have the tickets were not in general in the secret for no proposition of this kind is talked of publicly till the Budget is open'd. In the course of the winter many people apply to have a share in such subscription or lottery as may be set on foot in the course of the Session, & bind themselves in some degree to embark, let the conditions be what they will. The greater part of the loan is always distributed amongst the rich men in the City, who have been used to subscribing in times of war, & other public necessities. A small part is given to the subscribers at the West end of town. I am sorry I did not receive your application for Lady Frances earlier, but I do assure her that it has not been usual for the Chancellor of the Exchequer to give notice of an intended lottery to his friends, and that I had not myself in the last lottery, nor have I in the present, a single ticket. Whether I am doomed to the misery of continuing in my office another year I know not, but if I am I will venture to promise that it shall be as little profitable to me as the two last have been. Your Lordshp will be so good as to make my excuses to Lady Frances. If I could oblige her then I would, but it is too late. She will know, however, that she fares as well as I do myself.[7]

Apart from the intelligent adaption of lotteries North had little scope for other measures of fiscal enterprise. In the course of the first seven decades of the eighteenth century the proportion of total revenue raised by direct taxation fell steadily; by North's time as Chancellor it produced less than one fifth of the whole.[8] The land tax was the main form of direct taxation, normally levied at three shillings in the pound with occasional increases to four shillings in time of war, but the assessments of property values on which it was based were out of date and a suggestion for a realistic reassessment mooted during the American war was killed by parliamentary opposition.[9] Income tax was considered too radical until the exigencies of the war against Napoleon compelled its acceptance. North had to depend on indirect taxes, chiefly customs and excise duties, for the greater part of his revenues, and as he acknowledged 'the burden must [therefore] lie on the bulk of the people'. He was not insensitive to the claims of social justice, arguing that 'luxuries ought to be taxed ... because the first weight ought to fall upon the rich and opulent',[10] but in reality his scope for innovation was restricted and he could only raise the sums he needed by taxing commodities bought by rich and poor alike.

There was a brief moment when North seemed ready to contemplate a radical proposal for taxing a particular section of the rich. Irish revenues were stagnant and a proposal had gained ground in Dublin that a tax of two shillings in the pound should be levied on the rentals of Ireland's absentee landlords. The plan was not unreasonable as the absentees contributed little or nothing in any other way to the well-being of the impoverished kingdom. Early in 1773 Lord Harcourt, the Lord Lieutenant, wrote to North asking if the Privy Council would sanction such a measure if it was passed by the Irish Parliament. Despite, or perhaps because of, his lack of interest in or understanding of Irish affairs, North assured him that if Dublin approved the proposal it would be accepted in London.[11] He soon found himself in the middle of a major political row. The Marquis of Rockingham orchestrated a campaign among his fellow absentee land-lords and he, the Duke of Devonshire and three other senior peers despatched a letter of protest to North on 16 October which they subse-quently made public.[12] The letter was intemperate, almost hysterical in tone and referred to 'this extraordinary design' which the signatories maintained was 'without parallel in any civilised country'. The heart of their case was that it was grossly improper to discriminate against one section of the landed interest:

> My Lord, we find ourselves comprehended under the Description of those who are to be the Objects of this unprecedented Imposition. We possess considerable Landed Property in both Kingdoms; our ordinary Residence is in England. We have not hitherto considered such Residence as an act of Delinquency, to be punished; or as a Political Evil, to be corrected, by the Penal Operation of a Partial Tax.[13]

These were sentiments that might be expected to appeal to North but his initial reaction was cool. He sent a copy of the letter to Dartmouth describing it as 'very extraordinary and captious' and saying he was calling a Cabinet meeting to consider a reply.[14]

When North's relatively brief reply was sent three days later it main-tained (presumably with the support of his ministerial colleagues) the same objective stance. He explained that the absentee tax was one of a number of measures under consideration for the relief of Irish financial distress but conceded that on behalf of 'His Majesty's Servants' he had written to the Lord Lieutenant: 'That if the Irish Parliament should send over to England such a Plan as should appear to be well calculated to give Effectual Relief to Ireland in its present Distress, Their Opinion would be, that it ought to be carried into Execution, although the Tax upon Absentees should make a Part of it'.[15]

In taking this principled line North had some heavyweight support. Lord Chatham had refused to sign the peers' protest because he believed that 'the Commons of Ireland [were] acting in their proper and peculiar sphere, and exercising their inherent, exclusive right, by raising supplies in the manner they judge best', a view endorsed by Lord Shelburne.[16] North also had the backing of the King, who told him he was 'much pleased with the answer to the Strange letter from the five Noblemen, it is candid and at the same time void of compliments, which their Manifesto could not have deserved'.[17] The opposition grew, however. If passed in Dublin the measure would, under Poynings' Law, require sanction only from the English Privy Council, but when North discovered that many of his regular parliamentary supporters, including a number of the Country Gentlemen, strongly resented the proposal, his resolve faltered.[18] George III was also having second thoughts and their correspondence during November strikes a note of panic as they searched for plausible reasons for backtracking on their earlier sympathy for the measure.[19] North's rather unheroic solution to their dilemma was to persuade Harcourt, the Lord Lieutenant, to lean hard on the Irish Parliament to reject the proposal to ensure it never even reached London.[20] He was successful, though only by the small margin of fourteen votes, and it was five years before North again took much interest in Ireland.

Lord North's failure of nerve over the absentee tax is easy to regret, but in the face of gathering opposition and uncertain support from the King it was probably inevitable. He was a politician to his fingertips and well understood the merits of timely retreat from an exposed position.

There was, however, one area in which his firmness at the Treasury produced permanent benefits. One of the conundrums about North is that he often appears personally disorganised yet well able to see the virtues of efficient and honest administration elsewhere. His dedication to sound national finances made him question the working of much of the Treasury machine.[21] Morale among staff was low, there was no proper career structure, and absence without leave, at least for the more junior clerks, was commonplace.

North's reforms at the Treasury date from his later years in office but it is easier to consider them at this point. In February 1776 the Lords of the Treasury were having trouble filling a vacancy among the four chief clerks because no one wanted to accept promotion to a post that required more work and therefore fewer opportunities for outside earnings. They responded by pensioning off the two clerks who had so far refused advancement and decided that a reorganised team could manage perfectly well without replacing them. Under North's guidance the Board then laid down three principles for governing the future operation of the department. First, each official was to be allocated specific responsibilities, which precluded passing them on to an obliging colleague during unofficial absence. Secondly, all clerks would receive regular training in the execution of their duties. Thirdly and most importantly, merit not seniority would govern rewards and promotion. On this point the Board minute reads:

> And my Lords think fit to declare that in all future regulations of this office and distributions of the business they shall regard the ability, attention, care and diligence of the respective Clerks, and not their seniority, and that in their opinion this rule at all times hereafter ought to be attended to, and pursued, in order the better to conduct and carry on the public business.[22]

In an age when army commissions were bought, and bishoprics handed out to aristocratic mediocrities like North's half-brother Brownlow, that was a radical departure from custom, but from then on it became central to Treasury practice.

Towards the end of North's ministerial career pressure grew for better control across the whole spectrum of government finance. Resentment against corruption and extravagance, coupled with increased taxation due to the American war, led in 1779 to a national movement for 'Economical Reform'. Early in the following year this found expression in Parliament.[23] North was faced with repeated demands for the abolition of sinecures and other wasteful or corrupt forms of expenditure. The Opposition pressed for a parliamentary committee which would, it was hoped, find plenty to condemn in the administration's use of the nation's money. North countered by successfully moving for the appointment of a statutory Commission on the Public Accounts with extensive powers to summon witnesses and examine confidential papers.[24] Crucially his Bill laid down that the six commissioners were to be financial and legal experts, not politicians. Only six reports were produced before North left office, but one historian's comment highlights the importance of the initiative he took: 'The fifteen reports of the Commissioners for examining, taking and stating the public accounts, presented between 1780 and 1786, permanently influenced the character of British government'.[25] If it were not for America, North might have been remembered and honoured chiefly as an able and innovative Chancellor of the Exchequer.

Lord North should also be remembered as the statesman who played an important part in keeping Canada for the British Crown. With the defeat of the French in the Seven Years War and the subsequent Treaty of Paris, the province of Quebec had in 1764 become a British dependency. Unlike the American colonists, whose language, culture and religion were largely shared by the imperial power, the French settlers, comprising 98 per cent of the population of the province, had little in common with their new masters.[26] In particular they were Catholics, which in Britain would have debarred them from any part, no matter how minor, in the service of the state. The best form of government for the new colony had been a matter of debate for British administrations for some years, but no final conclusions had been reached. In August 1773 North and his Ministers decided the time had come to act. They drew on proposals prepared by the government law officers, and also on the advice of the able Governor of Quebec, General Sir Guy Carleton, proceeding with resolution and speed. Whether North consciously associated the need for settlement in Canada with the threat of trouble further south is arguable. The decision to initiate the Canadian legislation was taken before the news of colonial defiance in the form of the Boston Tea Party had reached Lonodon. Moreover, although the coercive legislation consequent on the Tea Party was completed before the final passage of the Quebec Bill, there is little evidence that North or his supporters justified the latter by reference to the situation that had necessitated the former. Nevertheless, over Canada North combined expediency with understanding in a way he never achieved with America.[27]

The Quebec Bill was introduced first in the Lords and did not reach the Commons until 26 May 1774.[28] Apart from extending Canadian territory southwards and westwards, to embrace additional French settlers, the measure had three principal and contentious provisions. First, Roman Catholics were to be allowed full freedom of worship, together with the right to levy tithes to support priests and churches. Secondly, French civil law was to be retained, even though it did not allow for trial by jury. Thirdly, the Bill provided for the government of the province by a nominated council rather than an elected assembly. On the first two provisions North was able to counter opposition by arguing that they were what the vast majority of Canadian settlers wanted, in which he was supported by General Carleton who was called to the House at the committee stage to give evidence.[29] On the question of the nominated council he was on more difficult ground, but he pointed out quite fairly that if the franchise was restricted to English-speaking settlers the French majority would object: 'The bulk of the inhabitants are Roman Catholics, and to subject them to an assembly composed of a few British subjects would be a great hardship'.[30] On the other hand North was able to appeal to the fears of his audience in arguing the case against an assembly elected under a wider suffrage. Having referred to the great imbalance in numbers between French and English settlers, he continued:

> The fair inference, therefore, is that the assembly would be composed of Roman Catholics. Now, I ask, is it safe for this country – for we must consider this country – to put the principal power into the hands of an assembly of Roman Catholic new subjects? I agree with the honourable gentleman, that the Roman Catholics may be honest, able, worthy, sensible men, entertaining very correct notions of political liberty: but I must say, there is something in that religion that makes it not prudent in a Protestant government, to establish an assembly consisting entirely of Roman Catholics.[31]

Largely because of an undercurrent of religious prejudice much more pronounced than his own, North faced strong and sometimes abusive parliamentary opposition to the Quebec Bill, at one point causing him to rise 'in a terrible passion', which was not his normal form.[32] In the nine days of debate it took to get the Bill through the House he is reputed to have spoken seventy-two times and 'undertook the defence of the measure almost single-handed'.[33] Due to the time of year and the wish of Country Members to return to their estates, the debates took place in thin Houses, but every division went strongly in North's favour and the Opposition never mustered more than forty-nine votes. To say that he personally saved Canada for the British Empire would be an exaggeration, but had he not faced down his opponents in those gruelling debates this part of the Empire might have proved far harder to retain.

As well as his successes during his early years as Prime Minister North suffered a minor parliamentary rebuff on 25 February 1774 when Grenville's Election Act, shortly due to lapse, was indefinitely extended by the large majority of 250 to 122.[34] This was against North's wishes and also those of George III, as had been the case when the Act was first passed four years before in the early days of his premiership.[35] For a trial period the Act had removed adjudication on disputed elections from the whole House of Commons to a committee of Members chosen by ballot, a change that reduced the influence of the government on the decision reached. As there had been no general election since the Act was passed it had not been put to very much use, but North was facing one within the next year and would much have preferred the measure to disappear. He made a short, rather feeble speech against it – ending 'jocularly' according to Cobbett, which must have referred to delivery rather than content.[36] Although there is no direct record he seems immediately after his defeat to have offered his resignation to the King, the first of many occasions to follow, but it is hard to believe he expected it to be taken very seriously over such an unimportant issue. The day following the vote Lord Suffolk, Secretary of State for the North, wrote to George III:

> Lord North having walked out to breakfast I had not an opportunity of seeing him as soon as I wished, but have now the happiness to assure yr Majesty that you will find him perfectly disposed to submit himself to your Majesty's pleasure; if he is not thoroughly convinced that he has abilities sufficient to carry on your Majesty's service, he is however satisfied that the event of yesterday does not lay him under an indispensable necessity to distress your Majesty, & throw this Country into confusion.[37]

It has been suggested that North's offer of resignation may have been influenced by his father's decision to vote in the Lords in favour of extending the Act, contrary to the wishes of his son, something Lord Temple told Lady Chatham was 'the greatest piece of fun'.[38] As, however, the main debate in the Lords did not take place until 8 March, ten days after Suffolk's letter,[39] it seems Guilford cannot be held responsible for his son's action on this occasion.

During the first half of the 1770s North's personal life was not yet clouded by the political troubles ahead, and there was time to spend week-ends at Bushy and to pay regular visits to Wroxton and Dillington. Writing from Bushy in August 1772 he told his father: 'Our venison & our melons are excellent, & notwithstanding the heat of the days we find proper times for walking & playing at skittles in our new skittle ground'.[40] His pride and delight in his young family remained strong, as seen from a postscript about his eldest son in a letter to his father in June of the same year: 'I must just add, that I am sure you will be pleased with George's exercise; It was almost entirely his own; the alterations were very few & inconsiderable. I have seldom seen better verse even from the best scholars in the 6th form'.[41]

There was a brief setback to North's happiness in August 1773 when his wife had a miscarriage, but he assured his father she was recovering well,[42] and she later bore him one more child, his adored son Dudley. The end of that year brought great pleasure to the whole family when the yearning of the elderly Lord Guilford for a court appointment was at last satisfied by his installation as Treasurer to the Queen at a salary of £900 a year.[43] North no doubt played a part in securing the position for his father – and it would have been thought not only odd but improperly unfilial if he had not – but he must have been delighted to be able to satisfy the old man's vanity. According to Walpole there was some laughter in London drawing-rooms and a joke went the rounds that the reversion of the post was promised to Lord Bathurst, who at eighty-nine was twenty years older than Guilford.[44] The duties could not have been very demanding as he continued to spend much of his time at Wroxton or Waldershare, but he evidently took his role as courtier seriously. There is a glimpse of him at the age of seventy-one in a letter James Harris, the British Minister in Berlin, received from his mother in England: 'His Majesty's birthday was very brilliant ... Gertrude got a pretty light brown coat for your father, lined with blue and trimmed with a gold net set on blue ribbon. We thought him quite gay, till Lord Guilford came here to carry him to Court. His Lordship was dressed in light green, the cuffs turned up with a flowered silk with silver, pink and green flowers'.[45]

North was able to assist the promotion of another member of his family a year later. On 26 November 1774 a report reached London that Dr James Johnston, the Bishop of Worcester, was dying following a fall while taking the waters in Bath.[46] Without delay the King informed North he proposed to give the see to his half-brother Brownlow. Next day, however, the news from Bath was better so he had to tell him: 'It is rather extraordinary if the Bishop of Worcester should recover, but at least the accident has shewn my desire of doing that which must give you pleasure'.[47] By the 29th Dr Johnston's death was no longer in doubt and the King could write again to North confirming Brownlow's preferment.[48]

Meanwhile North's own honours had continued to accrue. Two years earlier, in the middle of his problems with the East India Company, North had referred in a letter to his father already quoted to 'all the honours I receive'.[49] He particularly had in mind his installation as Chancellor of Oxford University at Downing Street the following day, a ceremony attended by Benjamin Franklin, the agent in London for the colony of Pennsylvania.[50] Although his election by Convocation, the governing body in which all properly qualified masters of art could vote, had been officially unanimous, an attempt had in fact been made to block it at an earlier stage, a reflection of the arguments that had troubled the university for the past four years.[51] In 1768 six members of St Edmund Hall had been expelled for attending unauthorised prayer meetings. In the row that followed reformers demanded the removal of subscription to the Church of England's Thirty-Nine Articles of Religion as a precondition of entry to the university,[52] and on 6 February 1772 a petition in favour of the change was presented to the House of Commons. Unsurprisingly most speakers opposed the petition and it was heavily voted down, but the strength with which North attacked it was uncharacteristic of his normal good-humoured style:

> how can we comply with the desires of a few petitioners, when the whole body of the clergy oppose them, and treat their project not only as mad and frantic, but as irreligious and anti-Christian? The peace of society ought with us to be the first object ... Wake but the many-headed hydra, religious controversy, and she will be more difficult laid asleep than the Hesperian dragon. Not all the opium, not all the mandragora, or perfumes of the east, will lull the monster to rest. Check then such a mad project in the bud, and give not the least countenance to the Petition. Its object seems to be the absolute overthrow of the church.[53]

There was therefore general pleasure among traditionalists at Oxford when, as soon as the existing Chancellor Lord Lichfield died at the end of August, North allowed his name to go forward as a candidate for the vacancy.[54] No doubt the pleasure was enhanced by the knowledge that North could make speeches in Latin without the need of notes,[55] but the main reason for satisfaction came from his standing as a powerful politician who would always defend the connexion of the university with the Church of England, and discourage dangerous experiments. The few reformers failed to agree before the election on a rival candidate, and North took up an office he was to hold until his death twenty years later.

North's loyalty to the Church of England was undeviating; he opposed the mildest suggestion for change. In his speech just quoted he asked: 'How then, as statesmen, can we, with any degree of prudence, make innovations in a religious institution, which has stood the test since the Revolution?'[56] It is, however, extremely difficult to judge the extent to which the religion he professed had any effect on his personal philosophy or his behaviour. In all the hundreds of his letters to his father that have survived the only references to God come in such expressions as: 'Lady North is recovering, thank God', and there is never a hint of an un-completed conversation on spiritual matters. It is true, of course, that apart from occasional exceptions like Dartmouth, Newcastle or the mature Grafton, eighteenth-century noblemen took their religion for granted, and did not usually allow it greatly to influence or inform their lives, but North's faith, though unarticulated, may have been more than superficial. Towards the end of his life, when he was unwell and going blind, his wife had no doubt of the support it gave him:

> and tho' his eyes are not better he is now quite compos'd and resigned to the Will of God, who if he should think fit to deprive him of the Blessing of sight, he trusts will at the same time give him strength of mind to bear that misfortune with proper Fortitude and Resignation.[57]

During these early years in office personal financial affairs continued to worry North (there is a reference in a letter to his father in September 1773 'to the trouble you have had about my money),[58] but the predominant impression is of man for whom the anxieties of position and office could usually be relieved by the satisfactions of private life. As he entered the sixth year of his premiership in 1775, a year which marked a turning-point for both the ministry and his reputation, North does not seem a very different man from the one who became First Lord half a decade earlier. Despite his often debilitating self-doubt, he had already survived longer than most other eighteenth-century Prime Ministers and had several achievements to his credit. Thereafter the picture starts to darken, but the biographer of North faces a difficulty. After 1774 the stream of letters to Guilford slows down, and North's unofficial voice is therefore heard less often. There is no reason at all to think this betokened any lessening in North's love for his father. The simplest explanation is probably the best: with the American war on his hands North was often too busy or too tired to take up his pen to the man he had treated as has confidant ever since he had grown up.

10

The Thirteen Colonies

In his *History of England,* first published seventy years ago, G. M. Trevelyan looked back on the American struggle for independence with wistful regret that such bloodshed should ever have happened: 'A way out could have been found by men of good will summoned to a round-table conference ... '[1] He went on to explain why such retrospective optimism was misplaced, but the mostly peaceful dissolution of the remaining British Empire in the present century lends point to his sense of an opportunity lost. There were considerable reserves of mutual good will between the American colonies and the mother country, but in the end they proved insufficient. What went wrong? The question is important not only for its own sake, but also because no assessment of Lord North's role in the loss of America can properly be made in isolation from the historical and psychological background to the whole story.

North America, particularly its eastern seaboard, first attracted organised English interest during the second half of the sixteenth century. In 1578 Queen Elizabeth I granted a charter to Sir Humphrey Gilbert, authorising him to set up a trading colony in any part of North America not already inhabited. He appears to have been the first English adventurer who envisaged America as a land suitable for permanent communities, not simply as a base for privateering or a staging point on the route to Asia.[2]. His attempt to found a settlement on Newfoundland was unsuccessful, and he was lost when his ship sank on the return journey; nevertheless, the charter granted him by the Queen had lasting results. Among its provisions it laid down that any laws enacted in the territories acquired should as closely as possible resemble those of England, and that the colonists were to enjoy the same privileges 'as if they had been abiding and born within this our Realm of England'.[3] This principle was followed in subsequent charters, providing a shared inheritance that strengthened the sense of affinity between the new settlements and their homeland, but also encouraging future generations of Americans to resist attempts at their exploitation.

The first successful attempt at settlement by the English in North America was initiated by the chartered London Company in 1607, at Jamestown on the James river, forty miles upstream from Chesapeake Bay. Despite great hardships, an appalling death rate from disease and bloody conflict with neighbouring Indians the settlement survived and, as newcomers started to establish themselves further inland, the colony of Virginia was born. Nevertheless, by 1618 it only numbered some 600 people, a figure that had not reached 900 by 1620.[4] In 1619 a representative assembly met for the first time, and after 1624 the Governor and Council were appointed by the Crown, making Virginia the first of the so-called Royal Colonies in America.[5] The impetus behind the new colony was primarily commercial, the desire on the part of both the promoters in London and the adventurers who crossed the Atlantic to find gold and to make money, an aim some achieved in due course, but through the cultivation of tobacco. No doubt many of the immigrants had additional reasons for embarking on a new life, but at this stage gain was the principal spur.

The hope of earning a living, if not always a fortune, was (and remained) an important attraction for aspiring colonists, but a parallel stimulus was the wish to escape religious intolerance under the first two Stuarts. In 1608 a small group of Puritan farmers, artisans and working folk, mostly from East Anglia, fled to Holland. After twelve years they decided they could not remain indefinitely in a foreign (though friendly) country, and must look for a permanent home further afield, where they could earn their living and continue to worship God in their own way. They returned to England and were offered support by the Plymouth Company, first chartered in 1606 by James 1. They were joined by a number of other Puritans, and in September 1620 102 men, women and children set sail for America crammed into the 183 ton *Mayflower*. Those who survived the passage finally set foot on American soil at a spot known as New Plymouth, well to the north of Virginia, on 20 December.[6] Others of similar beliefs and temperament followed. The colony of Massachusetts Bay with its capital at Boston was founded in 1630, and by 1640 there were some 14,000 independent-minded settlers in the young New England colonies.[7] Towards the end of the seventeenth century there was a further influx of Dissenters, particularly Quakers, who mostly settled south of New England, in areas where William Penn had been granted exclusive rights by Charles II and his brother James, Duke of York. Gradually a continuous strip of

English settlement was established from Canada (still French) to the 'Old Dominion' of Virginia.

To the south of Virginia, in the territory stretching to Florida and the lands claimed by Spain, the English colonies developed in rather different ways to the communities further north. Shortly after his Restoration Charles II granted the entire area to a small group of his friends and courtiers, who encouraged settlement on their new domains primarily in the hope of commercial benefits. Charleston was founded in 1670 and was soon followed by the colony of South Carolina, and later by its namesake to the north. In 1732 Georgia received its charter, the last of the initial thirteen colonies to achieve official recognition.

Unlike many of the men and women who had put down their roots in Pennsylvania, Delaware and the New England colonies, few of the new-comers to the southern settlements had fled intolerance at home; most were members of the Church of England, and the Anglican Church became established in both Carolinas. In one particular respect, however, they followed their neighbours in Virginia: the extensive employment of slave labour. By Independence over a third of the population in the south was negro, and a way of life particular to the region had evolved.[8] There has been a tendency to use the term aristocracy when considering elements of this southern society, with the larger plantation owners cast as the new nobility, but it is a misnomer; plutocracy is more apt. Although there was a greater proportion of Loyalists in the south during the American war than in the middle colonies and New England, few southern colonists saw any reason to defer to the claims of a genuinely hereditary elite living in secure comfort 3000 miles away.

At the outbreak of the American war in 1775 the population of the thirteen colonies was around 2,500,000.[9] (The comparable figure for Great Britain was in the region of 11,500,000.) The five southern colonies (Maryland, Virginia, the Carolinas and Georgia) accounted for nearly half that figure, a proportion, however, that included some 500,000 slaves. The white, free population was fairly evenly distributed throughout the colonised territories, though it was by no means homogeneous in culture. The New England colonies retained a Puritan ethos; extravagance and marked inequalities were distrusted, and a considerable measure of religious intolerance practised. To the south, in Pennsylvania, where the Quaker inheritance was strong, there was much less pressure to conform, and in the other two middle-Atlantic colonies of New York and New Jersey the presence of Dutch settlements, founded before the arrival of the English, encouraged variety in worship and way of life. Further to the south again, with its plutocratic milieu, the culture was clearly different to that of the colonies centred on Boston or Philadelphia. Moreover, the problems of communication and travel, especially by land, had done little to blur these differences in the century and a half since the first settlers arrived, allowing Lord North and his Ministers to cherish the belief that the American colonies were incapable of collaboration in the face of a common enemy. In North's defence it should be noted that many years later it seemed even to the second President of the United States that colonial cooperation had been little less than a miracle. In 1818 John Adams, reflecting in a letter to a friend on the events that led up to Independence, wrote: 'thirteen clocks were made to strike together – a perfection of mechanism, which no artist had ever before effected'.[10]

English statesmen were not well-informed about the situation in America. Transatlantic communications were slow and uncertain. Even with favourable weather and the benefit of the prevailing westerlies, the voyage from America to Britain rarely took less than four weeks; the opposite journey, in ships unable to sail close to the wind, could last two or even three times as long. Moreover, no senior Minister who served under North had ever crossed the Atlantic, and government opinion was largely dependent on reports from colonial Governors and administrators sent out from England. On the whole they were not a very distinguished lot of men, mostly non-entities accepting office unwillingly for the sake of a salary grudgingly paid by the local assemblies. In 1754 Benjamin Franklin commented that 'Governors often come to the colonies merely to make fortunes, with which they intend to return to Britain, are not always men of the best abilities and Integrity, have no estates here, nor any natural Connections with us, that should make them heartily concerned for our welfare'.[11] Twenty years later, when he was the agent for Massachusetts in London, his opinion of Governors – and of their value as sources of information – does not seem to have improved much:

> Their office makes them insolent; their insolence makes them odious; and, being conscious they are hated, they become malicious. Their malice urges them to continual abuse of the inhabitants in their letters to Administration, representing them as disaffected and rebellious, and (to encourage the use of severity) as weak, divided, timid, and cowardly. Government believes all; thinks it necessary to support and countenance its officers. Their quarreling with the people is deemed a mark and consequence of their fidelity.[12]

A good example of misinformation passed to the government in London appears in a letter written in March 1774 to William Knox, Under Secretary in the Colonial Department, by Henry Ellis previously Governor of Georgia, but at the time the colony's agent in England: 'We know the real inability of the Americans to make any effectual resistance to any coercive method which might be employed to compel their obedience. They are conscious of it themselves, but may well give scope to their insolent licentiousness when they have so long been suffered to practise it with impunity'.[13] These are the views English Ministers wanted to hear; there were some others available which they preferred to ignore. In the same year as Ellis made his optimistic comments, Charles Lee, an American by birth who had held a commission in the British army and was later a major-general under Washington, wrote to Edmund Burke:

> I have now run through the whole colonies from the north to the south. I have conversed with every order of men, from the first estated gentleman to the poorest planters, and cannot express my astonishment at the unanimous, ardent spirit reigning through the whole. They are determined to sacrifice everything, their property, their wives, children and blood, rather than cede a tittle of what they conceive to be their rights ... There is one more circumstance that we gentlemen in red never choose to remember, viz, – that in all our defeats, particularly in those in Ohio, the provincials were the last to leave the field. But be these things as they will, if I have any judgement, the people of New England are, at this day, more calculated to form irresistible conquering armies, than any people on the face of the globe.[14]

Governments in London tended to underrate two aspects in particular of the common American experience that encouraged cooperation among the colonies, especially in opposition to overseas interference. The first was of a general nature, best described as the frontier spirit. Even by the middle of the eighteenth century few Americans were more than three or four generations distant from original settlers, and many were much closer. The memory of hardships and dangers successfully overcome bolstered both distrust of authority, not least when far distant, and respect for the virtues of mutual support. It was not merely due to convenience that by the 1760s the inhabitants of the thirteen colonies, whether Yankees, Pennsylvanians or Carolinians, had become collectively known as Americans, a description increasingly used by the colonists themselves.[15]

The other aspect of American life that English politicians either ignored or mistrusted was the vigorous growth of representative government. The system varied a little from colony to colony, largely depending on who appointed the Governor, his Council and the judges. In eight of the colonies the right lay with the Crown; in Pennsylvania, Delaware and Maryland the original proprietorial families, the Penns and the Baltimores, still held the responsibility; and Connecticut and Rhode Island were virtually autonomous.[16] In every case, however, fiscal and legislative authority lay with the colonial assemblies, bodies elected under a franchise that usually included all free men able to satisfy a fairly modest property qualification. The levels varied from colony to colony, and may have been raised in some cases during the century prior to Independence, but nothing comparable was achieved in Britain until the Reform Act of 1884.[17] Eighteenth-century statesman in London watched with concern as the assemblies steadily encroached on the powers of the appointed officials.

In December 1742 a new royal Governor, James Glen, arrived at Charleston, capital of South Carolina, to take up his post. He had been appointed five years earlier, but had preferred during this period to leave his responsibilities in the hands of the Lieutenant Governor, an American by birth called William Bull, while he busied himself with his Scottish estates and offices. It is hardly surprising that within two months of his arrival Glen was writing to the Secretary of State, the Duke of Newcastle, complaining that 'he found the whole frame of government unhinged, and the Governor divested of the power placed in him, which power was parcelled out to many hands ... ' To make matters even more difficult for him, Mr Bull preferred to reside on his plantation sixty miles distant from Charleston, and had only found time to pay a brief visit of one day to the new Governor since the latter's arrival the previous year.[18]

Glen appears to have made little progress in asserting his authority. Five years later he wrote to a subsequent Secretary of State, the Duke of Bedford, saying that 'little by little the people have got the whole administration in their hands and the crown is by various laws despoiled of its principal flowers and brightest jewels'.[19] The flowers and jewels were, of course, various rights of patronage so important to the success of eighteenth-century administrations. This vignette of gubernatorial frustration in South Carolina in the 1740s is well-documented, but there is no reason to think the picture was very different in other colonies. In 1763 Sir Jeffrey Amherst was appointed Governor of Virginia, a colony he never visited during his five-year tenure of the office.[20] Almost by default, badly-informed English governments allowed power to transfer to local hands, and as the colonies increasingly became makers of their own decisions they had less and less intention of seeing the process reversed.

There was, however, one important sphere where this apparently indifferent (or indolent) attitude on the part of the government in London did not apply: trade relations between Britain and America. Throughout the seventeenth century and for much of the eighteenth it was assumed by almost everyone that colonies were planted for the benefit of the home country. As it was once put by an American historian: 'The aim was not to transplant English men and women to new homes across the sea where they might create a greater Britain, but to transport some laborers to a plantation in a distant land whose natural products were such as England could not raise herself'.[21]

Many individual settlers may have been driven by the yearning for new (and better) horizons, but in the eyes of the entrepreneurs and politicians promoting them they were a means to an end: the generation of more wealth in English pockets. At first this difference of motivation did not greatly matter; expectations of finding gold were disappointed, and most of the early colonists had trouble enough providing for their own needs without trying to produce a surplus for export. With the success of tobacco-growing in Virginia, however, this changed.

In 1621 the government of James I decreed that all tobacco available for export must be traded with British merchants, a policy that continued unchanged until the American war, when the colonies were exporting 100,000,000 pounds of it to Britain every year.[22] Later in the seventeenth century various Navigation Acts extended this policy to other commodities, forbidding direct third-party dealing and restricting transatlantic trade to British or American ships. In practice the impact of these regulations was softened by smuggling, and American shipping may even have gained from the exclusion of all foreign competition. Furthermore, although the sale of tobacco from Virgina or Maryland was confined to Britain, the market was protected and no imports were permitted from the rest of the world. Finally – and something English politicians did not forget – it was the imperial power that policed the trade routes of the north Atlantic, providing military protection against the French in Canada (prior to the end of the Seven Years War) and against attacks by local Indians. The point was politely but clearly put in a letter sent to all thirteen colonial Governors in March 1775 by the American Secretary, Lord Dartmouth:

> I am unwilling to suppose that any of the King's subjects in the Colonies can have so far forgot the benefits they have received from the Parent State, as not to acknowledge that it is to her support, held forth at the expense of her blood and treasure, that they principally owe that security which hath raised them to their present state of opulence and importance. In this situation, therefore, justice requires that they should in return, contribute, according to their abilities, to the common defence; and their own welfare and interest demand that their Civil Establishment should be supported with a becoming dignity.[23]

The scales were not as unevenly weighted as Americans came to believe: in the years prior to the outbreak of hostilities nearly 4 per cent of the entire

British budget was spent on maintaining the army in America.[24] By the time of the Boston Tea Party, however, emotion had taken the place of logic on both sides of the Atlantic.

11

The Gathering Storm

In the late summer of 1773 the East India Company hastened to take advantage of North's recent Act and shipped consignments of tea to New York, Philadelphia and Boston. In the first two cities much of the trade had been contraband, in the hands of merchants who were in effect smugglers. As they could hardly expect to be chosen as consignees by the East India Company for the new and potentially cheaper supplies, and saw themselves threatened with serious loss of business, they whipped up their local communities to oppose the importations. They protested that the tea monopoly was only the thin end of the wedge, which would later be widened to cover other imported commodities; and that the whole project was a ruse to gain acceptance of taxed tea.[1] In these two cities they were successful in deterring any rival merchants from accepting consignments, and the ships eventually returned to Britain with their cargoes.

The prospects for the consignments shipped to Boston were on the face of it more promising. Considerable quantities of legally taxed tea had been passing through the port already, and the merchants who handled it were those selected for the new (and cheaper) consignments.[2] Increased business would presumably be welcome, and serious trouble was not expected when the aptly named vessel *Dartmouth* tied up in the harbour on 18 November, followed within days by two further ships with tea in their holds, the *Eleanor* and the *Beaver*. There was, however, a radical element among the citizens determined to expunge the shame of Boston's recent record as an importer of taxed tea,[3] which tried to intimidate the merchants not to take delivery of the new consignments. The merchants fled to military protection (some to Castle William, an island fort in the harbour), and refused to capitulate.

A complicating factor was that under local regulations a ship's cargo had to be unloaded and the import duties paid before the Governor was authorised to sign clearance papers; there was, moreover, a time limit of twenty days, after which the cargo was liable to forfeit.[4] The limit for the *Dartmouth* expired on 17 December. Governor Thomas Hutchinson, two of whose sons were among the merchant consignees holding out for their rights, believed he could weather the storm with the support of most of the richer and more respectable members of the community. He declined to waive the rules and allow the ships to depart with their cargo on board and the duty unpaid.[5] Meanwhile the radical element was concerned that the duty might be paid secretly, thus releasing the tea for legal sale if it could be subsequently landed.[6] On the night of 15 December a number of Bostonians, some dressed as Red Indians, forced their way onto the three vessels in the harbour and dumped their tea overboard. New York and Philadelphia may have presented a more determined and united front against accepting the tea consignments, but it was Boston that made the headlines.

The destruction of the tea was essentially an irrational act. The tea carried a lower overall duty than previous consignments and its importation threatened few local trading interests. As a baffled North said in a debate a year later: 'it was impossible ... to foretell the Americans would resist at being able to drink their tea at 9d. in the pound cheaper'.[7] The Tea Party was an outraged protest against the British government's readiness to manipulate tariff levels for the benefit of a private company, without any reference to the people most concerned; an act of defiance against insensitive imperial rule. Unfortunately, North and most of his Ministers never seriously considered what lay behind such behaviour.

News of the Tea Party reached London in January 1774. At a Cabinet meeting on 29 January it was agreed 'that in consequence of the present disorders in America, effectual steps be taken to secure the dependence of the colonies on the mother country'. At the next meeting, on 4 February, North was given unanimous backing for a punitive response against Boston and the colony of Massachusetts.[8] It was decided to close the port of Boston by placing the customs facilities elsewhere, and to amend the Massachusetts constitution by emasculating the Council. It was at first believed by Dartmouth, the Colonial Secretary, that these measures could be put into effect by simple administrative decree, thus avoiding both delay and the provocation associated with further legislation, but when doubts arose about the legality of this course of action it was decided to proceed by Act of Parliament. North introduced the Boston Port Bill in the Commons on 14 March, the committee stage was taken on 23 March, it passed the House two days later without a division, and after a similarly easy passage through the Lords became law within a few days.[9] But, as Burke explained in a letter

The *able Doctor, or America Swallowing the Bitter Draught.*

The Lord Chancellor, Lord Mansfield, holds down the figure of America, North pours the contents of a teapot down her throat, and Lord Sandwich peers up her skirts. The figures on the left represent France and Spain. *London Magazine,* 1 May 1774. (*British Museum*) to the Committee of Correspondence of the General Assembly of New York, the measure did not lack opponents: 'There were not indeed wanting some few persons in the House of Commons, who disapproved of the Bill, and who expressed their disapprobation in the strongest and most explicit terms. But their Arguments upon this point made so little impression that it was not thought advisable to divide the House'.[10]

In the course of the debates North adopted a tone of resolute but fair-minded determination, telling the House: 'I am by no means an enemy to lenient measures, but I find that resolutions of censure and warning will avail nothing; we must therefore proceed to some immediate remedy; now is our time to stand out, to defy them – to proceed with firmness, and without fear; they will never reform until we take a measure of this kind'.[11]

It is clear from his speeches that North underestimated the unity of the colonies in the face of British coercion. He thought 'Boston alone was to blame for having set this example, and therefore Boston ought to be the principal object of our attention for punishment',[12] and that if this course was followed the other twelve colonies would not rally to the offender's side. There were plenty of reasons for questioning this comforting belief. John Gooch, an expatriate Englishman living in Boston, wrote to his friend George Cumberland in May 1774 saying that 'the shutting up of the Port is Pernistious [sic] to both Parties as the Colonies are united in the Common Cause'.[13] The Colonial Secretary Dartmouth had also been told by a correspondent in America that confidence in the failure of colonial cooperation was misplaced: 'if the Boston port bill and the other proceedings against that Province have been founded on a supposition that the other Colonies would leave them to struggle alone, I do assure your Lordship there never was a graver mistake'.[14] If that warning was ever passed on to North he was evidently in no mood to listen.

Hard on the heels of the Boston Port Act came two further measures to coerce the colony into submission, the Massachusetts Government Bill and the Massachusetts Justice Bill. The first was intended to strengthen the powers of the new Governor General, Thomas Gage, who had succeeded Hutchinson in April, at the expense of the Council whose members, (previously elected) he would in future appoint. Introducing the Bill on 28 March North explained: 'I propose, in this Bill, to take the executive power from the hands of the democratic part of government; I would propose, that the governor should act as a justice of the peace, and that he should have the power to appoint the officers throughout the whole civil authority'.[15]

North was also responsible a few days later for the introduction in the Commons of the other measure, the Justice Bill. It allowed the Governor to remove criminal cases involving servants of the Crown from Massachusetts to another colony or even to Great Britain on the grounds, North said, 'that the juries of that country . . . were not established after the manner in which our juries here were and therefore were not so likely to give each offender impartial trial'.[16] It was an offensive proposal and condemned in forthright terms by Colonel Barré: 'It is proposed to stigmatise a whole people as persecutors of innocence, and men incapable of doing justice; yet you have not a single fact on which to ground that imputation'.[17]

North got his two Bills through with large majorities in both Houses but signs of disquiet were growing. Barré could be ignored as a maverick, but there were others who, while supporting the Boston Port Bill as a reasonable punishment for the wilful destruction of private property, were yet made uneasy by the two later measures which seemed to seek the unnecessary humiliation of the entire colony. Among the doubters was Dartmouth himself, who as American Secretary should have held a key position in the making of colonial policy. As early as 15 March he shared his worries with Lord Shelburne, who passed them on to Chatham:

> I accidentally met Lord Dartmouth yesterday in a morning visit. Without entering into the particular measures in question, he stated, with great fairness, and with very little reserve, the difficulties of his situation, the unalterableness of his principles, and his determination to cover America from the present storm to the utmost of his power, even to repealing the Act.[18]

The Act he was referring to was North's Tea Act, the immediate cause of all the trouble. A few months later Hutchinson wrote to a friend about Dartmouth: 'I seldom see him but he laments that the people in the Colonies have put it out of his power what he never would have come into his office, if he had not hoped to do, towards a reconciliation'.[19] He was a more serious-minded man than his step-brother: having long since inherited his estates he remained in politics largely from a sense of duty combined with a considerable personal loyalty to North. Unfortunately he lacked ability as a fighter for unpopular causes and, despite the office he held, he was unable to exert a restraining influence on the Cabinet.[20]

Among more vocal critics of North's policies was the MP John Dunning, later famous for his motion on the increasing influence of the Crown. In the third reading debate on the Massachusetts Government Bill he strongly condemned the direction government action was taking: 'It does not appear to be either peace or the olive-branch – It is war, severe revenge, and hatred against our own subjects'.[21] At this stage, however, opposition to the ministry's American policies was scattered and ineffectual. As Burke warned the Committee of Correspondence in New York: 'That you may not be deceived by any idle or flattering report, he assured, that the determination to enforce obedience from the colonies to laws of revenue, by the most powerful means, seems as firm as possible, and that the ministry appear stronger than I have ever known them'.[22]

When Lord North successfully steered the Tea Act through the Commons in the spring of 1773, he was primarily concerned to relieve the financial position of the East India Company by rescinding the duty on its exports of tea to the American colonies. The logical corollary was the simultaneous abolition of the import duty, so that even smuggled tea would have no edge on the product legally brought in from the Company's warehouses; North refused to take that step, a decision that led directly to the riot in Boston Harbour on the night of 15 December. It then becomes easy to trace the sequence of events from the Tea Party to the onset of armed hostilities, thence to the Declaration of Independence and to the later disaster at Yorktown, and on to the loss of the American colonies nine years after North's Tea Act – easy but unjust to North. The débâcle was a much more complicated affair, owing as much to flawed political philosophy as to the misjudgements of one man.

Reference was made earlier to the principled constitutional position taken by many English politicians concerning parliamentary supremacy. In August 1774 former Governor Thomas Hutchinson, then back in Britain, wrote to a friend in America:

> I verily believe every step taken by the House of Representatives, and by the town of Boston, in opposition to the Governor [General Gage] and his system, has confirmed the King and his Ministers in their determination to shew no sort of favour whilst the authority of Parliament is denied. Indeed, I have not met with one person in the kingdom – and I have seen flaming patriots, as well as fawning courtiers – who thinks the avowed principles, either of the House or Council, admissible. Lord Chatham himself has most certainly allowed that there is no particular case, nor no particular part of the Dominions, which can be exempt from the authority of Parliament without a solecism.[23]

In general these views were endorsed by George III who, despite the attacks of some later historians, saw himself as a bulwark of the constitution rather than a monarch in pursuit of personal power. In a letter to North on 14 November 1774 he spoke of 'Supporting the Authority of the Mother Country',[24] a theme he several times returned to in his correspondence with his First Minister.[25] There was, nevertheless, an intransigent element

The Council of the Rulers and the Elders against the Tribe of ye Americans. North, left foreground, is buying support; the Speaker draws attention to a map of America bursting into flames. *Westminster Magazine,* December 1774. *(British Museum)*

in the King's thinking which North found difficult to counter and ultimately prolonged both the war and his own reluctant tenure of office. George III told North: 'We must either master them or totally leave them to themselves and treat them as aliens'.[26]

North's own attitude often seems ambivalent; he was caught between the determination of the colonists and the belligerence of the King, most of his parliamentary colleagues and much of the British population. As a result he tended to be inflexible when compromise might still have been possible and accommodating when it was too late. A letter dated 3 August 1774 from Hutchinson to his son in America makes North sound almost insouciant: 'Lord North gives himself no concern, or at least, he appears unconcerned; and says that order and government must take place in the Colonies, whether it be sooner or later depends upon themselves; in the meantime they can hurt nobody but themselves.'[27] By the middle of November Hutchinson wrote in his diary that whereas North had previously been hoping for an improvement in relations with America 'in his present view the case seemed desperate, Parliament would not – could not concede. For aught he could see it must come to violence. He had the Kingdom with him'.[28] A week later Hutchinson noted, 'It is whispered that Lord N. in the Cabinet, is more backward than most of the rest of the Ministers';[29] and, after the receipt of a petition from the illegally established Continental Congress in America, he wrote', 'I could plain perceive that it would have been very agreeable to him [North] to have found something in the Petition that would lead to an accommodation'.[30] Hutchinson was an interested and well-informed observer, and it is evident he found it hard to decide how North intended to handle the growing crisis.

Compounding the difficulties that stemmed from his inherently laissez-faire temperament was North's faulty analysis of the situation. First, he continued to believe long after it was correct that taxation was at the heart of the dispute and that concessions in this field alone could solve it.[31] As late as February 1775, only two months before the first shots were exchanged at Lexington, he informed the Commons, as a matter relevant to the quarrel, that Americans only paid on average six pence per year in taxation as against the comparable British figure of twenty-five shillings.[32] By then such comparisons were pointless. The Americans had become a nation and wished to order their own affairs.

North shared his other misapprehension with most of his countrymen. He failed to grasp the American readiness and ability to fight to defend their rights. On 14 March 1774 he had assured the Commons that 'the good of this Act is that four or five frigates will do the business [of closing Boston harbour] without any military force';[33] and in November he told

Hutchinson the colonies must be subdued, adding that 'he would not allow the thought that the Kingdom was not able to do it'.[34]

Parliament was prorogued on 22 June 1774 and North could go on holiday content that he had taken the necessary steps to contain the American problem. A general election was due by March 1775, and on 30 September the Cabinet decided to hold it without further delay. North self-protectively warned George III that such haste might reduce the effectiveness of the measures an administration would normally take to improve the prospects of a satisfactory outcome: 'As a premature dissolution of Parliament renders the necessary preparation almost impossible Government cannot expect to be so strong in the next House of Commons, as it were at the natural end of the Parliament, Lord North hopes that his Majesty will not think him to blame if some important elections succeed contrary to his wishes.'[35]

The reasons for the slightly premature dissolution of Parliament are clear. The government wanted a fresh mandate before facing any consequences arising from its intermittently hard-line American policies. As North told Thomas Hutchinson in November: 'Parliament was dissolved on this account – that we might, at the beginning of a Parliament take such measures as we could depend upon a Parliament to prosecute to effect'. [36] The King took a close interest in the election and throughout its course corresponded with North almost every day.[37] The results were better than either had feared and, although party loyalties were an uncertain factor in the eighteenth century, North could inform the King that the administration probably had 321 reliable supporters in a house of 558 MPs. [38] He suffered the irritation of John Wilkes's reappearance as the Member for Middlesex, but no attempt was made this time to unseat him and the new Parliament, which continued until 1780, sustained North and his ministry through the greater part of the American war.

Parliament met on 29 November 1774 and in the Speech from the Throne George III referred to 'the daring spirit of resistance and disobedience ... in Massachusetts Bay' and asserted: 'You may depend on my firm and steadfast resolution to withstand every attempt to weaken or impair the supreme authority of this legislature over all the dominions of my crown'.[39] In the debate that followed North argued 'that however necessary and agreeable a reconciliation with America might be, as no terms had been offered by America, England would not submit first'.[40]

He was speaking with the knowledge that, far from offering terms, the American colonies had in September taken a decisive step to coordinate their resistance to the Crown when the first Continental Congress had met in Philadelphia. The delegates were drawn from twelve of the thirteen colonies. Georgia, a frontier province very dependent on British support, did not join till the end of the following year,[41] but otherwise they covered a broad spectrum of colonial opinion, including initially a substantial number of moderates. These hardened their stance in the course of the assembly, probably under pressure from the local associations they represented where radical settlements were growing and Lord North 'was cursed from morn to noon, and from noon to morn by every denomination of people'.[42] The Congress called for the repeal of all legislation affecting the colonies passed since 1763 and sought to enforce their demands by imposing an embargo on trade with Great Britain. Independence was not included among their aims and it was agreed to send a respectful petition for the redress of grievances to the King, but the authors were evidently not too hopeful of results, as arms were already being secretly sought from Europe,[43] and men were drilling in much of New England, Virginia and New York.

At the end of August 1774 General Gage reported that the colony of Massachusetts, apart from Boston, was virtually out of his control.[44] Four weeks later he was sufficiently alarmed to hint, in a letter to his predecessor back in England, that the government should consider 'the suspension of the execution of the late Acts', a hint which he also dropped in a letter to Dartmouth.[45] Hutchinson noted North's response to the suggestion in his diary on 19 November: 'He did not know what General Gage meant by suspending the Acts; there was no suspending an Act of Parliament. How far it was necessary to temporise, from circumstances which he alone could know, he must be the judge ... The Acts must and should be carried into execution'.[46]

Nevertheless, North's mood by the end of November was again moving towards conciliation. He was never a man who allowed his sense of realism to be smothered by wishful thinking and, as Hutchinson had already guessed, he had begun to focus on the alarming prospect of civil war between Britain and her colonies, a conflict in which he could hardly avoid playing a conspicuous role. Prompted by Dartmouth, he therefore suggested the appointment of a commission to be sent to America to negotiate the framework of a settlement. This was intended as an olive branch, but silmultaneously he proposed the suspension of various economic regulations advantageous to America to exert pressure on the colonies. He discussed his ideas with George III, who predictably favoured the stick but queried the carrot:

I was much pleased with Your ideas concerning the suspension of bounties and other regulations that may be effected this Session towards bringing the Americans to their Duty, but am not so fond of the sending Commissioners to examine into the disputes; this looks so like the Mother Country being more afraid of the continuance of the dispute than the Colonies and I cannot think it likely to make them reasonable; I do not want to drive them to despair but to Submission.[47]

In the New Year the hopes of North and Dartmouth for a commission failed to win Cabinet support and were dropped, but conciliation was still in the air. At a Cabinet meeting on 21 January 1775 it was agreed that if any colonies were prepared to tax themselves to pay for their own 'civil government and administration of justice and for defence and protection' Great Britain would 'desist from the exercise of the power of taxation, except for commercial purposes only'.[48] This apparent concession was partly vitiated by the conclusion of the Cabinet minute which asked the King 'to take the most effectual methods to enforce due obedience to the laws and authority of the supreme legislature of Great Britain', but for a brief moment there seemed a glimmer of hope for a negotiated settlement.

That hope was dashed by the way the petition from the Philadelphia Continental Congress was handled when it arrived at the American Department in December before being passed on to the King. On Christmas Eve Dartmouth informed Bejamin Franklin and other American agents in London that 'His Majesty received your petition very graciously and, for its importance, would lay it before his Houses of Parliament when they met'.[49] In the event it was included among a bundle of other American papers sent to Parliament, formally introduced to the Commons by North on 19 January, ignored by the government and rejected for debate by a large majority a week later.[50] Whatever may have been the misgivings about the constitutional aims of the Continental Congress, that could hardly encourage dialogue with the American colonies.

What followed was no better. On 1 February Lord Chatham initiated a debate in the Lords on his Provisional Act for Settling the Troubles in America. His proposals upheld Britain's legislative authority but offered considerable concessions in return, including the suspension of the Boston Port Act and other laws offensive to American opinion. Initially Dartmouth, the American Secretary, was prepared to accept the Bill as a basis for discussion, but changed his mind under pressure from Cabinet colleagues. Chatham's motion was heavily defeated.[51] The next day North opened a debate in the Commons on an Address to the King upon the 'Disturbances in North America' and his tone had once more become uncompromising. He said that submission must come first, that the possibility of sending more troops was being considered, and that a Bill was in hand 'to put a stop to all the foreign trade of New England, particularly to their fisheries on the banks of Newfoundland, till they returned to their duty'.[52] He introduced the Bill in the Commons on 10 February.

Two days earlier Edward Gibbon had told John Baker-Holroyd, North's future son-in-law, 'in a few days we stop the ports of New England ... I am more convinced that with firmness all may go well; yet I sometimes doubt Lord N.'[53] This uncertainty about North's resilience was echoed by Hutchinson who, following a call on him, noted in his diary: 'I spent near an hour in conversation. He seemed overbourne with the weight of affairs; and tho' he evidently wished for something to take hold of to bring forward an accommodation, professed to be resolved never to concede to the present claims'.[54] A few months later another American, referring in a letter home to Philadelphia to a conversation he had recently had with North, relayed the Prime Minister's apparent lack of commitment to aggressive war against the colonies: 'He declared he never entertained any idea of subduing America, properly speaking; if he had, he said, he should have sent a much greater force. What was sent was only what was thought sufficient to protect the friends of Government'.[55] North's moderation was commended in a letter to his father from his old headmaster, Dr Dampier, now Dean of Windsor: 'This is an epoch which will render Ld North's name immortal in our English history. Whatever the event be, he has acted wisely, politically, firmly, moderately'.[56]

To the government and its supporters the New England Trade and Fisheries Bill of February 1775 was a properly reasonable response to the trade embargo imposed by the Continental Congress the previous September, but its timing could not have been worse. The Cabinet had agreed their concillation proposals on 21 January but North did not officially unveil them in the Commons until 20 February; the intervening four weeks having seen the churlish treatment of the petition, the rejection of Chatham's moderate attempt at mediation and, finally, the trade restrictions on the New England colonies. Beside these actions North's words carried little weight. He made a rather unconvincing speech outlining the various concessions he was prepared to make on taxation, but insisting on the prior acceptance by America of parliamentary supremacy: 'To be explicit ... that if the dispute in which the Americans have engaged goes to the whole of our authority, we can enter into no negotiation, we can meet no compromise'.[57] North was once again trying, though without any great confidence, to stand in the centre, with results that were predictable: he was shot at from either flank. He told the King after the debate that he had been in danger of losing some of his usual supporters who feared he was offering too much,[58] but from the Opposition benches he had to endure a scathing attack from Charles James Fox:

> What he has now proposed to you, does accordingly carry two faces on its very first appearance. To the Americans and to those who are unwilling to proceed in the extremes of violence against them, he holds out negociation and reconciliation. To those who have engaged with him on condition that he will support the supremacy of this country unimpaired, the proposition holds out a persuasion that he never will relax on that point; but, Sir, his friends see that he is relaxing, and the committee sees that they are all ready to withdraw from under his standard. No one in this country, who is sincerely for peace, will trust the speciousness of his expressions, and the Americans will reject them with disdain.[59]

Edmund Burke also had some harsh words on North's logic: 'The mode of argument, on the side of administration was the most ridiculous that had ever been known in parliament. They attempted to prove to one side of the House that the measure was a concession; and to the other that it was a strong assertion of authority'.[60]

Despite such critical speeches North's conciliation proposals were approved by 274 votes to 88 at the committee stage and confirmed a week later without a division. A year earlier they might have contributed to a settlement but the grudging spirit in which they were presented (and the march of events) ensured they were stillborn. In March news was received that more colonies had accepted the resolutions of the Continental Congress and were imposing an embargo on trade with Britain. Parliament retaliated with a new Trade and Fisheries Bill extending the restrictions to the latest rebels. The list did not include New York, which it was hoped could be separated from the rest.

Early in May the American Department received from the New York Assembly a petition to the King, a memorial to the Lords and a remonstrance to the Commons. The documents asked for the redress of grievances and the right of 'providing for the support of our own civil government, and the administration of justice in this colony',[61] but their tone was neither strident nor aggressive. Thomas Hutchinson reported both North and Dartmouth as reputedly ready to lend a sympathetic ear to the remonstrance,[62] but when it was considered in the Commons North argued 'that no paper should be presented to that House which tended to call in question the unlimited rights of Parliament'. The remonstrance was then rejected by 186 votes to 67.[63] The folly of slapping conservative New York in the face seems incomprehensible until it is remembered that at this stage few informed people believed a professional British army would not easily prevail over American irregulars. Furthermore, as North said in a semi-official note attached to his conciliation proposals which came before the Second Continental Congress in May: 'The Temper and spirit of the nation are so much against concessions that if it were the intention of the Administration they could not carry the question'.[64]

On succeeding Hutchinson as Governor of Massachusetts Bay, Gage had remained Commander-in-Chief of British forces in America. Not so much through incompetence as through a tendency to send despatches home that were honest and realistic about the situation in America he had, however, lost the confidence of the King and his Ministers. He had failed to subdue Massachusetts by force, and appeared to government eyes to have little enthusiasm for the task. He told the American Secretary: 'It had been suggested that it was highly necessary to apprehend a certain Number of Persons, which I believe wou'd have been a very proper Measure some time ago, but at present it wou'd be the Signal for Hostilities, which they seem very ripe to begin'.[65] At the end of the following January Dartmouth had written to him on behalf of the Cabinet and, although leaving him with a degree of discretion, he was urged to pursue a more active policy against dissidents, arresting the ringleaders and confiscating arms.[66]

Dartmouth's letter, dated 27 January 1775, was delayed by bad weather, and it did not reach Gage, and then only in the form of a copy, until 14 April.[67] Probably wisely, Gage ignored the American Secretary's appeal for the arrest of a few prominent rebels as, even if feasible, it was likely to be provocative and do little to defuse colonial resistance. Instead he decided to seize the arms that the Massachusetts Provincial Assembly had collected at Concord, a small town sixteen miles to the north west of Boston. He acted fast and within a few days organised a picked force of some 700 grenadiers and light infantry under the command of Lieutenant-Colonel Francis Smith of the 10th Regiment of Foot, with an experienced marine major, John Pitcairn, as second-in-command. Late on 18 April the troops were ferried across the Charles River estuary to the Charlestown peninsula, an operation not complete till midnight, and before dawn the next day Smith and his force set out for Concord.[68]

Although its precise objective was not supposed to be public knowledge, it had been impossible to keep the preparations for the expedition a complete secret. As a sensible precaution the colonists therefore put in hand the removal of the arms stored at Concord, and they also placed a small contingent of seventy militiamen at Lexington, a village across Smith's likely line of march. When Pitcairn, leading the advance guard, approached the village at dawn he found the colonists drawn up in three ranks on the green. It is probable they were there as a gesture of protest rather than to offer serious resistance; both sides were under orders not to open fire unless attacked.[69] Heavily outnumbered, the militia reluctantly began to disperse. Which man from which side ignored orders and fired the first shot of the War of Independence still remains in dispute. On resuming their march to Concord, Smith's soldiers left behind eight Americans killed and ten wounded, together with one British casualty. The news of the deaths spread rapidly through the surrounding countryside.

On reaching Concord the British troops destroyed the few arms the colonists had not already removed, then set out back to Boston. Angry and vengeful Americans gathered along the route and, according to a British officer who was present for the final stages of the withdrawal, 'took every advantage the face of the Country afforded them ... Our men had very few opportunities of getting good shots at the Rebels, as they hardly ever fired but under cover of a Stone wall, from behind a tree, or out of a house; and the moment they had fired they lay down out of sight until they had loaded again, or the Column had passed'.[70] Despite attempts by Smith to send out flanking parties, by the time the British force got back to Lexington it was in serious trouble. It was rescued there by a relief column of 1200 men under Brigadier-General Lord Percy sent out by Gage. The combined force then fought its way back to the Charlestown peninsula, where it could rest secure under the guns of the fleet.[71] Seventy-three British soldiers were killed that day and 174 wounded; American losses were forty-nine dead and thirty-nine wounded.[72] War had begun.

The first news of the fighting came not from Gage's official despatches but from an account in a Boston newspaper, hurried across the Atlantic to enlist sympathy for the American cause and to propagate the contention that it was the British who had fired first.[73] It reached London on 27 May, the day after the King in his speech at the close of the session had congratulated Parliament on its handling of the American situation.[74] After a visit to Lord Dartmouth four days later Hutchinson confided to his diary: 'He read me a card from Ld N., which says the beginning of action in America was rather inauspicious; but hopes the account in the *Massachusetts Gazette* was exaggerated. There appears a degree of that apathy which I think Lord N. has a great deal of'.[75]

It is apparent that the American Secretary also had little stomach for the further bloodshed he feared; his support for Gage, in a letter he wrote to him after he learnt of Concord, was distinctly equivocal, despite his earlier pressure for a more aggressive policy:

I am to presume that the measure of sending out a detachment of your troops to destroy the magazine at Concord was taken after the fullest consideration of the advantages on the one hand, and hazards on the other, of such an enterprise, and of all the possible consequences that were to result from it. It is impossible for me to reflect on this transaction, and upon all its consequences, without feelings which, although I do not wish to conceal them, it is not necessary for me to express.[76]

North's part in the course of events from the Boston Tea Party to the outbreak of fighting at Lexington has probably harmed his later reputation more than anything else that occurred while he was in office. The case against North rests on the belief that there was a chance, a window of opportunity, during those eighteen months, when a more skilful handling of the colonies could have resolved the crisis without bloodshed. Independence in all but name might still have been the outcome, but not at the unnecessary cost of British and American lives. It is impossible to deny that North was temperamentally unsuited to the responsibilities of office at a time of crisis. He was, in Hutchinson's words, 'overbourne with the weight of affairs', and his innate tendency to shrink from conflict (whether private or public) led him to misjudge colonial determination. Essentially, however, the condemnation of North has depended on the assumption that in the crucial months before Lexington he vacillated between coercion and conciliation, without any principles to guide his steps. That is untrue.

North's freedom for negotiation with the colonies was constrained by political realities. He did not operate in a vacuum. The general mood of the country was unsympathetic to American demands, a mood fully reflected in Parliament. As North had explained to the King after the debate in February 1775, in which proposals for allowing the colonies to tax themselves were put forward, he feared a loss of support if he seemed to offer too much – nor was he likely to receive any encouragement from George III if he considered doing so.[77] The one man on whom he might have leant in attempting to push through a negotiated settlement was the American Secretary, Lord Dartmouth. He was in the unique position of being both officially responsible for relations with the American colonies and being also step-brother and friend since childhood of the Prime Minister. There is little doubt he personally favoured a conciliatory policy and shrank from the prospect of war, but he was not a man on whom North could rely to fight for an unpopular policy. It is clear from his letters to Gage that Dartmouth preferred other people to take decisions and accept responsibility, and it is hard not to conclude that he was known as 'The Psalm-Singer' for his lack of punch as much as for his Methodist leanings. Benjamin Franklin remarked that Dartmouth, having initially been in favour of Chatham's 1775 Reconciliation Bill, subsequently withdrew his support on discovering the weight of opinion against it. Franklin continued:

> I am more particular in this, as it is a trait of that nobleman's character, who from his office is supposed to have so great a share in America's affairs, but who has in reality no will or judgement of his own, being with disposition for the best measures, is easily prevailed with to join in the worst.[78]

North's wish for a peaceful resolution of the dispute was fundamental to his American policy in the eighteen months after the Tea Party, but he was not prepared for peace at any price. He could (and did) offer substantial concessions on taxation, but he would not sacrifice the principle of parliamentary supremacy over all the King's subjects: something he believed to be the safeguard of liberty could not be traded to accommodate the colonies. The constitutional settlement reached with the Glorious Revolution was of tremendous importance to North, and to most of his contemporaries. He was old enough to remember the threat posed to it by Prince Charles Edward in 1745, perhaps even to recall his father's anxious communications with the old Lord Dartmouth about their children's and grandchildren's safety at the time.[79]

The Declaratory Act of 1766 had specifically confirmed that the doctrine of parliamentary supremacy was valid for the American colonies, a measure North had supported. Much as he wanted a negotiated end to the dispute with his fellow-subjects, and hard as he tried to find an acceptable way of reaching it, he could not jettison a principle that was central to his political philosophy. North's good faith and the reasonableness of his proposals were acknowledged by an American correspondent writing home to New York in March 1775, shortly after the debate on his 'Propositions for Conciliating the Differences with America':

> Whatever the enemies of both countries may say, the resolution which was moved for by Lord North is founded in the truest policy and benevolence. While it reserves and maintains the just and necessary sovereignty of Parliament, it invites the colonists to an amicable settlement of the dispute. It draws a strong line between the seditious and honest (the misguided) citizen, and, while it leaves the former to be checked by the sword of justice, leads the latter to obedience by granting him all the indulgence he could ask with safety to his own happiness ... The necessary and just authority of Parliament will be preserved, and the Americans gratified in their wish of being taxed by their own representatives.[80]

12

Wartime Prime Minister

In May 1775 the second Continental Congress met in Philadelphia and, as a last and rather reluctant attempt at persuading Britain to soften her policies, it agreed to send a petition to the Crown, later known as the Olive Branch Petition. It was formally approved on 8 July – though only after strong opposition by radicals – and signed by all the delegates present. No specific demands were included, but the King was respectfully urged to initiate a plan for mutual reconciliation. Its general tone was set in the opening paragraph:

> The union between our Mother Country and these Colonies, and the energy of mild and just Government, produced benefits so remarkably important, and afforded such an assurance of their permanency and increase, that the wonder and envy of other nations were excited, while they beheld *Great Britain* rising to a power the most extraordinary the world had ever known.[1]

The petition was despatched to London with Richard Penn, a former Governor of Pennsylvania, but Lord Dartmouth on behalf of the government declined to accept it and later told Penn there could be no official reply to a communication from an illegal assembly.[2] More significantly the Congress voted for the formation of an American army, appointing George Washington its Commander-in-Chief and, in response to an appeal from Massachusetts, passed a measure for the 'adoption' of the forces besieging General Gage in Boston.[3]

Since their return from Concord the British troops had been cooped up in Boston awaiting reinforcements by sea before they could confidently challenge their besiegers, reinforcements that began to arrive towards the end of May. On 25 May Gage received a long letter from Dartmouth urging him once again to adopt more aggressive tactics, though again warning him he would be held responsible for their outcome. 'At the same time I must again repeat that the King entirely relies on your Discretion, forming your judgement upon the Spot ... '[4] The letter was brought across the Atlantic by no fewer than three major-generals, Burgoyne, Clinton and Howe, sent by the government to help Gage (a lieutenant-general) and to stir him into action. On 12 June he proclaimed martial law throughout the colony, and at the same time made a general offer of pardon to all rebels (apart from two of their leaders) who returned to their proper allegiance. The offer was greeted by the patriots with derision.[5] Of greater importance, Gage and his newly arrived advisers decided to march on the rebel encampment at nearby Cambridge. Before this plan could be put into effect, however, news of it was leaked to the Americans, who at nighfall on the 16th moved on to the Charlestown peninsula. Advancing past a feature known as Bunker Hill, the highest point on the neck of land, they entrenched themselves on an elevation called Breed's Hill, only a short distance across the water from Boston itself. Not only did they now threaten the route to Cambridge, but any artillery they were able to position there would dominate the city and make it virtually indefensible. The British commanders quickly saw it was imperative to dislodge the rebels, a task allotted to General Howe. In the event his courage proved superior to his grasp of tactics.

Howe responded methodically but without great urgency, and it was the afternoon of 17 June before his force of around 2300 men was ferried across the estuary to the peninsula. After an attempt to turn the American flank failed, a frontal attack, with Howe himself leading on the right, was launched against the enemy dug in on top of the hill. The British soldiers were carrying 70 pound packs and the temperature was 90 degrees.[6] Twice Howe's men were driven back but, with the Americans running short of ammunition, a third assault relying chiefly on the bayonet was successful. The surviving rebels retreated past Bunker Hill (which gave its name to the battle), and westwards across the isthmus.

This was a bloody encounter in which the British lost 228 dead and 826 wounded, the two figures together representing more than 40 per cent of the total number of British troops involved. (Moreover, those wounded who died later are not included among the dead.) The figures for the Americans were reported as 100 dead and 271 wounded.[7] In a letter home General Howe referred to 'this unhappy day', adding 'I freely confess to you, when I look at the consequences of it, in the loss of so many brave officers, I do it with horror – the success is too dearly bought'.[8] The British authorities on the spot now knew that Burgoyne's recent description of the American troops as 'an undisciplined rabble' was hubristic,[9] and they attempted no more adventures in the neighbourhood of Boston.

The news of Bunker Hill reached London on 25 July and led to a flurry of unusual summertime activity.[10] After North had told George III 'that the War is now grown to such a height, that it must be treated as a foreign war', the King replied, 'I am clear as to one point that we must persist and not be dismayed by any difficulties that may arise on either side of the Atlantick; I know I am doing my Duty and can therefore never wish to retract'.[11] Two days later he advised Dartmouth to recall Gage, ostensibly for consultation but in reality as a cloak for dismissal,[12] and he set about organising the embarkation for America of five battalions of electoral troops from Hanover.[13] North's role in these activities was largely passive and non-committal. On 31 July he wrote to Burgoyne: 'Our wish is not to impose on our fellow subjects in America any terms inconsistent with the most perfect liberty. I cannot help thinking that many of the principal persons in North America will, in the calmness of the winter, be disposed to bring forward a reconciliation'.[14] At the beginning of August he went off on holiday and his letters to the King on the 3rd and 15th are dated from Cheltenham, and one on the 8th from nearby Ross.[15] In the middle of the month he informed George III that he would be passing through London en route for Somerset, a journey discouraged by the King,[16] though a visit to Wroxton two weeks later was made with his approval.[17] It was not until 9 September that North was back at his desk in Downing Street, and even then he spent much of the time at his semirural retreat at Bushy.

After receiving the news of Bunker Hill George III's immediate concern was to press for a Proclamation of Rebellion, in effect a declaration of war on his American colonies. North dragged his feet, referring the matter for advice to his legal officers Edward Thurlow and Alexander Wedderburn, respectively Attorney General and Solicitor General, who could be relied on to disagree and thus hold things up,[18] and his qualms about the Proclamation may well account for a wish to keep away from London. On 18 August, in the same letter that queried his trip to Somerset, the King complained to North:

> There has been much delay in framing a Proclamation declaring the conduct of the Americans Rebellious, and warning persons from corresponding with them ... it is now I think got into a good train, I have directed Lord Suffolk to have it shewn to you and if it meets with your concurrence in its present State to take such further Steps as may be necessary for having it read and ordered to be published by the Privy Council on Wednesday.[19]

George III had successfully manoeuvred North (and Dartmouth the American Secretary as well) into a course of action North only half-supported but which he could not find the conviction to oppose. The Proclamation was issued on 23 August 1775, two days after the first copy of the Olive Branch Petition had reached the American Department.[20]

There were a few senior politicians who continued to doubt whether treating aggrieved fellow-subjects as contumacious rebels was either wise or just, though their number and influence remained small for some years to come. Among them was North's predecessor, the current Privy Seal, the Duke of Grafton. He got wind of the administration's intention of rejecting the Olive Branch, and on 31 August this somewhat despised statesman wrote to North pleading for one more attempt at reconciliation. He accepted that the Petition from the Congress was 'inadmissible by His Majesty' but asked whether there might not be 'sufficient matter in the contents to encourage individuals to come and state to the whole legislature the wishes and expectations of the different colonies in order that harmony may be restored again'.[21] With considerable prescience he then warned North about the underestimated military capacity of the Americans: 'The training of their men during the winter cannot fail to form them into better troops, and their behaviour already has far surpassed the expectation of every one. In short, my lord, many consider the event for us not only to be hopeless, but bringing on certain disgrace and ruin'.[22]

North took seven weeks to reply to that letter. When he did, he gave Grafton a summary of administration policy, reiterating the familiar line that colonial submission must precede British concessions; he remained unmoved by the Duke's arguments. He also enclosed with his reply a draft of the King's Speech at the forthcoming Opening of Parliament on 26 October;[23] this was entirely concerned with the situation in America and the refusal of the colonists to recognise 'their subordinate relation to Great Britain'.[24] In the debate in the Lords that followed, Grafton explained that he had supported administration policy as long as conciliation had seemed its object but he could do so no longer. He called for the repeal of all Acts relating to America passed since 1763, and received support from a number of other peers.[25] The next day Lady North wrote to her father-in-law that Lord North 'vexes ... very much and he feels his situation grow every day more disagreeable, indeed it will be impossible for him to bare [sic] it much longer'.[26] On 8 November Grafton again attacked government policy, lamenting 'in the most pathetic terms the fixed determination ... of administration ... to rush headlong on their own ruin'.[27] The following day he was ordered by George III to return his seals of office.[28]

Grafton's dismissal occasioned a ministerial reshuffle, not because he was a particularly important member of the government but because Dartmouth took the opportunity to offer his own resignation as American Secretary, and to request Grafton's post of Privy Seal in its place. He could

North holds up a dispatch containing good news (the capture of New York by General William Howe). His arm is in a sling following a fall two months earlier when riding in Bushy Park. The figures on the right are Lord Sandwich and Lord George Germain, pointing in derision at Wilkes and other patriots. *London Magazine*, November 1776. *(British Museum)*

no longer doubt that Britain was fully at war with her American colonies and he had no wish to be the man who bore responsibility for its conduct. Dartmouth was prepared to support North by remaining a member of the Cabinet, but in a position of his own choosing. He was a stubborn man and would not be fobbed off with anything that seemed merely decorative. Lady North seldom obtrudes in the story of her husband's career, but she must have been interested and well-informed to have written the following letter to Guilford recounting the musical chairs that had ensued:

> The King took the Privy-Seal from the Duke of Grafton yesterday & it is now settled that Lord Dartmouth is to have it and Lord George Germain to succeed him. Lord North was very far from wishing Lord Dartmouth to give up his place, but it was his own desire to have the Privy-Seal and as that was the case Lord North thinks it lucky that Lord George Germain is to succeed him, as it will be a great ease to him to have a responsible Person in the House of Commons for the three Secretaries being all in the House of Lords, made his Situation in the House of Commons more disagreable. There was a little rub at first which made Lord North very uneasy for after it was agreed Lord Dartmouth should have the Privy-Seal, Lord Weymouth claimed a prior promise of it from the King. Lord Dartmouth was then offered the Groom of the Stole which was to be a Cabinet place, but he did not like it and desired to remain where he was; but Lord George Germain had then had the promise of Lord Dartmouth's place. This put Lord North under the greatest difficulties, but very luckily Lord Rochford [the Southern Secretary] (who has been very ill) desired to retire upon a Pension, upon which his place was offered to Lord Weymouth, who with a great good nature said (though he did not like the place) he would take it and let Lord Dartmouth have the Privy-Seal, so now everything is I hope settled to their mutual satisfaction. It is not yet known who is to succeed Lord Weymouth as Groom of the Stole. Lord North is as well or better than could be expected considering all his vexations. [P.S.] I think Lord Dartmouth will soon find himself happy in his good quiet place, but at present he seems a little uneasy for fear he should be thought to have run away in time of danger.[29]

This letter had been preceded by four days of correspondence between the King and North in which they searched for ways of squaring the ministerial circle, North hinting at resignation and George III becoming increasingly tetchy about Dartmouth's uncooperative attitude.[30] The King was worried about the effect the uncertainties were having on the morale of his First Minister, and not for the last time played on his sense of loyalty, telling him: 'You are my sheet anchor and Your care and comfort I shall in the whole transaction try to secure'.[31]

The resolution of the crisis had, as his wife noted, provided welcome support for North in the Commons as the new American Secretary sat there and not in the Lords. Lord George Germain (as Lord George Sackville) had been disgraced for disobedience after the battle of Minden in 1759 but had long since rehabilitated himself. Rich (through his wife) and well-connected (his brother was Duke of Dorset), he was self-confident to the point of arrogance, energetic and capable, though Brownlow North warned Guilford: 'I am not indeed without my fears that Lord George may be an unpleasant partner for Lord North. He is not a popular man and is reckonned very impractical and ambitious'.[32] Unlike Dartmouth, he quickly established that his office was in no way inferior in importance to those of the other two Secretaries and took the control of American affairs firmly into his own hands.[33] He was also a strong advocate of bringing the Americans to heel by armed force and his appointment shifted the administration further away from negotiation and towards coercion. Germain effectively became Minister of War as far as American land operations were concerned, complemented at sea by the abilities of Sandwich at the Admiralty. These two men remained in office as North's principal aides until the final débâcle nearly six years later. An earlier biographer of North has said the war became their war 'before it could be considered, if indeed, at all, Lord North's war'.[34]

On 20 November 1775, with his new Cabinet safely in place, North introduced a further coercive measure, the American Prohibitory Bill. It replaced much of the earlier piecemeal legislation with a complete naval blockade of the thirteen colonies, allowing the seizure of all American goods found on the high seas and the empressment of men taken on American ships into the Royal Navy. The Bill had tacked on to it a proposal for despatching a Peace Commission,[35] but as Lord Folkestone pointed out in a subsequent debate on the Bill: 'there were thirty-five clauses that aimed at desolation, and one only, a single one, that pretended to be pacific'.[36] North maintained his stance that submission must come before reconciliation, but much of his speech was devoted to explaining and defending his own position as First Lord. He had evidently given the impression in an earlier debate (probably on the King's Address) that he was ready to resign: 'what he said the other night, under a state of fatigue and indisposition, had led people to conceive he was so far tired out with this business, that his administration was drawing to a period'. He then went on to acknowledge that his abilities might be unequal to the task but he concluded on a resolute, confident note: 'he did declare, that unless the King dismissed him, or a majority of the House, disapproving his conduct, desired his dismission, he would not give up the conduct of this business to any body else'.[37] This was North in his upbeat mood but it contrasts oddly with his increasingly frequent pleas for release from the burdens he bore.

While North was rejecting petitions and strengthening legislative sanctions against the colonies, American forces were advancing into Canada.

On 13 November 1775 Montreal fell and by 5 December Quebec was under siege. The British Governor and Commander-in-Chief in Canada, General Sir Guy Carleton, conducted the defence of the city with determination and skill. His efforts were helped by the winter conditions suffered by the besiegers, and also drew on the support of those Canadians who remained loyal, possibly influenced by North's Quebec Act. Their number was small but it was sufficient to ease Carleton's task of holding Quebec and Canada for the Crown. Lack of positive local support soon compelled American withdrawal from Montreal. In the first months of 1776 10,000 British and German soldiers were sent as reinforcements to Carleton,[38] and by June the last of the invaders had been driven from Canada.

Under Germain's vigorous direction reinforcements were also despatched in increasing numbers to General William Howe, who had succeeded Gage as Commander-in-Chief in America, and by the autumn of 1776 his army totalled some 36,000 men.[39] Howe had spent the previous winter in Boston but in the spring the Americans had strengthened their forces and he found himself outgunned. On 17 March, after having evacuated his troops by sea to Halifax, he was instructed by Germain to establish himself in New York. He landed on an undefended Staten Island on 2 July and was joined ten days later by his brother Admiral Lord Howe and a fleet of warships and transports from England. In the course of the next two months Long Island and New York were captured and Washington's army severely mauled, though crucially Howe failed to destroy it. Nevertheless, in late June North was feeling confident and told General Howe there was 'a fairer prospect of seeing an end to the American disturbance than we could have flattered ourselves with a few months ago'.[40] By the end of the year, with Canada safe and a base secured on the eastern seaboard at New York, his tempered optimism did not seem misplaced.

British defeat in the War of Independence had many causes, but underlying them all was a strategic failure to identify clear objectives and to concentrate on them to the exclusion of sideshows. This failure had been much in evidence at both the military and political levels in the early months of 1776. While Howe was preparing to leave Boston for Halifax and New York, General Clinton received orders from home to mount a seaborne expedition to the Carolinas, where it was hoped local Loyalists would flock to his support. His force included men removed from Howe's army, but he was mostly dependent on fresh drafts shipped out from England. Loyalist support proved disappointing and ill-coordinated, an attempt to storm Charleston from the sea failed and, at the end of June, the expedition sailed off to New York to rejoin Howe. Nothing had been achieved and

Howe had been deprived of reinforcements at a time when they might have helped him defeat Washington decisively.

At the political level an instance of muddled thinking was the proposed Peace Commission which, probably as an afterthought, had been added to the other provisions of North's Prohibitory Act. The two Commissioners appointed were not very obviously men of peace. One of them was the admiral, Lord Howe, who on the rejection of his demand to operate on his own, had assumed joint command with his brother the general, recently promoted Commander-in-Chief in America.[41] Moreover, their terms of reference restricted them to offering an amnesty to Americans who submitted to British rule, with no scope for negotiation on the wider issues. On 4 July 1776, eight days before Lord Howe landed, the Second Continental Congress meeting in Pennsylvania approved the text of the Declaration of Independence. It is doubtful if any peace proposals short of the offer of complete autonomy could thereafter have had much chance of success, but those offered by North and his Ministers made a bad situation worse. They were rejected outright by Washington. Lord Howe's pronouncements on his peace mission were circulated by the Continental Congress in the belief that they would bolster support for the rebel cause.[42]

Throughout the war the British effort suffered from a lack of purposeful direction. The generals were brave and professional soldiers (though of no outstanding military talent), but they lacked the guidance and control a clear-sighted statesman might have provided. Germain's vision was too limited – and too sanguine – and the dislike of his colleagues was a barrier to any extension of his responsibilities as a war leader, while North's tolerant, easy-going nature disqualified him from assuming a role that might have come naturally to either Pitt.

The effects of inadequate long-term planning by the government in London were exaggerated by the slowness and unreliability of transatlantic communications. The information available to North and his Ministers was always out of date, and the recommendations they issued were received in America sometimes several months after the events that occasioned them. Most official despatches were carried by Post Office packet-boats, light craft that could make the crossing faster than merchantmen or men-of-war; on average they took two months to reach America, and one month on the eastward return. There were, however, never enough of them, partly because forty were lost by storm or capture in the course of the war.[43] Frequently, therefore, the Admiralty had to be asked to supplement the service but, as it was reluctant to provide ships solely for that purpose, despatches could wait several weeks before sailing. An examination of Germain's correspondence with General Sir Henry Clinton, the

Commander-in-Chief in America during the closing years of the war, showed that, over the period May 1778 to February 1781, sixty-three letters were sent, but only six reached Clinton in under six weeks, forty took up to three months, and the rest anything up to seven months.[44] North's administration was responsible for the conduct of the war but, in the absence of both sound strategic thinking and good communications, its control over the course of events 3000 miles away was inevitably restricted.

The closing months of 1776 were unsettling for North at a more personal level. On 9 September his wife wrote to her father-in-law telling him the King and Queen had visited them the day before at Bushy and stayed for over three hours. She said: 'The King insisted on Ld North sitting in his great chair, indeed it would have been quite impossible for him to have stood all the time'.[45] The implication is that North was no longer capable of staying on his feet for an extended period although he was then only forty-four. Eighteen months earlier Thomas Hutchinson, considering the possibility of a change of ministry, had noted that if old Lord Guilford died North would find himself translated to the Lords, but he added 'Ld N. himself is not long lived – corpulent etc'.[46] While riding in the park at Bushy a fortnight after the royal visit North was thrown from his horse; he fell heavily and broke his right arm.[47] He recovered sufficiently to be in his place in the Commons when Parliament reassembled on 31 October,[48] but the shock of the fall had pulled him down and led to a loss of weight. His friend Jack St John informed Guilford he was 'the better for the accident for it has reduced him very much',[49] a point acknowledged by North a few months later in an anecdote retailed by Walpole: 'Dr Warren, his physician, asking his Lordship what he felt, he, who was very gross, replied, "What I have not felt a great while, my own ribs" '.[50] His fall marked the onset of a gradual decline in his health which became increasingly apparent as he grew older.

The other personal matter that concerned North at the end of 1776 was the possible marriage of his eldest son George, who was only just nineteen. From North's letter to his father on the subject it almost sounds as if he was quietly sitting in Downing Street one early November day when a complete stranger was ushered in who proceeded to suggest that his daughter would make a suitable wife for George. The visitor was Mr James Egerton, an immensely rich Cheshire landowner. His daughter was his only child and he intended to settle £100,000 on her when she married, with a further £300,000 to follow on his death.[51] North must have had some advance warning of the visit but there is no suggestion that the two families had ever previously met or even corresponded. North, however, had an unromantic, eighteenth-century view when the possibility of a good match was in sight. He decided to consult his father without delay and his arm was evidently sufficiently mended to write a long letter in his own hand which in part read:

> Whether the young people will like one another is as yet uncertain, but all that I hear to the disadvantage of the young lady is, that she has a bad complexion, and is rather inclined to be fat but that she is not deformed, and has nothing disgusting in her appearance. That she is sensible, prudent, good tempered, & well educated seems to be the opinion of all that have any acquaintance with her. To be sure, on our side, we are rather too young, but so great an Establishment, if it can be acquired with a good & virtuous wife, who has no defect in character, temper & understanding, is an advantage not to be lost, & this opportunity appears to me not to be neglected. I, therefore, can not help hoping that the persons the most concerned will like one another. If this match goes on, which, I think, it will, we shall stand much in need of your Lordship's advice.[52]

Inevitably the news of the proposed marriage got out, and among those who heard the rumours was one of Mrs Delany's gossipy correspondents Frederick Montagu: 'P.S. I have opened my letter again to inform you that Mr North, Lord North's eldest son, is going to be married to *Miss Egerton, the great Cheshire heiress.* Old Sam [James] Egerton gives her *one hundred thousand pounds.* I don't write in figures, for you should think I put an 0 too much'.[53] The Norths would probably have preferred to keep the matter quiet for the time being, as there was a hurdle to be overcome. Mr Egerton had made it absolutely clear to North that as far as his daughter was concerned 'he would never think of obliging her to marry any man against her will' and that George had therefore to win her approval.[54]

Some sympathy may be felt for the nineteen-year-old George, pressed to woo a girl who was not only three years older than him but whom he had never met. Before travelling to Cheshire to embark on the enterprise he sensibly warned his grandfather: 'She is so suspicious that her money is the pursuit of all her admirers that I own I cannot help entertaining the greatest doubt of success'.[55] Guilford then took a hand in the affair, rebuking his grandson for passing his time at university and in London 'in a constant state of dissipation',[56] and implying that a satisfactory outcome to the siege of Miss Egerton would do much to restore his good standing. It is clear from George's report to his grandfather that his visit was not a success,[57] and by April Egerton had to inform Guilford that Mr North had not 'made himself agreeable to my daughter'.[58] It is nice to record that when George finally married ten years later it was entirely for love, to his grandfather's intense displeasure.

In February 1777 North caught a cold which developed into something more serious and kept him confined at Bushy for several weeks. On 20 March, referring to his duty at the Treasury and in Parliament, he told the King 'that he can not yet say when he shall be able to return to it, as he recovers his strength & spirits very slowly'. George III chose to interpret that statement optimistically, replying the next day: 'It is with infinite satisfaction that I find myself now enabled to express to You my Dear Lord the pleasure that arises to my mind from finding You are daily recovering the bad effects of your late severe illness'. He then reminded North that he had ordered Lord Guilford 'to keep you at Bushy till the end of the Easter Holidays', perhaps evidence of the King's awareness of Guilford's influence over his son, though maybe no more than a private joke at the expense of the old man.[59]

While North was ill, important decisions were being taken by his ministerial colleagues about that year's plan of campaign in America. These decisions were coloured by an unjustified optimism reflected in a letter Brownlow North wrote to his father early in the year: 'Our letters from Sir George [an unidentified army officer] are written in high spirits, & he seems to consider the work which the army had to do, as nearly completed & imagines they shall scarcely have an enemy to meet the next campaign'.[60] The general thrust of operations was agreed by the Cabinet on 24 February, a meeting at which North was almost certainly not present. On the same day the King wrote to him recommending '*Abstinence* and *water* as the ablest and safest physicians' for his increasingly bad cold.[61] In any event there is no reason to think he played a significant part in shaping the military strategy pursued over the next few months. It originated in America with Generals Burgoyne and Howe and was endorsed in London by Germain. It envisaged the invasion of the colony of New York by a large force from Canada under Burgoyne, while a rather smaller force under Howe (Sir William since the capture of New York) pushed up from New York City to join him at Albany on the Hudson River. A third more limited expedition from Canada under Lieutenant-Colonel Barry St Leger would provide a diversion by marching round the far end of Lake Ontario before turning eastwards to join the other forces at Albany. The object of the plan was to take control of the New England colonies and isolate them from the others.

The strategy had two weaknesses. The first sprang from divided control. Neither Howe nor Burgoyne was in overall command (at least until their forces met), which increased the already existing difficulties of coordination due to stretched communications. The other was a failure to appreciate the logistical problems presented by the terrain through which both

Burgoyne's army and St Leger's diversionary expedition had to advance. Nevertheless, if the plans had been carried out as originally conceived they might have been successful, though whether the overall British position in America would have been significantly strengthened is open to question.[62] Instead only half the plan was implemented, Burgoyne's and St Leger's advance from Canada. Howe, far from moving troops up the Hudson in their support, persuaded Germain to authorise a seaborne expedition to Philadelphia. Germain failed to inform Burgoyne of this change of plan in time for any modification of his own operations,[63] though on 18 May he ordered Howe to complete his capture of Philadelphia in time to cooperate with the the force advancing from Canada.[64] In the event Howe, with a force of over 260 ships and some 15,000 troops, did not set sail until 23 July and he departed without leaving any instructions for his deputy in New York, General Clinton, to assist Burgoyne.[65] After several changes of plan his men finally disembarked on 25 August 1777, pushing Washington back at the battle of Brandywine Creek and entering Philadelphia on 25 September. Hopes that this success would encourage a rush of Loyalists to the British cause in Pennsylvania proved completely unfounded.

Further north, on 14 June, General Burgoyne had begun his advance at the head of a force of 9500 men, 138 cannon and a large baggage train, and a week later St Leger had set out on his diversionary march round Lake Ontario.[66] Burgoyne was a dashing cavalryman. Years earlier he had eloped with a daughter of the Earl of Derby, but his possibly exaggerated reputation as a rake was balanced by undoubted courage and contempt for the second-rate. Unfortunately his judgement was easily clouded by an overconfidence verging on arrogance, and his underestimate of the difficulties involved in his route south was at least partly responsible for the final disaster.[67] On 5 July Fort Ticonderoga, only seventy miles north of the planned rendezvous at Albany, fell to his troops, though its American garrison managed to escape under cover of darkness.[68] The news of this success reached London at the end of August causing much rejoicing,[69] only to be followed by growing concern as no further victories were reported, and as Howe and his seaborne army appeared to have vanished.

Meanwhile, St Leger's progress had been halted and he was forced to turn back to Montreal, while Burgoyne's resumed advance on Albany met increasingly tough resistance and was impeded by serious supply shortages. He had heard, however, there was an American magazine at the lightly defended village of Bennington some thirty miles to the east of his line of march. On 11 August he despatched an ill-assorted body of British and German soldiers, American Loyalists and local Indians, commanded by the

Hanoverian Lieutenant-Colonel Frederick Baum, to march to Bennington and seize the stores. On approaching the village they discovered that, far from being undefended, it was held by a strong contingent of New Hampshire militia. On 16 August Baum's outnumbered and surrounded troops were routed: Baum was killed with around 200 of his men, and 696 were taken prisoner.[70] This was a disaster for Burgoyne, both in terms of the losses and of its effect on the morale of his whole army; it was not until 13 September that he resumed his advance on Albany.

After other fiercly contested but inconclusive encounters in which the British suffered heavily, Burgoyne tried to retreat across the Hudson River. Finding his way blocked, he took up his position on rising ground surrounded by open country at a spot called Saratoga, hoping the Americans would exhaust themselves attacking him. Instead they surrounded his position and waited. With his route back to Canada cut off, little prospect of relief from the south, his food running out and his army demoralised, Burgoyne was trapped. On 17 October 1777 he formally surrendered, together with his remaining force now totalling less than 6000, one of the most humiliating rebuffs British arms had at that date ever suffered.

While events in America were moving towards disaster, North spent an uneasy summer in London.[71] His wife had had a difficult delivery of their last child, Dudley, at the end of May, and it was far from certain that the child would live;[72] North himself was not fully recovered from his recent illness. Walpole reported that when he opened the budget on 14 May he did so 'languidly, and appearing ill'.[73] The King was robustly optimistic about the outcome of the war, telling North: 'In my opinion the Americans will treat before Winter',[74] but North did not share his confidence and sank into a mood of deep depression. In August he wrote from Downing Street to his father:

> In the course of ten years' hurry and vexation, I have never been so hurried and vexed as I have been for these last two or three months. Indeed, I am almost worn out with continual fretting. It may very possibly be that my uneasiness proceeds from my own faults, but the fact is that so long a continuance in a situation which I dislike, and for which I am neither adapted by temper or capacity, has sunk my spirits, weaken'd my understanding, impaired my memory, and fill'd my heart with a kind of uneasiness from which nothing can deliver me but an honourable retreat. I am sorry to say that I do not foresee the moment when that happiness will fall to my lot.
>
> To this state of mind and to a more than ordinary hurry of business, your Lordship will be so good as to attribute your having waited so long for an answer to your letters, and not to any want, duty and respect, and affection, where I am

sure I owe them by every tie, and where I trust I have been always ready to pay a debt ...

My letter ends rather more pleasantly than it began, thoughts of seeing your Lordship at Wroxton have enlivened me, but my heaviness will, I fear, soon return.[75]

George III was concerned about his First Minister's state of mind and he sought the advice of John Robinson who was both Secretary to the Treasury and one of North's closest political confidants. Robinson told the King: 'His Majesty's discernment certainly perceived what oftentimes preys on Lord North's mind; it is the situation of his private affairs'.[76] He explained that North's net income was well under £2500 a year, that Guilford, whose own income was four times that figure, only helped with a very small allowance to George, his eldest grandson, and that North's accumulated debts totalled £10,000. Robinson ended by informing the King that Lord North's 'delicacy and reservedness' had inhibited him from making an approach himself, which suggests that North was not averse in principle to seeking royal help.

On receiving Robinson's letter George III wrote to North. He started by explaining that having recently settled all arrears due from the Civil List his own financial position was 'perfectly at ease', and he continued:

You have at times dropped to Me that You had been in debt ever since Your first settling in life, and that You had never been able to get out of that difficulty. I therefore must insist You will now state to me whether 12, or £15,000 will not set Your affairs in order if it will, nay if £20,000 is necessary I am resolved you shall have no other person concerned in freeing them but myself; knowing now my determination it is easy for You to Make a proper Arrangement, and at proper times to take by degrees that Sum. You know me very ill if you do not think that of all the letters I have ever wrote to You this one gives me the most pleasure, and I want no other return but Your being convinced that I love You as well as a Man of Worth as I esteem you as a Minister.[77]

It was a generous letter and the King's offer was gratefully accepted. During the next five years North drew a little over £16,000 of the sum the King had made available to settle his debts.[78] The money came from the Secret Service Account, a fund viewed with considerable suspicion by the Country Gentlemen as the figures were never presented to Parliament.[79] Under the overall supervision of the First Lord of the Treasury, the account was used partly to bribe foreign politicians and for other forms of subversion, and partly to provide pensions (supposedly under a cloak of confidentiality) for worthy but impecunious gentlemen like Dr Samuel Johnson.[80] Strictly speaking it was not therefore his own money that George III made available to North but, as under the circumstances he was the only person who could initiate this particular item of expenditure, North's gratitude was in no way misplaced.

This transaction between King and Prime Minister has been much discussed both in terms of the motives behind it and for its effect on the recipient. The suggestion that George III made his offer with the deliberate intention of restricting North's freedom to oppose him or to resign has rightly been dismissed.[81] The King was often demanding but seldom devious and the offer was made for straightforward reasons. He was fond of North but aware of his weaknesses, and he was concerned that his First Minister would break under the burden of his worries; he happened to be in a position to alleviate one of the most pressing. Whether North was afterwards influenced in his attitude to the King is harder to say. It would have been out of character if he had not felt a strong sense of obligation to the man who had so handsomely come to his rescue. Moreover, an expression of this obligation comes in a letter he wrote to Thurlow, the Attorney General, only six weeks after the offer was made: 'I certainly always have wished and do still wish, to quit my present situation, & will take the first fair & honourable opportunity of doing it, but I am under such obligations to the King that I can never leave his service, while he desires me to remain in it'.[82]

North's talk of resignation must always be regarded with a degree of scepticism but the King's generosity added one more strand to the rope that bound him. Although he had been the King's hard-working Prime Minister for over seven years, and could have fairly considered the help as recompense for faithful service already rendered, he regarded it also as a claim on future loyalty.

13

After Saratoga

At the end of October 1777 news reached London via Paris of St Leger's enforced withdrawal to Montreal, but the disappointment was mitigated on 3 November when confirmation was received of Sir William Howe's success at Brandywine Creek.[1] North pondered the right tone to take in the King's Speech at the forthcoming Opening of Parliament. He consulted William Eden, a senior civil servant and like John Robinson a member of his confidential circle:

> How shall we mention America? Shall we be very stout or shall we take advantage of the flourishing state of our affairs to get out of this d—d war and hold a moderate language? ... My pen is wretched and I am very melancholy notwithstanding our victory. My idea of American affairs is that if our success is as great as the most sanguine politician wishes or believes, the best use we can make of it is to get out of the dispute as soon as possible.[2]

North and the King decided the speech should sound a note of sorrow rather than anger. Although the King referred to 'that constitutional subordination' which with God's help he hoped to uphold throughout his dominions, he also said he would 'ever be watchful for an opportunity of putting a stop to the effusion of blood of my subjects ... and I still hope that the deluded and unhappy multitude will return to their allegiance'.[3] Significantly there was no mention of Burgoyne and his army, presumably because in the absence of any reliable reports there was a growing fear that something had gone seriously wrong.

In the debate that followed Fox declared 'that the idea of conquering America was absurd' and condemned the strategy which 'placed the two armies in such a position as from their distance made it utterly impossible that one should receive any assistance from the other'.[4] The main Opposition attack was directed at Germain, who was rightly accorded responsibility for the strategy adopted in America. North made a short speech in which he defended General Burgoyne, whom he described as 'that military senator' (he was an MP), and also dismissed the fear that either France or Spain had any warlike intentions towards Britain.[5] Whether he was being honest in making this last assertion is questionable. Before the end of December he was warning George III of 'the growing disposition of the Court of France to support [American independence] openly and by force of arms if necessary'.[6]

In the early evening of 2 December Captain Moutray of HMS *Warwick* reached London from Quebec carrying the first reliable reports of the events at Saratoga. The despatches were addressed to Sandwich as First Lord of the Admiralty, who passed them to the King the same evening.[7] Copies must also have been sent to North and Germain. There appears to be no first-hand account of North's reaction on hearing the news but it is clear from a letter he wrote to George III two days after Captain Moutray's arrival that he had at once and in person offered his resignation.[8] This was refused and when he faced the Commons later that same day he had recovered his composure. Early in the debate on a motion on the army estimates Germain was compelled to confirm the rumours of Burgoyne's surrender, and opponents of the administration then turned the rest of debate into an inquest on the conduct of the war.[9] The main object of attack was Germain. He was defended rather obliquely by North who said: 'He could not possibly make any objection to the enquiry into that noble Lord's conduct, as he made no doubt that he would acquit himself before that House'. In the rest of his short speech he presented himself once again as a man of peace, and moreover someone who had 'been dragged to his place against his will', a place he a would gladly lay down if it would advance the cause of reconciliation.[10]

At the end of the debate the government won by a comfortable majority and the following day the King wrote to North to thank him: 'The Manly, firm, and dignified part You took brought the House to see the present misfortune in its true light, as very serious but not without remedy'.[11] Over the next week the government continued to defeat critical motions on American affairs without much difficulty: when the Commons adjourned for the Christmas recess it seemed relatively secure. It was and it was not. North's administration still had four years to run but Saratoga marked a watershed in political matters even more than in military.[12]

Saratoga was a major reverse for British arms but there were still large undefeated royal forces in America; nevertheless, after Saratoga the confidence of most of the ruling establishment that untrained colonial levies could not withstand a professional British army began to erode. The votes in the Commons immediately after the news of Saratoga were deceptive. Many Opposition Members feared that a vote against the administration was indirectly a vote in support of Britain's foes (which would soon include France and Spain), a dilemma that helped to sustain North's ministry. His majorities hid a growing disenchantment with the conduct of the war and a growing disbelief in the prospect of eventual victory. There is no question that North shared these doubts and that the best outcome he thought possible was an honourable stalemate. His personal dilemma – and it became his purgatory – was that George III remained one of a diminishing band whose confidence was unshaken.

Aware of shifting sands under his feet, North decided over the Christmas recess to make one last attempt at a negotiated peace. He had already secretly tried and failed to reach an agreement with three American agents, Benjamin Franklin at their head, who were in Paris successfully seeking French support,[13] and he realised that the only hope was to deal directly with a body he had previously stigmatised as illegal, the American Congress. He worked on his peace proposals without consulting the Cabinet, but he kept in close touch with the King and, after apologising for a memory lapse over a matter of minor importance, his letter of 29 January continued:

> Indeed, the anxiety of his mind for the last two months has deprived Lord North of his memory and understanding. The promise he has made of bringing forward a proposition for peace with America, and the necessity he thinks there is, from the situation of affairs, of endeavouring to draw some of the Colonies from their claim and plan of independancy upon Great Britain make him think it necessary to take some step of a pacific kind in Parliament but the former opinions, the consistency, and the pride of his political friends and himself stand in the way of everything that would be effective, or, indeed, have the appearance of a proposition likely to be accepted in any part of America.

North then explained to George III the extent of his difficulties: how if he was too accommodating to the Americans he would lose the support of 'friends of government', and if he offered too little his plans had no hope of success. He knew he was in an impossible situation and in a long final paragraph he spelt out the political implications of failure. He ended his letter:

Lord North is in such a situation that, whatever he does must be attended by some disgrace, and much misery to himself, and, what is worse, perhaps, with some detriment to the public. In this case, perhaps, a change which might bring into his room some person less pledged than himself might be of advantage to his Majesty's service. He submits the whole to his Majesty's pleasure, and, though his health and his understanding are greatly impaired by struggling so long in office, and in circumstances to which he has always been unequal, he would not on that account suggest a thought of retiring, unless the singularity of his present situation did not make him think it his duty to mention it.[14]

In his response George III used a familiar combination of emotional blackmail and flattery to block North's escape route, tactics North was quite incapable of resisting:

I should have been greatly hurt at the inclination expressed by you to retire, had I not known that however you may now and then be inclined to despond, yet that you have too much personal affection for me, and sense of honour, to allow such a thought to take any hold on your mind.

You must feel how very entirely I have confided in you since you have presided at the Treasury, how fairly you have been supported by your Colleagues in the Administration, how sincerely you are loved and admired by the House of Commons, and how universally esteemed by the Public; indeed these reflections must rouze your mind and enable you to withstand situations still more embarrassing than the present.[15]

The King also made it clear that he was not enthusiastic about North's peace initiative, fearing it would fail to impress the Americans while upsetting loyal supporters at home. That is what precisely happened.

North introduced his plans in the Commons on 17 February 1778. He proposed not only the repeal of most of the existing coercive legislation but at the same time the permanent suspension of Parliament's claim to tax America, the original cause of the war. His other proposal was the appointment of Commissioners with large discretionary powers to negotiate with Congress 'as if it were a legal body'.[16] When he sat down after speaking for nearly two hours he was, according to the contemporary *Annual Register*, greeted with 'a dull melancholy silence' while 'astonishment, dejection and fear overclouded the whole assembly'.[17] Neither supporters nor opponents could fully credit that North's somersault over his American policy was genuine; they feared it was a smokescreen for more calamitous news he was hiding from them.[18] In reality it more truly reflected his outlook than the repressive measures he had promoted in earlier years.

The legislation to implement North's proposals passed both Houses without much debate. He then seems to have lost interest in the project and played little part in selecting and briefing the three Commissioners.[19]

These were William Eden, who had probably first put the scheme into North's head,[20] and who saw his appointment as a clever career move, George Johnstone MP, a former Governor of West Florida who had publicly declared his opposition to independence,[21] and, as leader of the party, the twenty-nine-year-old fifth Earl of Carlisle. This was an extraordinary choice to head the Commission and one which Walpole said was 'universally ridiculed'. He was a young man-about-town who 'was totally unacquainted with business and though not void of ambition, had but moderate parts, and less application'.[22]

The Commissioners set sail for America on 17 April 1778. When they reached Philadelphia in early June they were astonished to discover that General Clinton (who had succeeded Howe) was about to evacuate the city, transfer his forces to New York and mount an expedition against the French-held West Indian island of St Lucia. Astonishment turned to anger when they learnt that although orders for this move had been despatched by Germain, more then three weeks before their own party had left Portsmouth, they had not been told of them. Eden only half forgave North for what he regarded as duplicity, and for scotching any chance of success for the Commission.[23] The evacuation of Philadelphia looked to the Americans a sign of British weakness; as it followed by a few weeks the entry of France into the war on their side their determination not to negotiate was strengthened. Congress told the Commissioners that a peace treaty would only be discussed when either independence had been acknowledged or all British military and naval forces had been withdrawn, conditions they were not authorised to consider.[24] After further fruitless and humiliating attempts at negotiation, Johnstone flounced out in August, having been caught trying to bribe members of Congress,[25] and the two remaining Commissioners sailed for home in November.

The obvious criticism of the Carlisle Commission is that it came too late, but that is reasoning after the event. Before Saratoga it is most improbable that North could have persuaded either the King or Parliament to accept such radical proposals and the fact that he did not try to do so is therefore irrelevant. His true failure lay in not taking the Commission under his personal wing and ensuring it had a more high-powered membership, and particularly in refusing to recognise that its only valid role was to sue for peace. He had told Eden he wished 'to get rid of this d ... d war', but so long as George III believed he could retake his American empire by force there was little North could do.

While the Carlisle Commission was still on its way to America North made another unsuccessful attempt to lay down the burdens of his office. Writing early in May to the King, who was visiting the fleet at Portsmouth, he told him: 'Your Majesty's service requires a man of great abilities, and who is confident of his abilities, who can chuse decisively, and carry his determinations authoritatively into execution ... I am certainly not such a man ... This is not false modesty; my ancient indolence is much increased ... '[26] In his reply the King dryly reminded North that 'the last words you used were that you did not mean to resign',[27] but twice more over the next four days North reiterated his inadaquacy for the position he held, and for a brief moment on 10 May George III seemed prepared to contemplate 'the retreat of Lord North from the Treasury'.[28]

In view of these heartfelt pleas for release it comes as something of a shock to find North asking the King a week later to be appointed the Lord Warden of the Cinque Ports.[29] Like all the best eighteenth-century offices reserved for the nobility and their relations, the Wardenship carried a stipend but only vestigial duties. The former was reckoned at the large sum of £4000 a year,[30] while the latter consisted of little more than an occasional visit to the Warden's official residence at Walmer Castle, where the local great and good were suitably entertained. The King had already promised North he could have the place when the present incumbent, Lord Holdernesse, died, an event which occurred on 16 May.[31] The next day North reminded George III of his promise,[32] but there seems to have been an element of misunderstanding over the King's offer.

North saw the Cinque Ports as insurance for the future, providing security when he left office, a view supported by his rather surprising refusal to accept more than £1500 of the full salary while he was still at the Treasury. After he had met the expenses of maintaining Walmer Castle and entertaining the locals this would leave him with less than £1000 in his own pocket.[33] North was therefore very anxious to be given the position for life, as had been the case with almost all previous incumbents, and not simply 'during pleasure', as the King had offered. He told George III that 'it would be a disgrace to me to have that office upon a less respectable footing than my immediate predecessor'.[34] The King persuaded him he need not worry about his security of tenure and he climbed down, but he also pointed out to North that when offering him the Cinque Ports he flattered himself that 'this fresh mark of my regard would have stimulated you to continue at the head of the Treasury ... '[35] There is no reason to believe that the King was crudely trying to bribe North. As with his relief of North's debts, George III wanted to bolster his First Minister's rather unreliable self-assurance in the interest of maintaining his administration in office. Nevertheless, North had been put on notice that in the King's mind there was an understandable linkage between favours offered and services expected.

George III comes out of this episode rather well. Lacking in imagination and subtlety, he does not always appear a very sympathetic man, but on this occasion he handled his Minister with sensitivity, even if sometimes with exasperation. He accepted the salary arrangements North wanted, and explained patiently that tenure 'during pleasure' was no reflection on North but followed a decision he had taken about all such appointments; on 2 June he used their discussions to offer North some friendly advice:

> I cannot help touching on another point, but at this hour it would neither be right nor friendly towards You, to conceal a single idea, the greatest part of Your difficulties arise from entering too far with others in plans of business but particularly arrangements of Employments, without fairly stating Your sentiments unto Me; if on the contrary You sounded my opinion first You would save much trouble and vexation to both of us, and where can you repose Your undigested thoughts more safely than in the breast of one who has ever treated You more as his friend than Minister, and who would perhaps frequently put You on Your guard against things which if consented to from Your being hampered disgrace my service, or if refused distress Your mind.[36]

North lost no time in taking possession of his new dignity. He probably received the official appointment on 18 May,[37] and by the 30th Lord Guilford's steward at Waldershare was writing to his master at Wroxton: 'I am happy to acquaint your Lordship that there was a general discharge of cannon from the Ships in the Harbour, and Fortifications at Dover yesterday; and that Lord North had every other mark of proper respect shown him there'.[38] It is also clear from the letter that, although North visited Walmer Castle, he and his family preferred to stay in the civilised comfort of the mansion at Waldershare set in its rolling deer park than occupy the dark, somewhat cramped quarters of his official residence.

North's attention in the early summer of 1778 was by no means wholly engaged by his attempts at resignation or his enjoyment of his new dignity. Irish problems had again come to the fore. Reduction in colonial trade due to the American war was causing economic hardship, and the example of the American revolt was increasing the pressure for political reform at home. Due to the withdrawal of British troops to fight in America the government had reluctantly agreed to the establishment of a local defence force. By May 1778 the new and mostly Protestant Irish Volunteers had attracted 8000 recruits and within a year the figure was thought to have risen to 20,000. No one believed that the rush to enlist indicated a sudden desire to defend English supremacy.[39] As his initial support for the Absentee Tax had shown, North was not unsympathetic to the need for new measures in Ireland. He told Lord Buckinghamshire, the Lord Lieutenant, to send him full reports and then ignored them. Perhaps he had no real desire to read them; his interest in Ireland was fitful and lacking in urgency.

In April 1778 the government brought in a Bill to relax Irish trade restrictions. Speaking in its support North made the apt comment that although most people agreed something must be done for the relief of Ireland they usually differed over what form it should take.[40] At first the Bill progressed satisfactorily but it came under growing attack from English commercial interests that feared Irish competition. On 25 May North made no effort to intervene when the Bill was lost on an adjournment motion,[41] but he was beginning to receive warnings of the possibility of an Irish rebellion. A year later he again tried with little more success to persuade Parliament to accept relief measures, but new developments strengthened his hand. The Irish organised a boycott of British goods which proved much more effective than anyone expected. Opposition to North's proposals melted away and by early 1780 he had got his Irish Trade Bills through Parliament. He was much relieved when the Acts were well received in Dublin.[42] When two years later the Irish question next troubled an English government North had left office, but his failure to achieve a permanent settlement of an intractable problem should not be held against him. He was certainly not prepared to contemplate serious constitutional reform, but he was ready to adapt his mercantilist orthodoxy in the interests of a more prosperous and hence less discontented Ireland, a flexibility which put him in advance of many of his opponents.

The major change on the international scene during the years 1778–79 was the entry first of France, in June 1778, and then a year later of Spain into the American war as enemies of Great Britain. Both hoped to repossess territories lost in earlier conflicts, Spain particularly seeking the return of Gibraltar taken by the British in 1704, but in other respects their policies were dissimilar. France believed that the detachment of the American colonies from the mother country would advance her own commercial prosperity and she therefore provided active support. Spain, on the other hand, with her extensive colonial empire to the south, was wary of encouraging republican independence; although the Spanish gave financial aid, they recognised America as a co-belligerent only at the very end of the war.[43]

The involvement of France was the more serious matter. For the last three years of the war a substantial French fleet was stationed either on the American seaboard or in the West Indies and, although it failed to achieve a decisive defeat of the British naval forces, its presence hindered British operations and finally made a critical contribution to American victory at Yorktown in October 1781. Britain was faced with the threat of invasion and with the far greater demand on resources that a sea war with two major continental powers made inevitable. Patriotism was at a premium, but confidence in the administration was beginning to slip.

In describing someone's life there is a danger of overemphasising the bad times as against the good, if only to add contrast and interest to the narrative. It seems nevertheless legitimate to describe 1779 as the low point in North's time as Prime Minister. In the closing months of the previous year he had again tried to persuade the King to find another First Minister, though his letters lack the pleading tone of the previous spring. Like other men he was no doubt inconsistent; sometimes he pined for the peace of his family life and the peach houses at Bushy but at others was unable to resist the pull of power and the excitements of office. At the end of October he told George III of his fears that in the forthcoming parliamentary session his support would weaken and that 'nothing will mend the matter, but a change in the appearance of Public affairs or a change in the administration'.[44] He also promised the King his thoughts in writing on how to maximise government support. A few days later the King testily referred to this 'Plan on Paper' and told him: 'This you promised to draw up; yet the Week has elapsed without Your producing it, and Your aversion to decide would lead You to postpone it till too late, unless forced by me to what I look upon not only as essential to the conducting public affairs with credit, but as necessary for Your own ease of mind'.[45] There is a distinct impression that George III was starting to lose patience. He kept North because he had no alternative if he wanted to avoid a government of Whig grandees, but the King was beginning to treat him as an only moderately useful servant.

On 10 November North, in the course of a long letter to the King, made another appeal for a change:

> Lord North upon the positive injunctions of his Majesty, remains in a situation for which he was never fit, & for which he is now less fit than ever, but he can never pretend to like it, or hold any other language than his wish of retiring. He has already declared to his Majesty, & thinks himself obliged in conscience to repeat the declaration, that he considers his continuance in Government in his present station as highly prejudicial to his Majesty's affairs, &, therefore, he intreats his Majesty to continue his search after a better arrangement.[46]

George III replied with a brief, rather incoherent note ignoring North's arguments but telling him: 'I think it the duty [to] my personal honour of those in public station [that] must prompt them with zeal to make every effort to assist me who have unreservedly Supported them'.[47] Four days later North made one more attempt:

> He will certainly bear patiently the misery he feels from continuing in office because it is his Majesty's pleasure that he should continue there, but he thought it his duty to state to his Majesty, & he thinks it is his duty once more to repeat that he is conscious & certain that he has neither the authority nor abilities requisite for the conduct of his Majesty's affairs at this time, & that he has every reason to apprehend that his Majesty will essentially prejudice his own & the public cause by obliging him to remain where he is.[48]

The King's answer extolled 'the beauty, excellence and perfection of the British Constitution' and asserted that his Ministers must show in their speeches 'that they will never consent to the Independency of America',[49] advice that North can hardly have appreciated. The question of North's departure was then dropped (at least for the time being) and he ended his next letter: 'On this subject he will trouble his Majesty no more, but leave it entirely to his Majesty to determine what is best for the public good'.[50] He had completely failed to influence the King's thinking and faced the difficulties of the ensuing year with that failure on his mind.

In March 1779 the Northern Secretary Lord Suffolk died, adding to strains within the administration that were to last for most of that year. As a study of North's relationship with John Robinson, the Secretary to the Treasury and his personal confidant, concluded: 'The stages of North's deepening depression – and the attendant creeping paralysis from which he suffered – can be shown to have had correspondence with the ascending steps of the ministerial crisis'.[51] Due partly to his own lack of resolve, and partly to bitter personal rivalries within the administration, it was seven months before he was able to fill the vacant place with a former diplomat, Lord Stormont. At the same time both Sandwich and Germain were under attack in Parliament, the former probably unfairly, as he had worked hard to improve the state of the navy, but Germain with far more justification. North concluded his government might be stronger without his American Secretary but was afraid to to sack him; he told the King that if Germain would resign of his own accord he would be ready to pass on to him the Wardenship of the Cinque Ports that he had so happily accepted only a few months earlier. George III was unenthusiastic about the idea and Lord George remained in office.[52] Meanwhile the deferred decisions and unread papers piled up around North.

On 17 June 1779 Spain formally declared war on Great Britain, and there were rumours of the combined French and Spanish fleets sweeping up the Channel.[53] Four days later George III took the unusual step (unprecedented in his reign),[54] of summoning a Cabinet meeting himself, at which he made a half-hour speech to his Ministers (including North) 'recommending unity of spirit in their several departments', and told them the advent of Spain into the war must not be made an excuse for a 'dishonour-able peace' with the Americans.[55] He had already given North the same belicose agenda, telling him the conflict could not be justified in terms of loss or gain as 'this is only weighing such events in the Scale of a Tradesman behind his Counter'.[56] After the Cabinet meeting he wrote to Sandwich that 'If others will not be active, I must drive', a clear reference to North's inertia.[57]

Three days earlier North had suffered a terrible blow when his youngest child, Dudley, died at Bushy aged two, followed by the collapse of Lady North.[58] The deaths of young children were too common to occasion much comment and the King's condolences were formal rather than heartfelt, a brief opening paragraph in a letter mostly devoted to more mundane matters, but North cared deeply.[59] Lord Carlisle told George Selwyn: 'Yesterday Lord North lost a favourite child, which he loved with a fondness you alone can conceive'.[60] On 25 June, in a debate in the Commons on doubling the size of the militia, his personal probity was bitterly attacked by Fox. In his reply North took the opportunity to explain in detail how few had been the rewards for his often reluctant service, mentioning in particular his refusal to accept the full salary accorded to his predecessor at the Cinque Ports. He also referred to his very limited private means and his 'pretty numerous family', at which point Cobbett comments: 'At these words his lordship struck his breast, and burst out into a flood of tears, probably from the casual recollection that one of his sons lay dead at that moment. The House, touched at the circumstance, called for the question, but his lordship, recovering himself, desired leave to go on'.[61] The same day John Robinson told Charles Jenkinson that North 'was now in better spirits & determined to go on',[62] but he left for his summer break in a mood of deep pessimism.[63] In August Sandwich told the King he had seen Robinson 'who gives but a desponding account of Ld North's disposi-tion'.[64]

To a certain extent the dangers of political paralysis in 1779 were contained by an arrangement that North soon suspected and then re-sented, the intimate relationship established between Robinson and Jen-kinson. John Robinson was North's trusted confidential adviser, a man with a rich wife, considerable integrity and not too many personal axes to grind.[65] Charles Jenkinson was an able and ambitious MP, recently ap-pointed Secretary at War, who had become almost as close to George III as Robinson had to the Prime Minister: 'sole confidant of the King' as Walpole described him.[66] With royal approval these two men talked and corresponded freely with each other about the problems faced by North and his ministry and how best they could be overcome, information that was then passed by Jenkinson to 'the Closet', in other words to the King.[67]

It is easy to criticise this backstairs way of doing things both on constitutional principles and on grounds of the betrayal of North's trust, but given the real responsibilities still held by the King for the good government of the country and the apparent incapacity of his First Minister, the only alternative would have been to reconstruct the ministry and allow in men who might want to recognise American independence. This George III was determined to avoid, an attitude shared by Robinson and Jenkinson. Robinson was additionally motivated by true affection for North and the desire to strengthen his faltering will and protect him from his own indecisiveness. His letters to Jenkinson in late 1779 reveal North's state of mind. In August he told him North was 'the most altered Man I ever saw in my life',[68] and in November wrote at length about his friend's miseries. In part the letter read:

> He told me … that he was sensible that every one was leaving him, and were plotting to desert him, and overturn the King's Government, but why should they do that, why need they do it when he said only come and take his place, he was ready to quit to any proper Administration that could be formed, but that he could not form one, as he was the man they all run at, that he saw clearly he should be deserted on some Question, perhaps some Collateral one to Government … it would endanger the King, that the dread of all this and that he should be the Cause of it distress'd him beyond Measure, that his Duty, His Honour and every tie of Regard, required him to state this to His Majesty and that it preyed on his Mind so much as rendered him incapable of anything, he had no Decision, he could attend to no Business, that his Sufferings were only felt by himself, but most sincerely felt, indeed with the greatest Torments of Mind but were impossible to be described and he could not bear to be the cause of the destruction of His Majesty's Power and Government, and perhaps the Ruin of his country – He then, my Dear Sir, fell into such a Scene of Distress, I assure you as made my Heart bleed for him and drew Tears from my Eyes. I pressed him to consult his friends. He said he had no friends he could consult. All seemed to have deserted, he was pleased to add except me.[69]

14

The Road to Yorktown

With the entry of France and Spain into the war the resources of the British navy were stretched to the limit. A fleet was retained in home waters to counter the threat of invasion, Gibraltar required supplies, transatlantic convoys and the British islands in the West Indies needed protection, and the freedom of movement of British forces along the American seaboard had to be ensured. It says much for the abilities of Sandwich at the Admiralty that defeat in the American war was held off for three years after the French entry into the conflict, and that ultimate French and Spanish gains from participation were minimal. Nevertheless, from 1778 the perspective shifted. Great Britain was now involved in an international war in which victory in America was no longer the sole or even the most important objective.

After Saratoga British strategy in America took a new direction. The main base remained New York, the French fleet having crossed the Atlantic too slowly to interfere with Clinton's move there from Philadelphia.[1] In the northern and middle colonies no decisive engagement took place during the last three years of the war. The British mounted punitive expeditions, with occasional support from Loyalists and local Indians, which Washington, aided by his new French allies, was able to contain. Stalemate was reached and might have continued indefinitely without the impact of events further south. The new plan was to reestablish British authority in the southern colonies of Georgia and South Carolina, with the prospect of a subsequent move into North Carolina and possibly Virginia. It was believed, not entirely without foundation, that Loyalist sentiment was stronger in the south, and it was recognised that any American troops advancing from the north would be handicapped by long and vulnerable supply lines while the British forces could normally expect to receive reinforcements and ordnance by sea. If a firm position was established in the south the reconquest of New England and the north became a possibility.

A seaborne force under Lieutenant-Colonel Archibald Campbell captured the coastal Georgian city of Savannah on 29 December 1778 and by the end of the following month the whole colony was in British hands. Holding it in the face of guerrilla harassment proved harder than expected, but the reinstated royal Governor, Sir James Wright, was able to maintain civil rule there for nearly three years.[2] Charleston, further up the coast in South Carolina, fell to General Clinton in May 1780, involving the surrender of 5000 American soldiers and 300 cannon.[3] In August an army led by General Earl Cornwallis, one of Clinton's subordinate commanders, won a major victory at Camden in South Carolina. Although an attempt to subdue North Carolina failed, at the end of the year the British position was deceptively encouraging. As before, however, the British government (and its commanders in the field) underestimated the resilience and determination of its opponents.

At the end of the previous year North's problems in Ireland were (at least temporarily) on the mend. He had also finally succeeded in rebuilding his Cabinet without the whole political edifice falling about his ears, and the war in America gave grounds for guarded optimism. It is true that 1780 was to produce its own crop of difficulties, but on the whole they were ones he was better fitted to handle. The movement for Economical Reform has already been discussed, together with North's successful deflection of demands for reformed national finances onto the Commission on the Public Accounts.

Arising directly out of the reform petitions, however, the House of Commons on 6 April 1780 considered John Dunning's famous motion that 'The Influence of the Crown had Increased, is Increasing, and Ought to be Diminished'. The rather abstract, general nature of the motion was well calculated to appeal to a broad spectrum of Members who for one reason or another had growing doubts about the administration, and its close support from the King, but still hesitated to oppose it on specific issues in the middle of a war. North did not give one of his best parliamentary performances. He was viciously attacked by Thomas Pitt, Chatham's nephew, who told him he 'had sunk and degraded the honour of Great Britain; the name of an Englishman was no longer a matter to be proud of ... but the noble lord had contrived to sink it almost beneath contempt'.[4] In his reply North made the now familiar comments about his lack of abilities and his readiness to retire but then uncharacteristically lost his temper,[5] accusing the Opposition of 'pursuing measures likely to overturn the constitution'. Challenged to withdraw the words North, demanded whether he was to hear himself 'charged as the author of our present misfortunes', a question that was met from the benches opposite with a chorus of 'You are, you are'. After a period of uproar North made a half-apology and resumed his speech, but it was one of the few occasions when he lost control of the House.[6] At the end of the debate Dunning's motion was carried by 233 votes to 215, a serious set-back for the administration.

The day following the vote North once more offered George III his resignation; as on this occasion his administration had been defeated on something akin to a vote of confidence he perhaps had little choice. The King declined the offer, pointing out that the motion had not primarily been aimed at North but at himself.[7] A week later Jenkinson told the King that North was 'too fond of having it believed that He continues in Office contrary to his Inclination … ', repeating a view he had expressed the previous December.[8] The significance of these comments may have been overstressed by historians seeking a consistent pattern in North's numerous ineffectual attempts at resignation. The King was convinced the ministry would survive, telling North 'a little time will I am certain open the Eyes of Several who have been led on farther than they intended … '[9] He proved correct. Many Country Gentlemen who had voted with Dunning became uncomfortable associating with men who supported American independence. Over the next two weeks reform measures were defeated with growing ease, and when Dunning proposed on 14 April that the King should be 'addressed' not to dissolve Parliament or prorogue the present session until the abuses 'complained of by the petitions of the people' had been corrected, the ministry defeated him by the comfortable margin of fifty-one votes.[10] In essence North had successfully fought off calls for constitutional change, in which he certainly did not believe, but had given a modest impetus to an important programme of financial reform.

The next challenge to the authority of North and his government was more direct and more brutal than the threat of parliamentary defeat. In 1778 the Catholic Relief Act had with North's support provided a slightly greater degree of toleration for Roman Catholics, though bigotry north of the border had prevented its application to Scotland.[11] On the heels of the various reform petitions Lord George Gordon, an unbalanced Scottish aristocrat who was virulently anti-Catholic, presented to the House of Commons on 2 June 1780 a petition from a group of like-minded Protestants demanding the repeal of the new Relief Act. Whether, as claimed by Gordon, 60,000 supporters besieged Parliament is unclear,[12] but when his petition was rejected by 192 votes to seven he took to the streets. He quickly raised a mob, which even conservative estimates put at 20,000, which for the next six days was in virtual control of the capital.

The ministry was slow to react to the violence. The maintenance of civil order was the responsibility of the City authorities but they seemed unable or unwilling to take any action, something the King condemned as 'the great supineness of the Civil Magistrates'.[13] Eighteenth-century respect for the forms of law caused further delay. While the mansions of the rich were burning and ordinary citizens were murdered, the Law Officers argued whether it was permissible to call out the troops to quell riots before a magistrate had read the Riot Act, a scruple given point by the judicious disappearance of all the City magistrates. George III seems to have played an important part in overcoming his Ministers' worries about the use of the military, and on 8 June Lord George Gordon was arrested.[14] Within a few days quiet was restored and a number of rioters were hanged. Gordon himself was tried for treason but acquitted.

Beyond acquiescing in the King's determination to suppress the disturbances by force, North does not seem to have been particularly active in promoting measures to restore order. He had rightly refused to be intimidated by Gordon's threats into repealing the Relief Act, and he remained calm, even casual, when the threats were fulfilled. Unlike some prominent figures, who left their well-known town houses, he remained in residence at Downing Street, guarded at the height of the riots by twenty grenadiers under the command of his son George, now Colonel North. On the evening of 7 June he invited a few people to dinner and in the course of the meal a mob gathered outside the house. When dinner was over messages were sent to the crowd outside that, with or without the Riot Act, the grenadiers would open fire the moment there was any trouble. The party then climbed to the top floor to get a better view of the fires blazing in various parts of London. In due course the crowd dispersed peacefully. When North was asked whether he had been frightened of the mob he answered he had not been half so much afraid of it as of the pistol wielded by Jack St John, one of his guests.[15]

The successful suppression of the Gordon Riots did nothing to persuade George III to reconsider his views on the best way of handling rebellion. He was, however, guardedly prepared to consider a broadening of the base of the ministry to strengthen its position in Parliament, though warning North that it could only be done 'if it can be attained without a violation of my Principles'.[16] At the end of June North approached Lord Rockingham to see if a coalition with his faction of the Whigs was feasible, but he discovered that the terms were too high. Rockingham not only demanded an acceleration of Economical Reform together with the dismissal of Sandwich and Germain but, more critically, insisted on a commitment from the King to negotiate American independence if this should prove expedient.[17] Jenkinson meanwhile told the King: 'Mr Robinson ... thinks I am a true Prophet in having always said that Lord North never meant to treat or to part with the smallest Degree of Power'.[18] But this is disingenuous. Jenkinson attributes to North a deviousness in the retention of office he never possessed; all the evidence suggests he tried to put the most favourable possible interpretation on Rockingham's terms in the hopes they could be accepted.[19] The King meanwhile sent North a long paper on the conditions he was prepared to consider, from which it is clear it was not his First Minister's love of power on which the negotiations foundered, but his own non-negotiable 'Principles'.[20]

Simultaneously with his discussions on a possible coalition North, together with his Cabinet, was weighing up the arguments for a snap election. An election was not due until the autumn of the following year, but the confidence induced by the defeat of Lord George Gordon, as well as the news from America of Clinton's capture of Charleston, which reached London on 15 June,[21] persuaded North he could strengthen his position in the Commons by an appeal to the voters. The Cabinet discussed dissolution on 30 June and again on 4 July without reaching a decision. It was agreed North should put in hand an analysis of the likely outcome of an election, and that meanwhile complete secrecy should be observed to catch the Opposition off-balance should one be called.[22]

John Robinson was assigned the role of North's election manager: in the course of July he and his assistants produced a forty-nine page report covering the probable result in each of the 314 constituencies and the likely views of the 558 members that would be returned for them.[23] While this work was in progress North was asked by one of his supporters on a visit to Downing Street if he could yet throw any light on the government's intentions, to which he answered: 'I really cannot say more than this, that the doctors are now met in consultation on the case in the other room, and you know the result on such occasions is generally death'.[24] The final prognosis, however, was optimistic and the King agreed to the dissolution of Parliament on 1 September 1780, to be followed by an election over the next few weeks.

To keep the Opposition in the dark, North and other Ministers set out on their holidays, North heading for Waldershare towards the end of August leaving word that he planned to spend three or four weeks there. He had already told Robinson: 'I have made it a rule this summer to allow myself no pleasure, no dissipation, nor vacation whatever'.[25] A few days later he returned inconspicuously to London and by the 29th was dating a letter to the King from Robinson's house at Sion Hill, conveniently close to Bushy.[26] The stratagem seems to have worked as the *Annual Register* reported: 'The Proclamation for dissolving parliament operated like a thunder clap, with respect to suddenness and surprise, on those who were not in the secret'.[27]

For North and Robinson the work was far from over. Local magnates with pocket boroughs but uncertain loyalties had to be persuaded to field candidates who would support the ministry, and money was judiciously distributed to subsidise election 'expenses' when a genuine contest was expected. Direct bribery by the ministry was not normal; it was easier to promise places or pensions in the event of a satisfactory result. Quite large sums were nevertheless disbursed to particular candidates to assist their own local efforts at influencing the electorate. Precise figures are hard to come by but it has been estimated that some £62,000 was provided by the government's election fund for this purpose in 1780; the extent of this indirect participation by North in electoral bribery should, however, be seen in context. Not only was he operating a system unquestioned by almost everybody in politics, but the sums involved were not enormous in relation to the totals spent by others on trying to influence the result. It has been suggested that £50,000 may have been distributed by the candidates themselves in just one constituency.[28]

It is the source of North's election fund rather than the use to which it was put that looks odd today. Starting in November 1777 George III put aside £1000 each month from his privy purse in anticipation of a future election, sums that were then subsequently (and presumably secretly) passed to North or Robinson. Despite this arrangement, however, the money accumulated proved insufficient for the requirements of the election and North with, he believed, the King's full authority borrowed £30,000 in his own name in December 1780 from Henry Drummond, the royal banker, to meet outstanding claims.[29] This loan had not been repaid by the time North left office, a situation that unhappily then developed into a bitter dispute between himself and George III.

Robinson's predictions of the results of the elections proved to have been optimistic. In the days when party lines were blurred and many Members sat as independent Country Gentlemen estimated figures for friends and foes were unreliable, but it was generally accepted that far from strengthening its position the ministry's support was probably weaker by five or six votes. More significantly the swing against the administration was greatest in the 'open' boroughs and the counties where popular opinion could influence the result. In the case of the counties this reflected a growing weariness on the part of the landed interest over increased taxation to pay for the war.[30]

The election was over by the end of September and, according to one of his biographers, North immediately became ill, 'perhaps as a result of it'.[31] The evidence for any illness at the beginning of October is slim and depends on a remark in a letter which may easily have been misdated.[32] Only a week later Walpole described North as 'very good company' at a party they both attended and where they shared a game of cribbage, and he also mentioned that North had just returned from a visit to Somerset.[33] This does not sound like a man convalescing from a stress-induced illness. At the end of the month, however, he did become seriously ill. He was in his place in the House when the Commons met to choose a new Speaker on 31 October, though he was criticised by Dunning for taking no part in the proceedings,[34] but he was almost certainly not present for the King's Speech the following day, as Walpole said he was 'very ill of a fever'.[35] On 2 November the King expressed his concern about North's health to Robinson and two days later wrote again urging him to borrow royal authority to insist that North took a few days to recover before returning to business. He also thought it worth while to ask Lord Guilford to advise his son to remain at home till he was better.[36]

North's recurring bouts of illness as he grew older can no doubt be considered partly psychosomatic in origin, an unconscious attempt to escape from the strains of his official life. He was nevertheless in poor physical condition. In 1782 Samuel Curwen described him as 'bulk greatly exceeding, large legs, walks heavily, manner clumsy . . . ',[37] a natural obesity probably abetted by overeating.[38] Even seven years earlier Thomas Hutchinson had not expected North to be 'long lived', a comment that was based on the outward and visible evidence of his state of health.[39]

After the debate on the Address on 6 November the ministry had a comfortable victory, with 212 votes to 130. The news from America was rather more encouraging and there had been little disposition among Opposition speakers to question the continued prosecution of the war.[40] The size of the ministry's margin was slightly misleading as over 200 Members, mostly independent-minded Country Gentlemen, did not bother to attend the brief pre-Christmas session, but the parliamentary outlook was moderately promising for North and his government. It has even been suggested that this was the one moment when he could with honour have laid down the burdens of his office and insisted on resigning.[41] He had served the King loyally for over ten difficult years, the American situation gave grounds for cautious optimism, he had just won an election, and he was ill. There is, of course, not the slightest indication that

North considered any such step. His thoughts turned to resignation when life was unpleasant not when the going was smooth. A few months later, however, in April 1781, the familiar complaints recur in a letter to his seventy-seven-year-old father. North was in penitent mood because he had forgotten the old man's birthday. After apologising for this lapse he wrote:

> I felt deeply your very affectionate expressions, & this additional instance of your constant & unremitting goodness to me, which has been one of my principal supports and comforts through Life. Your partiality leads you to think that my conduct has been creditable to myself & beneficial to the Public. I am afraid it has been otherwise, but, if I have not done well in my situation, I can truly say, it is a situation which I never sought, & I have been severely punished for all the harm I may have done by unceasing anxiety & weariness I have undergone.[42]

Despite North's complaints the first months of 1781 were relatively trouble-free. The period between Christmas and Easter was a vulnerable time for eighteenth-century ministries, as much of the session's most important business came before Parliament during those weeks.[43] The attendance of Members could be enforced or at least encouraged by a call of the House, a procedure by which on a predetermined day each Member had to answer to his name in the Chamber; any who were absent without a valid excuse were in theory liable to a penalty. The government seldom had need of such a device to rally their own supporters but it enabled the Opposition to secure a maximum turn-out of the Country Gentlemen, usually its best hope of victory. At the behest of the Rockingham party a call was taken on 31 January,[44] but despite full attendances the ministry survived every attempt to defeat it both then and through the spring and early summer. North had been very uneasy over the likely parliamentary reaction to the rising cost of supporting troops in America and the West Indies,[45] but on 24 January the vote for the necessary funds was carried by a large majority.[46] He had a similarly easy passage at the end of the month when the Commons were asked to approve the declaration of war on the United Provinces in response to the help the Dutch were giving the American rebels. There were grumbles, but patriotism overcame alarm at the prospect of the higher taxes that this extension of the war might entail.

The ministry's main danger arose from the renewed pressure for Economical Reform and in particular the reintroduction by Edmund Burke of his Establishment Bill, which prescribed a reduction in the number of placemen, pensioners and others whose salaries were charged to the Civil List or the Exchequer. At first North backed away from a confrontation, warned by Robinson of the uncertainty of the outcome,[47] but this was not a position he could sustain for long. He decided to fight on the second reading and on 26 February won the vote by the respectable margin of forty-three votes. If the Opposition could not run North closer on this issue at a time when reform was in the air, it was clear that only the failure of his American policy could dislodge him from office. In the spring of 1781 this did not look very probable. After the vote on Burke's Bill on 26 February until Parliament was prorogued on 18 July he had little trouble in resisting Opposition attacks, whether on his handling of a government loan, his reluctance to press for further reform of the East India Company, or his conduct of the war. For six months he enjoyed a political Indian summer, successful even if not always confident or relaxed.

The news from America was deceptive and deceived many in London. George III's belief that there were large numbers of American Loyalists waiting for a favourable opportunity to return to their true allegiance was widely shared, though the evidence for it had always been patchy. After the war Cornwallis complained bitterly of the lack of Loyalist support accorded him in North Carolina, commenting that 'the unexpected failure of our friends rendered the victory of Guilford of little value', but his superior, General Clinton, believed that Loyalist activity was at least partly dependent on the existence of secure British bases.[48] It was not lack of appropriate sentiments towards the Crown that held many colonists back so much as the fear of American patriot revenge if British protection was withdrawn. The realities of the situation were not appreciated at home: one historian has described the despatches of the American Secretary Lord George Germain at this time as 'an almost incredible picture of deluded optimism'.[49] On 7 March 1781, only a few months before the final defeat, he wrote to Clinton: 'So very contemptible is the rebel force now in all parts, and so vast is our superiority everywhere, that no resistance on their part is to be apprehended that can materially obstruct the progress of the King's arms in the speedy suppression of the rebellion'.[50] The British army had won some battles and captured a few cities but was realistically no nearer winning the war than it had been five years earlier.

This mood of unjustified optimism was given a boost at the end of May when news of the engagement at Guilford County reached London. On 15 March Lord Cornwallis, in the course of his attempt to subdue North Carolina, had defeated a body of American troops under General Nathaniel Greene but, as Cornwallis himself saw, this victory at Guilford achieved nothing. The British suffered substantial casualties and were soon compelled to withdraw to the coast at Wilmington.

Cornwallis then decided to advance northwards to occupy Virginia (with the possibility of inflicting a glorious and definitive defeat on the enemy probably in his mind), a move that caused General Clinton, the Commander-in-Chief, some disquiet when he heard of it. Clinton was more concerned about his own ability to hold New York, and favoured operations in the neighbouring colony of Pennsylvania. He saw Cornwallis's planned advance through Virgina to the Chesapeake as a diversion to which he could only give limited help, and one largely dependent for supplies and protection on British naval superiority.[51] Moreover, it weakened the British presence in the far south, and within three months only Charleston, Savannah and small adjacent areas were still in British hands.[52] American independence may have become inevitable, but it was hastened in 1781 by muddled strategy and indecisive leadership.

Lord Cornwallis had left Wilmington by the end of April. He was joined in Virginia in May by a British contingent recently reinforced by the small numbers Clinton could spare. He was now in command of an army of more than 6000 men, a force only exceeded in size by Clinton's at New York.[53] Towards the end of July his army encamped on the Williamsburg peninsula on the York River at the mouth of Chesapeake Bay. On 2 August he began to fortify Yorktown, a position on the north east of the peninsula with a deep-water anchorage but otherwise no natural advantages. He was well aware of the dangers of his situation, not least from naval blockade, but Clinton had urged him to retain control of the Williamsburg peninsula as a possible winter base for the fleet, and Yorktown was the least unsatisfactory of the sites available.[54]

Earlier Cornwallis had tried but failed to force a decisive battle with an American army already in Virginia under the French soldier of fortune the Marquis de Lafayette. When Washington, facing Clinton at New York, heard the news of Cornwallis's situation he hurried his men south to support Lafayette's efforts at containment of the British force. Washington's army reached the peninsula on 14 September, bringing the numbers opposing Cornwallis to some 16,000 men.[55]

During the summer a French fleet had crossed the Atlantic under Admiral de Grasse to assist the Americans by blockading New York, but Washington was persuaded by his French allies to agree to the diversion of the ships to the Chesapeake. They arrived there on 30 August, the day after a British fleet under Admiral Thomas Graves had sailed from New York to intercept them. On 5 September the two fleets met in an inconclusive engagement at the mouth of Chesapeake Bay, but many of the British ships were so badly damaged that Graves decided to withdraw temporarily to New York for repairs. De Grasse, subsequently joined by a smaller French squadron, was now free to establish a blockade of the bay; neither relief nor evacuation by sea was any longer available to Cornwallis.

The siege began in earnest on the night of 28 September when the encirclement of the British position was completed. On 9 October, after digging the necessary entrenchments, the besiegers brought up artillery and opened a bombardment with guns much heavier than the defenders could deploy, causing considerable damage and casualties. On 14 October two British redoubts were captured, and on the 16th an attempt by the defenders to break out across the York River failed. On 17 October 1781, four years to the day after Burgoyne's capitulation, Cornwallis asked for terms; two days later he led his troops out of their ruined encampment and surrendered.[56]

Fox and North share a two-handled tankard of beer. The froth spills over onto a copy of a petition from the Westminster Association, formed to press for parliamentary reform. Published by W. Humphrey, 2 May 1783.

15

The End of an Era

The news of Cornwallis's capitulation reached London on Sunday 25 November 1781, two days before the Opening of Parliament, the messenger going straight to Lord George Germain's private residence in Pall Mall.[1] Germain at once got into a hackney coach and went to Portland Place where the Secretary of State, Lord Stormont, lived. They then travelled together to the Lord Chancellor Lord Thurlow's house in Great Ormond Street. After a short discussion they decided that all three of them should go to Downing Street and lay the dreadful news before North. Probably the best-known account of this event comes from Wraxall:

> He had not received any intimation of the event when they arrived at his door in Downing Street between one and two o'clock. The First Minister's firmness, and even his presence of mind, which had withstood the riots of June 1780, gave way for a short time under this awful disaster. I asked Lord George afterwards how he took the communication when made to him. 'As he would have taken a ball in his breast', replied Lord George. For he opened his arms, exclaiming wildly, as he paced up and down the apartment during a few minutes, 'O God! it is all over!' Words which he repeated many times under emotions of the deepest consternation and distress.[2]

Germain's story shows North reduced to despair, but there are other assessments of his state of mind after the news of Yorktown reached him. In a letter which is undated but evidently written at the end of November, North's half-brother Brownlow (the recently appointed Bishop of Winchester) told his father: 'I was at Downing Street last night, all was hurry, the family well . . . They said Ld North was out of spirits but not as bad as he is sometimes.'[3] That picture of slightly unexpected resilience gains support from a letter written by Lord Loughborough (who as Alexander Wedderburn had caused North much trouble with his demands for employment) to his friend Lord Carlisle on 30 November: 'Lord North, I understand, has

shown firmness, in which I have seldom known him fail. Lord Gower and
Lord Sandwich were not thought to possess themselves so well'.[4] It was,
however, Germain not North who steeled himself to go to Kew and break
the bad news to George III.[5]

In his letter to his father Brownlow North also made the comment: 'In
general conversation I find that this will put an end to the American part of
our present war'. It is inconceivable that the Prime Minister, with his
sceptical, realistic mind, did not share that view and the prospect it brought
of approaching release from his burdens may have buoyed his spirits over
the next difficult few weeks. When the news of Yorktown reached London,
the King's Speech for the opening of the new session of Parliament two
days later had already been written; it does not appear to have been much
altered to take account of the new situation in America.[6] It made only
oblique reference to Yorktown, conceding that 'the events of war have
been very unfortunate to my arms in Virginia, having ended in the loss of
my forces in that province',[7] a rather muted acknowledgement of such a
humiliating reverse. The speech even expressed hopes that the King's
'deluded subjects in America' would return to 'that happy and prosperous
condition which they had formerly derived from a due obedience to the
laws' and ended with a call for the 'prosecution of this great and important
contest'.

For a while George III and most of his Ministers were in a state of shock,
seemingly unable to recognise that the loss of Cornwallis's army made their
previous expectations redundant, though North emerged from this fantasy
world a good deal quicker than the King. The day following the Opening of
Parliament George III told North that as soon as 'men are a little recovered
of the shock felt by the bad news ... they will then find the necessity of
carrying on the war, though the mode of it may require alterations'.[8]

In the debate in the Commons on the Address of Thanks, Fox attacked
the ministry on every aspect of its American policy, but he received only
limited support and the government won a handsome victory when the
vote was called.[9] North had, however, made an important concession
before the debate closed:

> The Address did not pledge the House to the continuation of the American war,
> or to any form, or shape, or size of it. The Address only declared to his Majesty,
> that they would support the measures which should be undertaken, or continued,
> for the preservation of the essential rights and permanent interests of the empire.
> There was no word of continuing the American war; it was not mentioned in the
> Address at all.[10]

A fortnight later an independent-minded MP, Sir James Lowther, put down a motion specifically demanding the end of the American war. By now public opinion had started to assimilate the news of Yorktown and its implications, and Lowther's motion was given substantial backing. The Address had been approved by a majority of eighty-nine, but the ministry defeated Lowther's motion (in a House of much the same size) by only forty-one votes, a result noted by the King with disappointment but not evidently with understanding.[11] The writing was on the wall and North could read it but George III would not.

North had appeared masterly in this debate, displaying insouciance in the face of calls for his impeachment,[12] while skilfully refusing to be pinned down on his future course of action.[13] He pointed out that Britain was still at war with France and Spain and that considerable British forces remained on the other side of the Atlantic. He may also have been concerned about the fate of those Americans who had stayed loyal to the Crown and had refused to take up arms against the mother country, if Britain in effect offered unconditional surrender. North knew independence was now inevitable but he neither wanted to negotiate from a prematurely weakened hand nor to indulge in pointless sabre-rattling. During a debate two days later in which Germain continued to demand the vigorous prosecution of the war against America, North ostentatiously rose from his seat on the Treasury bench and distanced himself both physically and symbolically from his American Secretary by taking one of the seats behind him.[14]

The pressure for Germain's removal grew over Christmas and the New Year, not least from some of his fellow Cabinet members who saw him as an obstacle to peace negotiations. North was half-inclined to keep him, as he valued his abilities as a government speaker in the Commons and hoped he could be persuaded to soften his tone on America, but when Henry Dundas, the Lord Advocate for Scotland, walked out of the House on 22 January, refusing to return until Germain had gone, the break-up of North's ministry had begun. Germain had the effrontery to demand (and get) a viscountcy from George III rather than the more usual barony offered to a retiring Minister; on taking his seat in the Lords he was greeted with a barrage of abuse and an unsuccessful attempt to deny him admission.[15]

North's slightly surprising readiness to retain Germain was matched by the equally unexpected willingness of George III to see him go. The King and the American Secretary were in disagreement over the man who should succeed Sir Henry Clinton as Commander-in-Chief in America. The King wanted Sir Guy Carleton, a man with whom the American Secretary was not on speaking or even writing terms,[16] but that was not the main reason for George III's indifference to the prospect of Lord George's departure from office. Although by mid December Germain was probably the only member of the Cabinet still determined to resist American independence, this was largely unimportant to the King. He was no longer interested in the opinions of his individual Ministers. Whatever their private convictions, he expected all of them to follow the line he laid down and oppose any moves towards American independence. Germain's voice in the Cabinet was not, therefore, of any special value.[17]

This was North's dilemma. He was pressed by the King to pursue a policy neither he nor most of his Cabinet any longer believed in, but at the same time George III refused to contemplate North's departure. So long as the First Minister felt bound to his monarch by ties of loyalty as friend and servant, only the defeat of the ministry in the House of Commons could bring that about. During December North had floated various ideas with the King for a solution that left the Crown with a vestigial sovereignty over the American colonies, but he had been brusquely rebuffed.[18] Immediately after Christmas the King told North that he would never agree to 'the getting of a peace at the expense of a Separation from America'.[19] Three weeks later on the day when Parliament met after the Christmas recess he returned to the point:

> I shall only add that on one material point, I shall ever coincide with Lord G. Germain, this is against a separation from America and that I shall never lose an opportunity of declaring that no consideration shall ever make me in the smallest degree an Instrument in a measure that I am confident would annihilate the rank in which this British Empire stands among the European States, and would render my situation in this Country below continuing an Object to me.[20]

North had never found it easy to say no to the King and after twelve years of devoted, perhaps over-deferential service, it was difficult to change. On the same day that he received the King's letter he replied:

> I am very sensible how unfit I have always been, and how much more unfit I am now to decide in matters of nicety and difficulty, and if I had not repeatedly laid before Your Majesty my incapacity, and humbly advised Your Majesty more than once a year during the past ten years to place your affairs in other hands, I should take to myself a much greater share of the blame for what Your Majesty's service has suffered by my indecision.[21]

That extract was, however, only part of a long, closely-reasoned letter in which he also said:

> Peace with America seems necessary, even if it can be obtained on no better terms than some Federal Alliance, or perhaps even in a less eligible mode. This is my

opinion, which I have the honour of submitting before Your Majesty, and I think it is my duty to suggest once more whether, if Your Majesty's sentiments coincide more with Lord Germain's than mine, you would choose that he should appear to give way to me.[22]

In the last two months of his premiership there is a calmer tone in North's correspondence with the King, and it is perhaps pertinent that, despite the pressures of his position, he still found time to enjoy the company of his friends. In the middle of February he was seen playing his regular game of whist at White's,[23] and a couple of weeks earlier Wedderburn told William Eden: Lord North 'has kept open house & his dinners have been very lively'.[24] He seems at last to have come to a firm conclusion about the inevitability of American independence and that nothing was any more to be gained from concealing his convictions or from worrying. He ended his long letter to the King with an unusually elaborate, almost emotive valediction: 'I beg leave to subscribe myself, with the utmost devotion and attachment, Sir, Your Majesty's most faithful and most obedient and most dutiful subject and servant, North'.

By early February, ten days into the resumed parliamentary session, it was clear to almost everyone except George III that North's ministry could not long survive. The Rockinghamites and the other Opposition factions smelt blood. The only question was when and how the kill would be achieved. The first Opposition attack was oblique rather than frontal. On 7 February 1782 Charles James Fox moved for an enquiry 'into the Causes of the Want of Success of the British Navy', an attempt to censure Sandwich, the First Lord of the Admiralty. North made a strong defence of his colleague, arguing that since Sandwich had come into office the state of the navy had much improved. This was true, but when the motion was put to the vote the ministry's majority was only twenty-two.[25]

Two weeks later Fox found a procedural device for resubmitting the same motion. There is no report that North spoke on this occasion but whether he did so or not his majority dropped to nineteen.[26] The next day the King wrote to North: 'I am very sorry to find so many persons could view the conduct of the Navy in so very prejudiced a light ... I trust they cannot have lost the feelings of Englishmen so much as to support the Motion of General Conway on Friday'.[27]

George III's inability to see the shift in political opinion on America was shown by his naive trust that Englishmen would not support General Conway's motion. He was referring to a resolution to be debated the following day in the Commons which urged that 'the war on the continent of North America may no longer be pursued for the impracticable purpose of reducing the inhabitants of that country to obedience by force'.[28] This effectively launched a more direct assault on the ministry. Despite North's assurance that he had always been in favour of peace, the ministry's majority dropped to one. Passions were roused when Fox immediately gave notice that the motion would be reintroduced. In the debate that followed that proposal Colonel Barré called North 'the scourge of his country', saying 'he had drained its resources, spent its cash, and reduced it almost to beggary'.[29] North rose to his feet in a rage, describing Barré's words as 'brutal and insolent'. Uproar followed and, after a lot of argument, North was persuaded to apologise for his use of unparliamentary language, but it is hard not sympathise with his anger. He had served his country as its First Minister for twelve years, and during that time he had only pursued policies that Parliament had approved. Retrospective criticism he knew was inevitable but he saw no reason to accept loud-mouthed abuse.

Conway's motion was reintroduced in the Commons on 27 February, essentially unchanged apart from the insertion of 'offensive' in front of 'war'.[30] Two days earlier North warned the King it was likely to succeed, to which he received the reply: 'I certainly till drove to the Wall do what I can to save the Empire, and if I do not succeed I will at least have the self-approbation of having done my Duty and not letting myself be a tool of destruction of the Honour of the Country'.[31] In the debate North's speech reiterated his wish for peace, but its most important passage reflected his belief that if the Opposition wanted to remove the ministry they should not do so by calling for negotiations with America but by tabling a motion of no confidence. He knew that was the only way to force the King's hand. He said:

> If the House should withdraw their confidence from him, it would be his duty, without waiting for an address for his removal, to wait upon his sovereign, and, delivering up to him the seal of his office, say to him, 'Sir, I have long served you with diligence, with zeal, and with fidelity; but success has not crowned my endeavours; your parliament have withdrawn from me their confidence; and all my declarations to them are suspected; Therefore, Sir, let me resign to you those employments, which I ought not to keep longer than I can be serviceable to your Majesty and your subjects'.[32]

The ministry was defeated by nineteen votes but did not resign. It was strictly only a defeat on a particular aspect of government policy, which could in theory now be modified without a change of Ministers. North, however, told the King 'that as the House of Commons seems now to have withdrawn their confidence from Lord North, it will be right to see, as soon as possible, what other system can be found'.[33] George III replied saying he was 'mortified Lord North thinks he cannot now remain in office', insisting that any new ministerial arrangements should be 'founded on keeping what is in our present possession in North America'.[34]

On 8 March 1782 Lord John Cavendish moved a formal motion of censure on the government and North accepted that if it was carried his resignation was inevitable.[35] In the event the motion was defeated by ten votes, partly because a number of Members who had earlier voted against the continuance of the war now wanted North to remain as the best man to bring in the peace. The next day, however, he told the King: 'After such division, Lord North is obliged to repeat his opinion that it is totally impossible for the present Ministry to conduct His Majesty's business any longer'.[36] George III asked for time to 'maturely deliberate'.[37] A further no confidence motion was tabled on 15 March. North made a dignified defence of his record, assuring the House 'he felt the most perfect calmness of mind' as he had 'the consciousness of having done no wrong'. He also alluded rather mysteriously to circumstances he could not explain which were preventing his resignation, presumably a coded reference to the King's refusal to face facts.[38] The ministry scraped home with a majority of nine and in a letter to North the King hinted at abdication.[39]

Yet another motion of no confidence was put down for 20 March. Meanwhile the King had instructed the Lord Chancellor, Lord Thurlow, to sound out the Marquis of Rockingham on his willingness to lead a broad-based coalition in the event of North's resignation. It quickly became clear to George III that Rockingham's terms were completely unacceptable, particularly the condition that there should be no royal veto on American independence, and he rejected them on 18 March.[40] On the same day North learned that a number of the Country Gentlemen, believing that 'vain and ineffectual struggles tend only to public mischief and confusion', were intending to withdraw their support from him.[41] North passed that information to the King, at the same time stressing what he had already expressed in an audience earlier that day, that 'the fate of the present Ministry is absolutely and irrevocably decided'.

North's letter on this occasion has been described as 'a significant document of modern British history'.[42] It was a remarkable *tour de force* for a busy, harassed man under constant parliamentary pressure and it set out the constitutional position in clear, firm and unambiguous terms. It is too long to quote in full but the main part of the letter reads:

> The torrent is too strong to be resisted; Your Majesty is well apprized that, in this country, the Prince on the Throne, cannot, with prudence, oppose the deliberate

resolution of the House of Commons; Your Royal Predecessors (particularly King William the Third and his late Majesty) were obliged to yield to it much against their wish in more instances than one; They consented to changes in their Ministry which they disapproved because they found it necessary to sacrifice their private wishes, and even their opinions to the preservation of public order, and the prevention of these terrible mischiefs, which are the natural consequence of the clashing of the two branches of the Sovereign Power in the State. The concessions they made were never deemed dishonourable, but were considered as marks of their wisdom, and of their parental affection for their people. Your Majesty has graciously and steadily supported the servants you approve, as long as they could be supported; Your Majesty has firmly and resolutely maintained what appeared to You essential to the welfare and dignity of this Country, as long as this Country itself thought proper to maintain it. The Parliament have altered their sentiments, and as their sentiments whether just or erroneous, must ultimately prevail, Your Majesty having persevered as long as possible, in what You thought right, can lose no honour if you yield at length, as some of the most renowned and most glorious of your Predecessors have done, to the opinion and wishes of the House of Commons.[43]

North's departure became him well, which is rather more than can be said of the King's behaviour. He replied to North's letter with a short, rather petulant note complaining that he felt hurt as North knew perfectly well that his 'sentiments of honour' did not allow him to treat directly with any of the Opposition leaders. This may well have been true but it was hardly something for which North was responsible. His reply ended: 'If you resign before I have decided what I will do, you will certainly for ever forfeit my regard'.[44] That was emotional blackmail. North had been trying to tell George III for some time that he must find a new First Minister. If the King had failed to take the warnings seriously he had only himself to blame.

North wrote again to the King on the 19 March urging him that, as Rockingham's terms were unacceptable, he should without delay send for Lord Shelburne, the other chief Opposition leader. He also made a moving plea for understanding. Referring to the following day's motion of no confidence he said: 'It is generally imagined that we shall be beat tomorrow; if it should happen, I must quit my place immediately, and shall remain in the Journals for ever stigmatized upon record by a Vote of Parliament for my removal, which I believe has seldom, if ever, happened to a minister before'.[45] He begged to be allowed to resign at once rather than wait till he lost the vote: 'I submit the whole to Your Majesty's kind consideration, hoping that you will permit me to save myself from disgrace'.

On the 20 March North had an interview with the King at St James's Palace. No official account is known of their discussions,[46] but Wraxall said North arrived for the interview around two o'clock, that it took at least an hour an a half and that no third person was present.[47] The implication from the length of the meeting, apparently extending well beyond the time at which the Commons was due to meet, is that George III was still reluctant to give way. In the end North's resignation was accepted, though according to Walpole grudgingly and with ill-grace, as he was dismissed with the words: 'Remember, my Lord, that it is you who desert me, not I you'.[48] It is legitimate to wonder how Walpole acquired this story, but whatever the truth of the matter there is no doubt George III parted from his dutiful and faithful servant with a singular lack of generosity.

North arrived at Westmister some time after four o'clock, entering a tense and crowded chamber in 'a full-dressed suit his ribband over his coat'.[49] Charles Howard, Earl of Surrey, rose to propose the motion that stood in his name for the removal of the ministry, the first business on the order paper. As he rose North also got to his feet and was given the floor by the Speaker at the expense of Surrey. North tried to speak to move the adjournment but his voice was drowned by clamour from the Opposition benches.[50] The Members opposite suspected what North was about to announce but wanted the satisfaction of his condemnation by a formal vote of censure. It was even believed Burke had prepared a motion for his impeachment.[51] For more than an hour Members wrangled over whose motion should take precedence until Fox formally proposed that 'Lord Surrey be now heard'.[52] This gave North the opportunity he needed because in exercising his right to oppose this latest motion he was also able to tell the House that Surrey's motion was now unnecessary. The ministry was no more and 'his Majesty has come to a full determination to change his ministers'.[53] That was bending the truth a little but it persuaded a majority of Members not to hound North to the humiliation he feared of a formal vote of censure. After some debate Surrey withdrew his motion and it was agreed to adjourn the House until the following Monday, to allow the King time to form a new ministry.

Wraxall compared North's departure favourably with that of his predecessor Sir Robert Walpole, writing that the First Minister of George II did not 'by any means display the equanimity, suavity, and dignity manifested by his successor'.[54] In his resignation speech North told the Common:

Before he took leave of his situation entirely, he felt himself bound to return his most grateful thanks to the House for the very kind, the repeated, and the essential support, he had for so many years received from the Commons of England, during his holding a situation to which he must confess he had at all times been unequal. And it was, he said, the more incumbent on him to return his thanks in that place, because it was that House which made him what he had been.[55]

As a result of the adjournment the Commons rose much earlier than expected. Outside it was snowing and bitterly cold and Members were impatiently awaiting the recall of their carriages which had been ordered to return much later. According to a contemporary account there was, however, one exception. Lord North's carriage was at the door. 'He put into it one or two of his friends, whom he had invited to go home with him, and turning to the crowd, chiefly composed of his bitter enemies, in the midst of their triumph, exclaimed, in this hour of defeat and supposed mortification, with admirable good humour and pleasantry, "I have my carriage. You see, gentlemen, the advantage of being in the *secret.* Good night".'[56] He went home with his friends to an enjoyable dinner party. One of them, the Scottish MP William Adams, later wrote: 'No man ever showed more calmness, cheerfulness, and serenity. The temper of the whole family was the same. I dined with them that day, and was witness to it'.[57]

North's departure from office ended a political partnership which had lasted for twelve years, that of himself and George III. Although there was still one short period to come when North was a Minister of the Crown, the King deeply resented the circumstances of his return to government, and dismissed him as soon as he had the opportunity to do so. During North's tenure of the Treasury, however, monarch and First Lord formed a successful team.

Like most successful partnerships, mutual regard, even affection, warmed the formal relationship between them. After the unsatisfactory outcome of his friendship with Bute, the King may have been wary of intimacy with anyone beyond his family circle, but there is no reason for scepticism when he told North that he had always treated him 'more as his friend than Minister'.[58] North's feelings for the King were inevitably coloured by deference, but again there is little doubt that the respect he felt for the office extended to the man. He was meticulous in keeping the King informed on everything relating to government business, and listened carefully – perhaps sometimes too carefully – to the advice he received in return. Above all, George III and Lord North shared two virtues: both men were deeply patriotic, with an unashamed pride in Britain and her institutions; and both aspired to decency in their conduct of life.

Good personal relations were without question a necessary ingredient in the vitality of the twelve-year partnership, but they were not on their own sufficient to ensure its success. The partnership was in essence political, and it was the political skills of both men that sustained it. In the case of North, a professional, such skills come as no particular surprise; his ability to manage the House of Commons and – for most of the time – his often fractious colleagues, speaks for itself. To attribute political acumen to the King, however, requires more justification; the traditional picture, after all, shows Farmer George, far more the bluff country squire than an astute man-of-affairs. It is true that his personal tastes were simple and included country pursuits, but George III also collected books, established the Royal Academy (and personally subsidised it), and greatly enjoyed music.[59] He may have lacked imagination, but he was not stupid, and he possessed the capacity to learn from experience. Having endured humiliation from George Grenville early in his reign, and then discovered the problems of finding a more sympathetic replacement, the King became determined to make full use of the discretion the constitution allowed him over the selection of his First Lord. In this he proved remarkably successful and shrewd. During the fifty years from his accession in 1760 to the establishment of the Regency in 1811, he was served for thirty of them by only two Prime Ministers, Lord North and Pitt the Younger, both his personal choices. Furthermore, in each case there was risk in the appointment; neither man could at the time be certain of the support of the House of Commons. In the event the King's instincts were vindicated: North quickly secured his position in Parliament; and Pitt was able to do the same after a substantial victory in the 1784 general election, called shortly after his acceptance of the seals. The King may have come to the throne as 'the veriest political simpleton',[60] but he grew into a man who understood how British government worked, and could use the system in what he honourably believed to be the best interests of the country.

George III wielded undoubted political influence. It was based on his experience, on his entitlement to select (and dismiss) his Prime Minister, and on his extensive rights of patronage, especially the creation and promotion of peers – but how much direct control did he exercise? The question is relevant to any attempt to apportion responsibility for events in America.

The King's authority, if not his influence, was severely circumscribed. First, it was impossible for any administration to survive for long without the support of the House of Commons, which in turn limited the scope for royal direction over government action. Secondly, the King was almost entirely dependent on Parliament for money since, following a precedent set in the time of William III, each monarch on his accession had exchanged the hereditary revenues of the Crown for a Civil List requiring parliamentary approval. This money not only had to provide for the personal expenses of the King and his family, but for all government expenditure, including salaries. Only the costs of the armed services were met directly by the Treasury.[61] Although not himself extravagant in his way of life, George III found the Civil List perennially inadaquate, and was compelled on occasion to seek supplementary help from Parliament. This, together with the ultimate sanction of a refusal by the Commons to vote supplies, was the practical check on royal power.

George III and Lord North shared many of the same political attitudes and assumptions: strong distrust of 'democrats' like Wilkes, belief in the merits of sound finance and low taxes, support for the position of the established church, and respect for the spirit of the mostly unwritten British constitution. They both accepted a world in which patronage played a large part, but wished to use it for recognisable political ends, not the enhancement of their own importance. It is therefore hardly surprising that when faced with the challenge of the American rebellion they reacted in harmony. The King regarded the colonists as his subjects, but he also believed, with equal force, that his jurisdiction must be exercised through Parliament, and that the ultimate authority of Parliament should never be compromised. This view was not only agreed by North but by almost everyone involved in politics, and by the nation at large. At least until the defeat at Saratoga, King, Parliament and people were united in their aim, even though there might be disagreements over methods. George III saw his roll as supporting the actions of his Ministers, perhaps spurring them to a greater sense of urgency, but not as the executant of an independent royal policy. A brief look at events on the political scene in the weeks immediately following news of the battle of Bunker Hill may illustrate the point.

The King entirely approved North's view that the troubles in America should now 'be treated as a foreign war', and he set about encouraging its prosecution with vigour.[62] Within a few days of receiving news of the engagement he wrote to North: 'I shall be extremely glad to see Lord Dartmouth and You as soon as it is convenient to You both that we may talk over whatever is still necessary towards forwarding the American business; a little Council of this kind will do more than several separate conversations'.[63]

Even before making this suggestion George III had sent orders to Hanover that five battalions of his German troops should be prepared for embarkation to America, a decision entirely within his powers as Elector. £10,000 was, however, required for equipping this force for overseas service, a sum which North explained to him, 'must in the first place, be taken out of the Civil List, & application must be afterwards made to Parliament to replace it'.[64] The government welcomed this proposed reinforcement of the British Army in America, but the King's action still required endorsement by his Ministers and retrospective approval by Parliament.

Another of the King's interventions at the time was to press for the recall of General Gage, and for a reordering of the command structure in North America, but his letter to North urging this action includes the qualifying phrase: 'if you are of this opinion'.[65] North and the Colonial Secretary, Dartmouth, almost certainly agreed with the proposal, and the cover provided by royal sanction was helpful; nevertheless, even in matters of senior military appointments, the King was not an independent agent.

One of the rare occasions when, on the face of it, George III did take semi-autonomous action during the American war also occurred in the aftermath of Bunker Hill: the Proclamation of Rebellion issued by the Privy Council on 26 November 1775.[66] The King was the driving force behind this, ignoring North's obvious reservations (which were probably shared by Dartmouth). On the other hand, the King's determination was backed by the Northern Secretary, Lord Suffolk, his Under-Secretary, William Eden and, in principle, by both the law officers, the Solicitor and Attorney Generals.[67] It seems difficult to argue that George III was abusing his constitutional position; with encouragement from senior Ministers he stepped in to resolve the indecision of his First Lord. Six years later, however, when the war had been lost, the King's outspoken wish to continue the struggle, even when coupled to tentative threats of abdication, had no influence on the outcome.

There is only one way in which George III might have had a marked and independent effect on the progress of the American war: he could have accepted one of North's repeated offers of resignation. It is unlikely that the King always took these offers very seriously, but that is rather beside the point; he was given several easy opportunities to drop his Prime Minister which, far from using, he ignored. It is idle to speculate in any detail on what might have happened had the King acceded to North's expressed desires. Much would have depended on the timing, but at no point during the critical years before and immediately after the opening of hostilities at Lexington was there any obvious replacement. It is hard to see Parliament later accepting the leadership of Germain, or even Sandwich, when British reverses called for a more vigorous approach to the war. Part of the strength of North's position lay in the competition's weakness; this also restricted the King's options.

If the King had replaced North during the early years of his premiership, it is just possible a statesman would have come to the fore who was more sensitive to American resentments, and more skilled at negotiating a settlement. It is, however, hard to see how he could have carried Parliament and country with him. If, on the other hand, a wartime replacement is assumed, a man to pursue the military solution, it is easy to envisage more bloodshed, but not a radically different outcome. The separation of the American colonies from the mother country was always going to be a messy business, but George III's Prime Minister presided over it with sorrow more than anger, and the legacy of bitterness was surprisingly small. Over the past two centuries both men have endured opprobrium for the parts they played; a greater recognition of their integrity, and of the difficulties they faced, would redress the balance.

16

The Coalition and the Last Decade

Lord North was once more a private gentleman. After twelve years as First Lord and a longer period as a Minister of the Crown, he could shed the worries of office and enjoy the gardens at Bushy and the company of his family without the shadow cast by his official responsibilities. He remained, however, one of the most influential players on the political stage; there were still more than 100 MPs who, though in no sense forming a party, normally continued to look to him for leadership.[1] He was only forty-nine and could reasonably be considered a statesman with a future as well as a past. Much would depend on his own inclinations; meanwhile he intended to make the best of his new freedom. He toured the north in August, visiting Buxton Spa, where Lord Loughborough told Eden that he had had supper with North and that he was 'in very good spirits and just as undecided in a party of pleasure as he is in any other party'.[2] When he got to Manchester the townsmen were so pleased to see him that they took the horses from his carriage and pulled it through the streets. His cousin Frederick Montagu, meeting him at Wroxton in September, described him as 'very good company'.[3] At the end of the month Edward Gibbon saw him in London and told a friend: 'The Warden [of the Cinque Ports] passed through on his way to Dover. He is not so fat, and more cheerful than ever'.[4]

On North's resignation the King, very much against his inclinations, was compelled to treat with the two main Whig factions, respectively the followers of Rockingham and Shelburne. He would have far preferred Shelburne as the new First Lord, but his party was the weaker of the two; after he had declined the offer the King gave the seals to Rockingham. The two Secretaries of State in the new Cabinet were Shelburne and North's articulate critic Charles James Fox. Fox's bitter hatred of George III, which was fully returned,[5] did nothing to enhance the stability of a ministry already split over Economical Reform and the pace and terms of negotiations for recognising American independence and ending the war. A crisis was precipitated by Rockingham's unexpected death on 1 July 1782. Shelburne became First Lord but some of the Rockingham Whigs, including Fox, departed into Opposition; it was seen to be most improbable that the ministry could long survive the reassembly of Parliament in December. This put North in an influential position, as neither faction could be sure of a majority without his support.

On 7 August the King wrote to North reminding him of his earlier assurances that after retirement he would give 'the most cordial support to such an Administration as I might approve of'. He asked him to use his influence with the Country Gentlemen in favour of Shelburne. He also told North he distrusted Fox more than ever after his brief experience of him as a Minister 'which has finally determined me never to employ him again',[6] words that North was to force George III to swallow a few months later. North replied coolly to this letter, doubting whether he could call upon the Country Gentlemen for their punctual attendance at Westminster and suggesting that he might offend them if he tried. The most he felt able to offer was to sound them out before Parliament met.[7] It is quite likely that North, enjoying his carefree summer, had not yet determined whether he wanted to return wholeheartedly to the political fray, but it is obvious that he no longer felt the same deep attachment and loyalty to the King as in earlier days.

When North resigned unhappy words may have passed between him and the King, but he was satisfied that in the end constitutional proprieties had been respected; on George III's side anger seems to have subsided quickly. He immediately arranged for North to have a pension commensurate to that awarded to Sir Robert Walpole and may have offered him a peerage. That is the inference to be drawn from his observation to the King that if he could be of any service to him it would most effectively be in the Commons.[8] Only a week after his resignation George III told him: 'The effusion of my sorrows has made me say more than I had intended, but I ever did and ever shall look on You as a friend as well as faithful servant'; to which North replied that it would be 'the business of his life in every station, to show his attachment to his Majesty to the utmost of his power'.[9] Unfortunately the two men fell out over money.

To help finance the expenses of the 1780 general election North had, on the King's authority, borrowed £30,000 from Drummonds the bankers, and at the time of his resignation the debt had not been settled. North had signed the promissory note but added a comment to his copy saying it had been shown to the King and was 'given by his order'.[10] Drummonds regarded him merely as agent for George III in the transaction, as it is most unlikely they would have lent so a large sum of money to the relatively impoverished North without a more substantial guarantor, but when they made enquiries about repayment of the loan (together with interest outstanding), after North's departure from office, the King accepted responsibility for only £13,000 of the total sum. The rest, he said, was North's liability. North gave vague undertakings about reordering his affairs to enable him to discharge the obligation over a period of years,[11] but in practice there was not the remotest chance he could do so and there is no evidence that he even attempted it. He did not believe he bore any responsibility for the money. The dispute remained unresolved for two more years until George III wanted another election loan from Drummonds, who refused to accommodate him until the earlier debt had been paid. He complied but very grudgingly, telling Henry Drummond that North had been guilty of 'the most bare faced fraud'.[12] North's accounting methods were sloppy and dilatory and the status of the loan was imprecise, but he understandably felt badly treated over this affair and it soured his relationship with the King in the months before his controversial return to office.

The King's Speech at the Opening of Parliament on 5 December 1782 explicitly recognised American independence, George III commenting: 'I have sacrificed every consideration of my own to the wishes and opinion of my people'.[13] In the debate on the Address of Thanks North gave a guarded welcome to the provisional terms of the treaty to formalise independence and to end the war with the continental powers. He put down a marker, however, which he later used to good effect, by ending his speech with the warning: 'He desired that, in not opposing the Address, he might not be hereafter deemed liable to [have] ... precluded himself from objecting to the particulars of the provisional terms with America, should they appear to him objectionable'.[14] The Address was approved without a division.

On 18 December Fox decided to test the parliamentary temperature by tabling a motion for more information on the articles of the provisional treaty as they affected America. North was critical of the ministry's handling of the negotiations but, for the present, was prepared to support its wish for diplomatic reticence. In the division the backing given by North and his followers allowed the ministry a vote of 219 while Fox could only muster forty-six.[15] This result demonstrated North's influence but otherwise solved nothing. Shelburne remained leader of a minority government, but one to which there appeared to be no viable alternative.

William Eden had reckoned the previous October that Shelburne had 140 followers, North 120 and Fox 90, with some 200 MPs uncommitted.[16] Only a combination of two of the three leaders could therefore provide a stable ministry, but this seemed impossible to achieve. Shelburne's young but much valued Chancellor of the Excequer, William Pitt, flatly refused to serve in any Cabinet of which North was a member;[17] as far as Shelburne was concerned, that ruled out any arrangement which included him. Fox, for his part, would not join any administration led by Shelburne, while his past unrestrained criticism of North was presumed to make an alliance in that direction unthinkable. A further complicating factor was George III's unrelenting hostility to Fox, which appeared to preclude the formation of any ministry of which he was a potential member. When Parliament met after the Christmas recess it was nevertheless obvious this political impasse had to be resolved before negotiations could be resumed on American independence and the terms of the peace treaty.

In the second week of February North sent his eldest son George, now also an MP, to call on George's friend Fox to suggest a meeting with his father. He was successful and the two men met at George North's house in Old Burlington Street on 13 February.[18] In several hours of discussion they found enough common ground to make an alliance workable. Fox had no difficulty accepting the constitutional doctrine North expounded that 'the King ought to be treated with all sorts of respect and attention, but the appearance of power is all that a King of this country can have',[19] and they concurred in their reservations about some of the provisions of the peace treaty. They differed on parliamentary reform but agreed it could be left to a free vote. With this alliance in place, they could topple Shelburne and compel the King to invite them to form a ministry. They could also satisfy the wishes of their followers for government posts.

The existence of the new partnership was quickly suspected, and it became public knowledge when Fox and North joined forces in an attack on the ministry on 17 February in a debate on the draft peace treaty. Fox was a little coy about the new relationship but did not directly deny it:

> That any such alliance has taken place, I can by no means aver. That I shall have the honour of concurring with the noble lord in the blue ribbon on the present question is very certain; and if men of honour can meet on points of general national concern, I see no reason for calling such a meeting an unnatural junction. It is neither wise nor noble to keep up animosities for ever ... my friendships are perpetual, my enmities are not so.[20]

The ministry was defeated by sixteen votes. On 21 February a motion of censure was tabled by Lord John Cavendish and the ministry was again

The Only Booth in the Fair. North stands on the stage passing money to Charles James Fox; the figures on the right are the Duke of Portland and Lord Shelburne. Shoe Lane, Fleet Street, 9 April 1783. *(Kenneth Baker)*

defeated, though still by the fairly small margin of seventeen. At the same time Shelburne was suffering resignations from his Cabinet; realising he could not properly continue, he resigned himself three days later.

The alliance between Fox and North, which a little later became their eponymous coalition, has since its inception been the target for vilification. There are numerous contemporary cartoons showing them with their fingers in the till or their snouts in the trough. The case for the defence has usually, though not always, gone by default ever since. Wraxall writing some years later said: 'The nation in general regarded the union formed between North and Fox as a mutual sacrifice of moral and political principles to ambition, or rather to love of office'.[21] North as well as Fox realised some justification was required for this union and he gave it in the debate which led to Shelburne's resignation:

> But there are certainly times and circumstances, and emergencies, when it highly becomes all honest men, of every party and description, manfully to relinquish their personal feuds and temporary animosities, and unite their serious efforts, by one generous exertion, in the common interest. It is, then, that mutually convinced of the integrity and honour of each other's intentions, however much they may have differed in carrying those intentions into execution, [they] could fairly meet in one cordial body for the public good. Every individual, inspired by the genuine love of his country, would then think it his duty to abate somewhat of the violence with which his former opinion was maintained, and form a junction at once honourable to himself, and serviceable to his country.[22]

This defence has been endorsed by at least two modern historians. In his political biography of North, P. D. G. Thomas wrote: 'The coalition was a mature approach to politics, but unfortunately for Fox and North it was too sophisticated for contemporary opinion';[23] and George III's biographer John Brooke believed 'a Fox-North coalition offered every prospect of a stable ministry and North felt there ought to be an end to political controversy over dead issues'.[24]

North's reputation suffered more than Fox's from the coalition, partly because Fox was deemed to have little in the way of reputation to lose. As he was dissolute, he was also unfairly regarded as unprincipled, whereas North had generally been considered a man of honour, moreover one who was constantly telling people how unfit he was for high office. The shock caused by the alliance can be seen in every contemporary account. It was all the more extraordinary in that it was opposed by most of North's family and in particular by his father, who according to George North had 'a rooted bad opinion' of Fox.[25] It is difficult to find any other major decision taken by North in which he ignored the views of his father and also of the King. Why did he do it?

One explanation that has been offered from time to time is that North felt safer from the threat of impeachment and even execution while he was in office.[26] Shelburne had indeed proposed to the Cabinet in April 1782 that he should be brought to a public trial for his conduct of the American war, but the proposal found little support and was never revived.[27] North's carefree demeanour during the summer of that year does not suggest he thought he was in imminent danger of prosecution, and it seems unlikely that the fear of it influenced his part in the events of the spring of 1783.

It is better to start from North's own explanation. He said he was acting in a public-spirited manner with no hope of personal advantage and from his wish to serve his country. This interpretation of his behaviour gains support from a shorthand memorandum which Guilford wrote and headed: 'What I said to the King from Ld N. upon Ld S[helburne]'s going out'.[28] The paper emphasises the difficulties of forming a stable ministry without Fox but doubts whether he and his party would join a government under a 'neutral person' as First Lord (a solution that might have made it more acceptable to the King). Various ministerial permutations are discussed and the paper ends:

> That if this could be settled to Your Majesty's satisfaction with them, & that he [North] could have the naming of the President of the Privy Council, the Privy Seal and the Secretaries of State & be himself of the cabinet without an office or emolument he would be willing to serve in that Capacity. He thinks a strong administration very necessary at this time & wishes Mr Pitt could be persuaded to give his assistance & take an Office now, or if he keeps his resolve of serving on no account with Ld N. if his Majesty could make an Administration with them now Ld Shelburne is removed, & take in some of his [North's] friends as a Testimony of his concurrence & leave him out of the cabinet or any Office he would support such an administration.[29]

Guilford may have wished to interpret North's thinking in a favourable light but it is reasonable to take the paper at face value. North's prime objective was to see a stable administration in office. As he ended an undated letter to his father around this time:

> I do not think I have much avarice. I have less ambition, &, if I do not flatter myself, still less malice. To see Peace established in the Country by a firm Coalition, to see my friends satisfied, to see my honour safe, &, a good government procured to this country by the sacrifice of my situation would be the most honourable, & the most eligible conclusion of my political warfare that I could possibly desire.[30]

North's motives in his political career may have been no purer than those of other men where public position is the prize. Perhaps he found time beginning to hang heavily in the year since he left office and, as memories of the stress faded, he regretted his loss of importance and power. The only valid reason for thinking he himself sensed his motives were not straightforward is that he later bitterly regretted what he had done. His son-in-law Lord Glenbervie, who admired him enormously, wrote in his *Diaries* that his wife Kitty had told him her mother had always opposed the alliance with Fox, and that North would sometimes say to her: 'O Nance, it would be happy for me if I had taken your advice. There is no action in my life that I have such cause to regret'.[31] It was an action that at the time did more damage to his good name than his entire conduct of the American war.

When Shelburne stepped down on 14 February the King began a desperate search for a ministerial solution that did not involve Fox. He first asked Pitt to form a government but, after a brief hesitation, he refused.[32] Then, using Guilford as go-between, he attempted to detach North from Fox by offering him a return to the Treasury or, if he declined, some other suitable Cabinet post and a key role in choosing the new Ministers.[33] The King warned Guilford, however, that if North was not to be the First Minister he reserved the appointment to himself: 'I have . . . declared that my Resolution is taken that the Treasury must be in the hands of no head of a Party but an Independent Peer named by Myself'.[34] This was completely unacceptable to Fox, who had agreed with North that their coalition would be led by the Duke of Portland, a comparative political lightweight but the official head of the old Rockingham party.

On or about 12 March George III finally accepted the principle of a Fox/North ministry under Portland,[35] but with resentment in his heart; resentment that was chiefly directed at North. Two weeks later he sarcastically referred to him as 'that *grateful* man'.[36] He then refused to receive Portland and insisted, through North, that he should first submit a complete list of his proposed ministerial team for royal approval. North had to tell him that Portland had no intention of complying.[37] The King then made one more attempt to persuade Pitt to accept office as First Minister writing to him: 'after the manner I have been personally treated by both the D. of Portland and Ld North it is impossible I can ever admit either of them into my Service'.[38] Pitt declined at once and the King 'much hurt' lamented his refusal 'to stand forth against the most daring and unprincipled faction that the Annals of the Kingdom ever produced'.[39] By 1 April he could hold out no longer and sent for North to tell him he would receive Portland and the proposed members of his Cabinet the following day,[40] though he left no one who would listen in any doubt of his hostility to his new ministry and his determination to be rid of it as soon as possible.[41]

In the new administration the two Secretaries of State (whose duties had been reallocated in 1782) were Fox and North. Fox's official responsibilities were concerned with foreign affairs while North's remit included home affairs, Ireland and India, but in practice Fox ran his colleague's department as well as his own. North's first biographer said that his 'return to office in 1783 involved his retirement from active political life. Fox was the predominant partner. North was literally and by metaphor the sleeping partner'.[42] He allowed Fox to correspond directly with the Lord Lieutenant of Ireland and, although North was an acknowledged expert on the East India Company, it was Fox who brought in the Bill for its reform. North's readiness to play second fiddle strengthens the case of those who believe that it was not primarily ambition that drew him back into office. He considered he had done his duty by his country and was now content with a back seat.

The coalition soon discovered the difficulties under which Shelburne had been working in negotiating the peace treaty, particularly the shortage of British bargaining counters but, after only minor revisions, it was signed in Paris on 3 September 1783. Earlier in the summer the ministry had drawn back from a confrontation with the King over the size of an allowance for the Prince of Wales, a matter which George III was considering using as an excuse to dismiss the government. The potentially divisive issue of parliamentary reform had been temporarily buried after a powerful attack on the whole notion by North. He argued that the demand for reform was not widespread and thus provided no justification for introducing radical change. 'To whom are we to pay respect', he asked, 'the few reformers or the contented multitude? Can this be a serious question? I perceive it cannot.'[43] The motion for reform was defeated by 144 votes.

The most important piece of legislation brought forward by the coalition was the East India Company Bill. It was introduced in the autumn and, although undoubtedly controversial in its aim of curbing vested interests, it did not look dangerous to the ministry. North's Act of 1773 had never achieved the intended improvement in the management of the Company, which was once again facing bankruptcy; the new Bill provided for a much greater measure of government control.[44] It was introduced in the Commons by Fox on 18 November and the second and third readings achieved majorities of 109 and 106.[45] North spoke on the second reading, explaining that he was always ready to support reform where it could be shown change was beneficial. He made some dry comments on the management of the Company:

The court of directors were the nominal ministers of the Company; they gave orders to the Company's servants in India; the Company's servants in India disobeyed those orders, and having an influence upon the court of proprietors at home, the court of proprietors over-ruled the court of directors. This was a perfect mathematical figure, but it was very far from being a perfect political one. The House has heard that the directors wrote fine letters; this certainly did them great credit; but, from the circumstances above mentioned, nothing was ever done in consequence, and all the important business of the Company ended where it began – in a fine letter.[46]

After the successful passage of the Bill through the Commons neither Fox nor North had any particular reason to fear its reception in the Lords. There were rumours that the King was intriguing to defeat it but Ministers did not credit them. Portland believed he had received a clear impression from George III of his support for the measure, but he was wrong.[47] The King let it be known through Lord Temple that 'whoever voted for the India Bill [in the Lords] were not only not his friends but he should consider them his enemies'.[48] The threat worked. On 15 December, on a motion for the adjournment, the coalition was defeated by eight votes; by the Bill's second reading two days later the royal wishes had become sufficiently influential that it was lost by nineteen.[49] That same day in the Commons North spoke to a motion that was indirectly critical of the King's behaviour: in the course of his speech he said that 'the responsibility of ministers was the only security which Englishmen had against the abuse of executive power'.[50]

Late the following evening, 18 December 1783, George III wrote to Lord North: 'Lord North is by this required to send me the Seal of His Department, and to acquaint Mr Fox to send those of the Foreign Department. Mr Frazer or Mr Nepean [the Under-Secretaries] will be the proper Channel of delivering them to Me this Night; I choose this method as Audiences on such occasions must be unpleasant'.[51] North obeyed, and left office for the last time.

George III's actions were constitutionally dubious and certainly shabby but neither consideration probably troubled him much. Unlike North, who was usually only able to hope he was right, the King never had any doubts about his rectitude. Moreover, on this occasion George III had success on his side. Before dismissing the coalition he had at last persuaded William Pitt to form a ministry, and on the day following North's brusque removal Pitt kissed hands as First Lord of the Treasury and Chancellor of the Exchequer. At first he had difficulty recruiting for a ministry that lacked a majority in the Commons but by the time Parliament reassembled after the Christmas recess, on 12 January 1784, his Cabinet was in place.[52] Over the next three months Pitt suffered a number of parliamentary defeats which, with the King's backing, he ignored. There was speculation that Pitt would invite Fox to join the ministry to strengthen Pitt's own position, but he made it clear that no such invitation would include North, a situation North himself accepted in the interest of stable government.[53]

At the end of March 1784 the King and Pitt played what they hoped was their trump card and called a general election. They rightly sensed that the coalition's parliamentary majority did not reflect public opinion, which in general suspected what appeared an unnatural alliance. Pitt had a triumph. Some ninety-six coalition supporters lost their seats or failed to stand; of these nearly half were reckoned personal followers of North. In the first division in the new House Pitt had a majority of ninety-seven.[54] He was now safe (and continued in office into the next century), but North's days as an influential politician were ended. There was no longer any prospect of power. Without the hope of employment or position his followers began to drop away, some attaching themselves to Fox. By 1788 a contemporary assessment gave their number as less than twenty.[55]

North continued to speak in the House from time to time, particularly in defence of the established order. As occasion arose he opposed both parliamentary reform,[56] and attempts to give relief to Dissenters and Catholics. He had a profound belief in the virtues of the British constitution, of which he considered the established church to be an integral part. It was impossible to restrict its privileges without endangering the whole edifice. He had spoken forcibly in the Commons in support of this view in March 1787 and a few days later a correspondent told Guilford that even the great scientist and nonconformist divine Dr Joseph Priestly had 'considered Lord North's speech in the highest terms, & to have declared that he "honoured Lord North above any man in England, because he spoke with the most perfect knowledge of the subject, & directly from the Heart" '.[57]

After 1784 North withdrew more and more into his family and social life and his attendance in the Commons was confined to debates on matters of particular interest to him.[58] His son George caused him a problem in 1785 by getting married without first asking his grandfather's permission. He had not told his parents either but that was far less serious than keeping Guilford in the dark, as the old man paid George an allowance which was virtually his only source of income. The girl was perfectly respectable, the daughter of the Earl of Buckinghamshire, but she had no money and, due to the secret nature of the marriage, there can have been none of the complicated negotiations over the details of a financial settlement so loved by eighteenth-century aristocrats.

George wrote to his grandfather, the day after his marriage, correctly predicting: 'I am very much afraid the Contents of this letter will raise your displeasure'.[59] Guilford curtly replied that he had no wish to see George or meet his wife,[60] but by the middle of October North had allowed them to come and live at Bushy. He wrote a typically apologetic and dutiful letter to Guilford, explaining that in taking them in he was in no way condoning their behaviour but wished to protect them from 'the consequences of that imprudence'. Lady North wrote a much better letter, calmer and less defensive,[61] and before long Guilford relented and invited the errant couple to visit him at Wroxton.[62]

North's sight, never good, deteriorated sharply in 1787.[63] When he attended a debate on 27 March on the repeal of the Test and Corporation Acts he was led into the Chamber by his son,[64] and another Member described him as 'very infirm and more than half-blind'.[65] A few weeks later Lady North wrote rather sadly to Guilford from Bushy: 'We shall return to London today, for as Ld North can not amuse himself as he us'd to do, with looking at the Peach House and Kitchen Garden he is in less spirits here than in London'.[66] Cures were tried at Bath and Tunbridge Wells (a spa first promoted by his ancestor the third Lord North) but nothing could give North back his sight.

His youngest daughter, Lady Charlotte Lindsay, later wrote that at times he became subject to 'extreme depression of spirits' and that at night her mother would often read to him until he went to sleep.[67] In general, however, he remained cheerful and discovered a fortitude in affliction that perhaps he did not know he possessed. In the autumn of 1787 Horace Walpole, who had not while North was in office been one of his particular friends or admirers, drove over from Strawberry Hill to dine at Bushy. He described the party in a letter to a friend:

> I ... never saw a more interesting scene. Lord North's spirits, good humour, wit, sense, drollery, are as perfect as ever – the unremitting attention of Lady North and his children, most touching. Mr North leads him about, Miss North sits constantly by him, carves meat, watches his every motion, scarce puts a bit into her own lips, and if one cannot help commending her, she colours with modesty and sorrow till the tears gush into her eyes. If ever loss of sight could be compensated, it is by so affectionate a family.[68]

He was prevented by his doctor from returning again to the Commons.[69] On 4 August 1790 his father died at the age of eighty-six and North entered on his inheritance, at last becoming a member of the House of Lords. It was too late. He was now a rich man with several country houses and estates but they were not much use to a man who was ill and blind. He took his seat in the Lords, making his maiden speech on 1 April 1791 on the subject of Pitt's intention of supporting Turkey in her war with Russia, which he opposed.[70] He had not lost his old sparkle. A subsequent speaker, Lord Stormont, justified the brevity of his own contribution by saying: 'Indeed, after a speech of such unanswerable reasoning, of so much information and eloquence, as the one they had just heard from his noble friend, nothing that he had to say could be of much consequence'.[71] He spoke on the same subject on 20 February of the following year, pointing out that his predictions from the earlier debate had proved correct;[72] this was his last appearance on the public scene.

In the early months of 1792 North's health rapidly declined, his legs became swollen and symptoms of dropsy appeared. At the end of July he asked his doctor for the truth and was told he had not long to live. His daughter Charlotte wrote: 'He received this news not only with firmness and pious resignation, but it in no way altered the serenity and cheerfulness of his manners; and from that hour, during the remaining ten days of his life, he had no return of depression of spirits'.[73] He died on 5 August. His last hours were described by Dartmouth's son Edward:

> No man ever met death with greater fortitude. When he found that he had but few hours to live, he desired all his family might be sent for to his bedside. When this was done, he said that with regard to his political life, though he could not have the presumption to suppose but what there had been much of error in many things he had done, yet it was a satisfaction which none but himself could in that hour conceive, that on no one act of it could he look back with regret. He then took leave of his family, after thanking them separately for their great kindness and attention to him since the loss of his eyesight, more particularly during his last illness; he expired without a struggle or groan.[74]

In his *Memoirs* the dramatist Richard Cumberland, who had known North reasonably well, wrote of him:

> I do not know the person, to whose society a man of sensibility might have given himself with more pleasure and security than Lord North; for his wit never wounded, and his humour never ridiculed; he was not disposed to make an unmerciful use of the power, which superiority of talents endowed him with, to oppress a weaker understanding; he had great charity for dullness of apprehension, and a pert fellow could not easily put him out of patience; and there was no irritability in his nature. To his acquaintance and friends he was all complacency; to his family all affection; he was generous, hospitable, open-handed, and loved his ease infinitely too well to sacrifice any portion of it to a solicitude about money.[75]

After her husband's death Lady North lost interest in life; she followed him to the grave five years later. They both lie in the family vault in the parish church at Wroxton.

Lord North was survived by six of his seven children, three sons and three daughters. The girls all made acceptable matches. The eldest, Katherine (Kitty), married Sylvester Douglas, a Tory MP, who for a short while held his father-in-law's old office of Paymaster General; he was created Lord Glenbervie in 1800. His *Diaries* provide useful anecdotal material about North, whom he much admired. In 1798 his second daughter, Anne, married as his third wife John Baker-Holroyd, first Lord Sheffield, when he was sixty-five and she was thirty-four. He held various middle-rank political offices, but is now chiefly remembered as the friend of Edward Gibbon and as the editor of his *Autobiography*. The youngest daughter, Charlotte, married the Honourable James Lindsay, son of the fifth Earl of Balcarres. Her brief memoir of her father, included by Lord Brougham in his *Historical Sketches*,[76] provides an attractive picture of North.

Lord North's eldest son, George, served as an MP from 1778 to 1792, for the last two years as succesor to his father in the family seat of Banbury. He was Under-Secretary at the Home Office during the Fox/North coalition, but otherwise achieved no particular distinction. In 1796, two years after his first wife's death, he married Susan Coutts, daughter and co-heiress of the banker, Thomas Coutts, thus adding to the family's already considerable wealth. Only three daughters survived from his two marriages; on his death in 1802, under the peculiar rules governing the inheritance of baronies by writ, the North title went into abeyance. After both her elder and younger sisters had died childless, the title was successfully reclaimed by the middle sister, Susan, in 1841.

Meanwhile, on George's death, the earldom had passed to his next brother, Francis, whose chief pleasures were found in the theatre and the company of actors. According to his brother-in-law, Glenbervie, he was good-natured but indolent.[77] When he died childless in 1817, North's youngest surviving son, Frederick, became the fifth Earl. He was a far more interesting man than his brothers: in fact Gilbert Elliot, Earl of Minto, described him as 'the only pleasant son of the family, and he is very remarkably so'.[78] Despite continual ill-health as a young man, Frederick lived an active and useful life. He served on the Viceroy's staff during the British occupation of Corsica in 1795–96, and two years later he was appointed Governor of the colony of Ceylon, recently taken from the Dutch. His attempts to impose even-handed and uncorrupt rule were not always successful, but his departure for home in 1805 was locally regarded with regret.[79]

During his time at Oxford, Frederick had become an enthusiastic and knowledgeable philhellene, and in 1791 had been received into the Greek Orthodox church; after his return from Ceylon the rest of his life was devoted to the cause of Greece. In particular, with the encouragement of his friend Count Capodistrias, the Greek statesman, he worked to establish the first modern university on Greek soil. This he achieved: in 1824 the Ionian University was inaugurated on Corfu (then a British protectorate), and Frederick was appointed Chancellor on the nomination of George IV. Three years later he died and, with the loss of his financial support and his personal influence, the university quickly declined into a small local college.[80] Nevertheless, it was a venture his father, with his love of classical culture, would have warmly endorsed. He never married.

17

Conclusion

When the blind Lord North lay dying in his house on the corner of Grosvenor Square he confessed to his daughter Katherine his fears for his posthumous reputation and for 'how he world stand with the world'. He said: 'this might be a weakness, but he could not help it'.[1] For much of the subsequent two centuries North's anxieties have proved well-founded. In particular his reputation has suffered from the attentions of Whig historians, not only (or even principally) for his mismanagement of the American war, but for connivance in what was assumed to have been George III's attempt to turn the clock back and be a King who ruled as well as reigned. In the high noon of Victorian parliamentary and institutional reform North's conservative instincts were unfashionable, and the difficulties with which he had had to contend were ignored. The nineteenth-century historian William Lecky stated that 'most of the measures he advocated were proved by the event to be disastrous and foolish', and a little further on he commented that 'through weakness of character he automatically subordinated his own judgement to that of the King ... '[2] In the 1920s G. M. Trevelyan could still bracket North with the ineffectual Lord Bute and refer to them both as 'puppet ministers',[3] having already condescendingly (and inaccurately) referred to North as 'the genial old gentleman who had done the King's dirty work year after year till America was lost'.

The allusion to puppetry was used by another historian, Dorothy Marshall, in 1962: 'At times North appears almost like a puppet held in position by George III's manipulation of the twin wires of Jenkinson and Robinson'.[4] Much the same point was made by J. H. Plumb, who confidently stated that North's 'fat, rounded body and soft pig-like face were indicative of more than ease, gentleness and affability; they bespoke an indolence that bordered on disease ... ' He then drew the remarkable conclusion that 'his body, lacking that hard muscular fibre without which no statesman can hope to dominate men or events, betrayed his temperament'.[5] North's recurring spells of inertia are well documented, but it is incorrect to deduce that they were his habitual reaction to his responsibilities or, for that matter, that all fat men are lazy.

During his lifetime North's reputation remained relatively intact. He was of course attacked, sometimes viciously, by his political opponents, but this was in the context of divided views on the right way to respond to a national crisis. What is significant is that his long tenure of office was not primarily due to the supposed manipulations of George III, but to the support he received from his fellow Members of the Commons, many of whom belonged to no party or faction and were proud of their capacity for independent judgement. A contemporary memorialist, Sir Nathanial Wraxall, elected to Parliament towards the end of North's premiership, probably reflected majority opinion when he wrote: 'Lord North excited affection as well as respect, and awakened admiration at the variety of his talents', though Wraxall added the reservation that 'he knew not how to inspire terror, like the first Mr Pitt ... '[6]

It is another contemporary, Horace Walpole, who bears much of the responsibility for the collapse of North's reputation, particularly with historians from the second half of the Victorian era and their successors. Walpole's *Memoirs of the Reign of George III* was written in the 1780s but, following elaborate instructions issued during his lifetime, not published until 1845. The last volume includes a three-page invective; the following extract suggests its flavour:

> As a Minister he had no foresight, no consistence, no firmness, no spirit. He miscarried in all he undertook in America, was more improvident than un-fortunate, less unfortunate than he deserved to be. If he was free from vices, he was void of virtues; and it is a paltry eulogium of a Prime Minister of a great country, yet the best that can be allotted to Lord North, that, though his country was ruined under his administration, he preserved his good humour, and neither felt for his country nor for himself.[7]

Such comments from a man who knew North well provided later writers with justification for the prejudices they already entertained.

In more recent times the tide has turned in North's favour. There has been more appreciation of the external constraints on his freedom of action, and also of his considerable achievements in fields away from the American war. Apart from a sympathetic study of his early career published in 1979,[8] one of the first modern historians to present a three-dimensional picture of North was P. D. G. Thomas in a short political biography which appeared in 1976.[9] Thomas's book is necessarily more concerned with

North's professional than his private life, but his balanced presentation of the former, setting out North's successes in the face of the difficulties he faced without denying his weaknesses, marked an important step in the reassessment of the Prime Minister. Another historian, John Brooke, in his biography of George III first published twenty-five years ago, wrote of Lord North: 'No statesman in our history has been so underrated'.[10]

North's long tenure of the highest political office in the country was not least among his achievements; his twelve-year period as Prime Minister was only exceeded in the eighteenth century by Sir Robert Walpole two generations earlier, and by William Pitt the Younger after the dismissal of the Fox/North coalition. The circumstances of Pitt's long hold on office were peculiar both to the man and the times in which he served, but a comparison between Walpole and North – provided it is not pushed too far – is more illuminating.

Both men reflected the prevailing temper of the contemporary English ruling class: conservative, suspicious of change and of proposals for reform. Walpole sprang directly from the group that most feared further upheaval, the landed gentry. They had emerged from the previous century as an important force in English politics; what they now sought was stability, continuing prosperity and low taxes. North came from a more aristocratic background than Walpole, but the dividing line between the aristocracy and the richer squires was always blurred. Guilford was pleased with his earldom and his occasional court appointments but, judging from his correspondence, much of his time was spent running his estates and socialising with his country neighbours. He apparently never aspired to a Guilford House in London, contenting himself with comfortable but not palatial terraced residences in newly fashionable Mayfair. His son, when in office, was happy to make use of the official accommodation provided in the Pay Office and later in Downing Street, but it was Bushy Park that became the family home. There North entertained his intimate friends, proudly showed off the fruit in the hothouses, and rode round the park inspecting the deer like any other country gentleman. Too much must not be made of North's rural roots. When he was in town he went to the theatre, played cards at Whites and mixed with fashionable society. Nevertheless, his political strength derived not only from connexions with the rich and powerful upper reaches of the nobility, but also from his instinctive understanding of the hopes and fears of the squires, and in particular of their representatives in the House of Commons, the Country Gentlemen. Despite growing uneasiness about his handling of American affairs, North remained Prime Minister for twelve years to a large extent

because the Country Gentlemen trusted him more than they were prepared to trust anyone else. This support was enhanced by his own mastery
of the House of Commons. He was a more civilised man than Walpole, but
the comment made by the fourth Earl of Chesterfield on the earlier Prime
Minister can equally well apply to North: 'He was both the best Parliament-
man and the ablest manager of Parliament that I believe ever lived. An
artful rather than an eloquent speaker; he saw, as by intuition, the disposition of the House, and pressed or receded accordingly'.[11]

North's parliamentary skills, allied to the trust (and affection) he inspired, were his greatest asset as a statesman. They were insufficient to
resolve the American crisis but, especially in the early years of the war,
nothing could have persuaded either Parliament or the English people to
accede to American demands without a struggle. In the case of other
seemingly intractable problems, such as Canada, the East India Company
and the Falkland Islands, North's handling of both the House of Commons
and the negotiations involved demonstrated ability and application. This
was recognised by contemporaries whose views were later ignored by
partial historians.

In the forty years that separate Walpole's resignation from that of North,
there was no statesman who could match North for integrity, selflessness
and the capacity for grasping complex problems. His understanding of the
nation's finances was never bettered by any of his predecessors, and his
impact on Treasury administration was both beneficial and lasting. In the
often unedifying world of eighteenth-century politics, North shone as a
beacon of decency, conscientiousness and competence; and when the time
came for his departure, he left with dignity and humour.

Appendix

Lord North's Letter to the King before his Resignation

Sire – Mr Grosvenor today in the House of Commons desired me to appoint an hour tomorrow morning, as he had a matter of importance to communicate to me, and I have since learned from good authority, that it is his intention to represent to me, in his own name, and in those of some other Country Gentlemen 'That, being now convinced that the present Administration cannot continue any longer, they are of opinion that vain and ineffectual struggles tend only to public mischief and confusion, and that they shall think it their duty henceforward to desist from opposing what appears to be clearly the sense of the House of Commons'. If these gentlemen persist in this resolution, Your Majesty will perceive that we shall infallibly be in a Minority even on Wednesday next, when the House will be moved, in direct terms, to resolve 'That it is their opinion that the management of public affairs ought not to be continued in the hands of the present Ministers'.

When I had the honour of an audience of Your Majesty this morning, I humbly endeavoured to state to Your Majesty my reasons for thinking that the fate of the present Ministry is absolutely and irrecoverably decided; The votes of the Minorities on Friday sevennight, and on Friday last contained, I believe, the genuine sense of the House of Commons, and I really think, of the Nation at large; Not that I suppose the minds of men in general exasperated against the individuals who compose the Administration, but they are tired of the Administration collectively taken, and wish at all events to see it alter'd. The torrent is too strong to be resisted; Your Majesty is well apprized that, in this country, the Prince on the Throne, cannot, with prudence, oppose the deliberate resolution of the House of Commons: Your Royal Predecessors (particularly King William the Third and his late

Majesty) were obliged to yield their wish in more instances than one: They
consented to changes in their Ministry which they disapproved because
they found it necessary to sacrifice their private wishes, and even their
opinions to the preservation of public order, and the prevention of these
terrible mischiefs, which are the natural consequence of the clashing of
two branches of the Sovereign Power in the State. The concessions they
made were never deemed dishonourable, but were considered as marks of
their wisdom, and of their parental affection for their people. Your Majesty
has graciously and steadily supported the servants you approve, as long as
they could be supported: Your Majesty had firmly and resolutely maintained what appeared to You essential to the welfare and dignity of this
country, as long as this Country itself thought proper to maintain it. The
Parliament have altered their sentiments, and as their sentiments whether
just or erroneous, must ultimately prevail, Your Majesty having persevered,
as long as possible, in what You thought right, can lose no honour if you
yield at length, as some of the most renowned and most glorious of your
Predecessors have done, to the opinion and wishes of the House of
Commons.

Your Majesty's desire is, I know, to form a Ministry on a broad bottom,
and such an arrangement would certainly be the best, but, in the present
moment, it is I fear, not attainable. In consequence of the disposition of the
House of Commons, a change in the Ministry is become absolutely necessary: There are no persons capable and willing to form a new Administration, except Lord Rockingham and Lord Shelburne with their parties: and
They will not act with any of the present Ministry but the Chancellor. It
follows then that the present Cabinet must be removed, and either one or
both of the before-mentioned parties must compose the new administration; or, that there will be no Ministry and the greatest confusion, with the
most pernicious consequences, will prevail in every part of Government. It
is with great reluctance that I presume to advise Your Majesty to send either
for Lord Rockingham or Lord Shelburne, but I shall not be an honest man
or a friend to my Country if I did not advise that step rather than that Your
Majesty, being no longer able to retain your present Ministers, should run
the risk of leaving the Nation at this time, without any administration, at
the mercy of all the evils and all the dangers which are naturally to be
apprehended in such an unsettled state of affairs. Your Majesty's goodness
encourages me to lay my poor but honest advice before you, and to submit
whether it will not be for Your Majesty's welfare, and even glory, to sacrifice,
at this moment, former opinions, displeasures and apprehensions (though
never so well-founded) to that great object (which is always uppermost in

Your Majesty's heart and which is at present in a degree of peril) The Public Safety.

Your Majesty's future Administration will be strong with respect to all the great measures of government, to the obtaining of supplies, to the conduct of war, and the conclusion of Peace. But, if Your new Ministers should attempt any dangerous innovations in the Constitution, they will, I believe, meet with a powerful and I hope, a successful opposition.

I have just seen the Lord Chancellor, who in consequence of a note received from Your Majesty today intends to call tomorrow morning upon Lord Shelburne. His sentiments I believe, agree with mine: He is sorry that the necessity of the times should oblige Your Majesty to take steps which cannot but be disagreeable to you, but he seems to think, with me, that no good purpose can be answered by a further contest. He desired me to remind Your Majesty that he had never own'd to Lord Rockingham his having mentioned his Lordship's four propositions to Your Majesty, but had always treated them as inferior, and subsequent considerations to be settled after the formation of a Ministry, and not as conditions of acceptance. He advises therefore that Your Majesty should not appear acquainted with that part of Lord Rockingham's conversation. I beg leave to subscribe myself, Your Majesty's most dutiful servant and subject. North.

Monday night [18 March 1782]

Source: *The Correspondence of George III, 1760–1783*, ed. Sir John Fortescue, v. pp. 394–97.

Notes

Introduction

[1] John B. Owen, *The Eighteenth Century, 1714–1815* (New York and London, 1974), p. 125; Paul Langford, *A Polite and Commercial People* (Oxford, 1989), p. 146n.; Henry Hamilton, *An Economic History of Scotland in the Eighteenth Century* (Oxford, 1963), pp. 3 et seq.

[2] Langford, *Polite and Commercial People*, p. 6.

[3] Estimates of the population of Ireland in the early eighteenth century are open to question; see K. H. Connell, *The Population of Ireland, 1750–1845* (Oxford, 1950), p. 25, table 4.

[4] Roger North died in 1734.

[5] *The Complete Peerage*, ed. Vicary Gibbs et al. 14 vols (London, 1910–40), ix. p. 659.

[6] Owen, *Eighteenth Century*, pp. 139 et seq; Langford, *Polite and Commercial People*, p. 142.

[7] Newcomen's engine used atmospheric pressure as motive force. Steam injected into the cylinder was rapidly condensed by the application of cold water to induce a vacuum.

[8] Owen, *Eighteenth Century*, pp. 309–10.

[9] Langford, *Polite and Commercial People*, p. 437.

[10] The author is much indebted to John Cannon, *An Aristocratic Century* (Cambridge, 1984).

[11] For a fuller discussion of the position of the eighteenth-century aristocracy see Langford, *Polite and Commercial People*, pp. 590–600.

[12] William Cobbett, ed., *The Parliamentary History of England*, 36 vols (London, 1806–20), passim.

[13] In 1750 the Irish peerage numbered 102 and the Scottish eighty-six, see Cannon, *Aristocratic Century*, p. 32.

[14] Ibid., pp. 1 et seq.

[15] Ibid., p. 2.

[16] Ibid., p. 132. Strict settlement was a form of entail intended to protect estates from feckless or extravagant heirs. It normally worked in favour of the eldest grandson.

[17] Bodleian Library, North Papers, D25, fols 98–102.

[18] Ibid., D23, fol. 173, North to Guilford, 10 April 1764.

[19] Ibid., Add. C4, fol. 211, North to Guilford, undated.

[20] *The Correspondence of George III, 1760–1783*, ed. Sir John Fortescue, 6 vols (London, 1927), ii. p. 249.

[21] Bishop North initiated, partly from his own resources, the restoration of both Winchester Cathedral and Farnham Castle; see *DNB*.

[22] In a Treasury seat a significant number of the electors depended on the government for employment. In the case of Harwich ten of the thirty-two electors held posts in the Customs House, and several others in the Post Office; see Sir Lewis Namier and John Brooke, *The History of Parliament: House of Commons 1754–1790*, 3 vols (London, 1964), i. p. 276.

[23] William Blackstone, *Commentaries on the Laws of England* (Oxford, 1765–69), iii. p. 328.

[24] Bodleian Library, North Papers, Add C4, fol. 47, North to Guilford, 18 December 1762.

[25] Lilian Dickins and Mary Stanton, eds, *An Eighteenth-Century Correspondence* (London, 1910), Guilford to Sanderson Miller [? November 1752].

[26] See, for instance, Kenneth Baker, *The Prime Ministers: An Irreverent Political History in Cartoons* (London, 1995).

[27] Langford, *Polite and Commercial People*, p. 391.

[28] Howard Robinson, *Britain's Post Office* (Oxford, 1953), p. 103.

[29] Bodleian Library, North Papers, Add. C4, fol. 132, North to Guilford, 30 May 1769. The envelope is addressed c/o Lady Eliazabeth Archer (North's mother's half-sister) at Hale, near Downton, Wilts. The lack of any further details of the journey implies Guilford was already in the picture.

[30] Ibid., D24, fol. 80, Lady North to Guilford, 11 August 1770. In the letter she refers to 'the following Saturday', which just could mean Saturday week, but does not alter the inference that road travel was no longer something difficult or uncertain.

[31] Langford, *Polite and Commercial People*, p. 409. The service ran between London and Bath, and was established by John Palmer, a Bath theatre owner, with the support of William Pitt.

[32] Robinson, *Post Office*, p. 35.

[33] Bodleian Library, North Papers, Add. C4, fol. 143, North to Guilford, 4 November 1769.

Chapter 1: Background and Upbringing

[1] The estate remained in the hands of Edward's decendants until the death of the thirteenth Lord North in action in 1941.

[2] North was ennobled 'by writ' rather than by 'letters patent'. Baronies created in this way can (under certain circumstances) pass through the female line, and in the nineteenth century the title was held by a woman. It fell into abeyance between the two sisters of the thirteenth Lord North on his death.

[3] The Lord Keeper was an alternative but less honorific title to that of Lord Chancellor. By the seventeenth century their functions were identical.

[4] The property had been acquired by Sir Thomas Pope, later Earl of Downe, at the time of the Dissolution. He presented it to Trinity College, Oxford, on condition his senior descendants could hold the property in perpetuity as tenants. This arrangement continued till 1932, when it was handed back to Trinity following the death of the eleventh Lord North.

[5] Bodleian Library, North Papers, B15, fol. 68, dated 1761; fol. 110, dated 1765.

[6] He married first, 1730, Lady Lucy Montagu (1709–34); secondly, 1736, Elizabeth, Viscountess Lewisham (1707–45); thirdly, 1751, Katherine, Countess of Rockingham (1714–66).

[7] Alan Valentine, *Lord North*, 2 vols (Norman, Oklahoma, 1967), i. p. 6.

[8] Horace Walpole, *Last Journals*, ed. A. Francis Steuart, 2 vols (London, 1910), i. p. 263.

[9] John, Lord Hervey, *Memoirs of the Reign of George II*, ed. Romney Sedgwick, 3 vols (London, 1931), iii. p. 817.

[10] C. D. Smith, *The Early Career of Lord North the Prime Minister* (London, 1979), pp. 90–92; Staffordshire County Record Office, Dartmouth MSS, D(W)1778/1.

[11] *The Autobiography and Correspondence of Mary Granville, Mrs Delany,* ed. Lady Llanover, 3 vols (London, 1861), 3 vols (London, 1862), 1st series, ii. p. 599, Delany to Mrs Dewes, 6 October 1750.

[12] Staffordshire County Record Office, Dartmouth MSS, D(W)1778/1.ii/761.

[13] Delany, *Autobiography,* 2nd series, ii. p. 476, Delany to Mrs Part, 10 October 1779.

[14] Bodleian Library, North Papers, Add. C4, fol. 97, North to Guilford, 12 October 1763.

[15] The property, which subsequently passed to Lord North, was adjacent to the manor of Sulgrave, the original home of the Washington family, a coincidence which George Baker in his *History of Northamptonshire,* 2 vols (London, 1822), i, p. 526, described as 'singular and interesting', which 'the local pride of the historian cannot suffer to pass unnoticed'.

[16] HMC, *Egmont MSS,* 3 vols (London, 1920–23), iii. p. 59, 'Diary of Viscount Percival, First Earl of Egmont'.

[17] Oxfordshire County Record Office, Wroxton Parish Registers.

[18] Valentine, *North,* i. p. 6.

[19] Egmont, *Diary,* i. pp. 207–8.

[20] Horace Walpole, *Memoirs of King George II,* ed. John Brooke, 3 vols (New Haven, 1985), i. pp. 52–53, 20 March 1751.

[21] Egmont, *Diary,* i. p. 235.

[22] Sir Nathaniel Wraxall, *The Historical and Posthumous Memoirs, 1772–1784,* ed. Henry B. Wheatley, 5 vols (London, 1884), i. p. 310.

[23] *Dictionary of National Biography,* s.n.

[24] William, Lord North, 'Lord North the Prime Minister', *North American Review,* 176 (1903), p. 736.

[25] Smith, *North,* p. 41. Smith reproduces a pamphlet published in 1787 which refers to North's relationship to George III. It is annotated in Walpole's hand: 'Falsely supposed son of the late Pr. of Wales'.

[26] E.g. Smith writes in *North,* p. 39: 'Whatever the fact, it was the supposition that was operative during the crisis of 1770 when Lord North became prime minister, even though that supposition may have been false'.

[27] *Catalogue of Political and Personal Satires Preserved ... in the British Museum,* ed. Mary Dorothy George, v (London, 1978), p. 127, no. 5132, 'The Assembly of the Grinders'; p. 514, no. 5855, 'State Cooks, or the Downfall of the Fish Kettle'.

[28] HMC, *Dartmouth MSS,* 3 vols (London, 1887–96), iii. p. 163. In a letter to her mother Lady Kaye, attributed to 1 September 1739, she expresses her disappointment that her husband will so soon be going 'into waiting'.

[29] Valentine, *North,* ii. p. 429.

[30] Oxfordshire County Record Office, Wroxton Parish Registers.

[31] Staffordshire County Record Office, Dartmouth MSS, D(W) 1778/1.ii/761.

[32] John Cannon, *Aristocratic Century* (Cambridge, 1980), p. 34. The four major schools were usually considered as Eton and Westminster, followed by Winchester and Harrow.

[33] *The Diaries of Sylvester Douglas, Lord Glenbervie,* ed. Francis Bickley, 2 vols (London, 1928), i. p. 299, quoting Sir George Yonge.

[34] Bodleian Library, North Papers, D5, fol. 139, Dampier to Guilford, 5 December 1746.

[35] Ibid., Add. C5, fol. 17, Dampier to Guilford, 17 September 1749.

[36] Ibid., D6, fol. 237, Dampier to Guilford, 21 December 1753.

[37] Ibid., C10, fol. 143, Guilford to North, 14 October 1749.

[38] Ibid., D6, fol. 13, Merrick to Guilford, 4 September 1750.

[39] Ibid., Add. C5, fol. 112, Merrick to North, 12 June 1750.

[40] *Musae Etonenses,* ed. William Herbert (London, 1817).

[41] When North became blind his elder daughters read him his favourite classics in the original Latin. John Cannon, *Lord North: The Noble Lord in the Blue Ribbon* (London, 1970), p. 6; Glenbervie, *Diaries,* i, p. 149.

[42] Wraxall, *Memoirs,* i. p. 371.

[43] Valentine, *North*, i. pp. 14–15.

[44] James Street, *The Mynster of Ile* (Taunton, 1904), p. 255.

[45] *The Correspondence of King George III, 1760–1783*, ed. Sir John Fortescue, 6 vols (London, 1927), ii. p. 249, King to North, 11 May 1771.

[46] Bodleian Library, North Papers, D6, fol. 22, Dampier to Guilford 15 April 1751.

[47] Ibid.

[48] Horace Walpole, *Memoirs of the Reign of George III*, ed. G. F. Russell Barker, 4 vols (London, 1894), i. p. 330.

[49] Wraxall, *Memoirs*, iii. p. 268.

[50] *The Letters of Horace Walpole*, ed. Mrs Paget Toynbee, 16 vols (Oxford, 1857–59), iii. p. 56, Walpole to George Montagu, 13 June 1751.

Chapter 2: Coming of Age

[1] Staffordshire County Record Office, Dartmouth MSS, D(W)1778/1.ii/793, Dartmouth to Huddersford, 28 July 1751.

[2] Ibid.

[3] Ibid., D(W)1778/1.ii/794, Dartmouth to Huddersford, 3 March 1752.

[4] *The Letters of Horace Walpole*, ed. Mrs Paget Toynbee, 16 vols (Oxford, 1857–59), iii. p. 24, Walpole to Sir Horace Mann, 19 November 1750.

[5] Horace Walpole, *Journal of the Reign of King George the Second*, ed. John Brooke, 3 vols (New Haven, 1985), i. p. 60.

[6] *Harcourt Papers*, ed. E. W. Harcourt, 14 vols (privately printed, 1880–1905), iii. p. 55.

[7] Bodleian Library, North Papers, Add. C4, fol. 1, North to Guilford, 23 April 1752.

[8] Peter D. G. Thomas, *Lord North* (London 1976), p. 7.

[9] BL, Add. MS 32728, fol. 317, Newcastle to North, 19 July 1752.

[10] Bodleian Library, North Papers, D6, fol. 209, Legge to Guilford, 16 September 1753.

[11] BL, Add. MS 32728, fol. 163.

[12] Staffordshire County Record Office, Dartmouth MSS, D(W)1778/1.ii/795, Dartmouth to Huddersford, 26 August 1752.

[13] Patshull House Papers, quoted Reginald Lucas, *Lord North*, 2 vols (London, 1913), i. p. 22.

[14] Henry, Lord Brougham, *Historical Sketches of Statesmen who Flourished in the Time of George III* (London, 1839), p. 391, appendix 3, letter from Lady Charlotte Lindsay.

[15] BL, Add. MS 32731, fol. 198/99, North to Newcastle, 18 February 1753.

[16] BL, MS 32731, fol. 199, North to Newcastle, 18 February 1753; Bodleian Library, North Papers, D6, fol. 212, Lambert to Guilford, 22 Sept 1753.

[17] Staffordshire County Record Office, Dartmouth MSS, D(W)1778/1.ii/798.

[18] Brougham, *Historical Sketches*, p. 391.

[19] *The Letters of Edward Gibbon*, ed. J. E. Norton, 3 vols (London, 1956), ii. p. 66, Gibbon to Dorothea Gibbon, 22 May 1775.

[20] *The Autobiography of Edward Gibbon*, ed. Lord Sheffield (London, 1978), p. 207.

[21] HMC, *Hastings MSS* (London, 1934), iii. p. 94, Revd Theophilus Lindsey to Francis, Earl of Huntingdon, 20 February 1755.

[22] *The Autobiography and Correspondence of Mary Granville, Mrs Delany*, ed. Lady Lanover, 3 vols (London, 1861), 3 vols (London, 1862), 1st series, iii. p. 336, Delany to Mrs Dewes, 22 February 1755.

[23] Westminster Archive Centre, St James's parish registers. The witnesses were Guilford, Dartmouth (presumably the best man), Dame A. Drake (the bride's mother, described as a widow, and always referred to by North as Lady Drake), and a Mr Geo. Williams (almost certainly a Somersetshire relation of Lady Drake's). If the date of 1753 given for the death of

Anne Speke's father is correct (see note 28 below), her mother had remarried and been widowed a second time in the course of three years.

24 *Harcourt Papers*, iii. p. 78, Countess Harcourt to George Lord Nuneham, 28 October 1755.

25 *Town and Country Magazine*, 10 (1778), pp. 121–23.

26 Horace Bleackley, *Ladies Fair and Frail* (London, 1909), p. 209.

27 *Catalogue of Political and Personal Satires Preserved . . . in the British Museum*, ed. Mary Dorothy George, v (London, 1978).

28 James Street, *The Mynster of the Isle* (Taunton, 1904), p. 153. There seems no particular reason to question the date given for Speke's death. He was a well-known local figure who had been an MP in four Parliaments.

29 HMC, *Hastings MSS*, iii. p. 94, Lindsey to Huntingdon, 20 February 1755; *Gentleman's Magazine*, 26 (1756), p. 262.

30 Bodleian Library, North Papers, D15, fol. 7.

31 Walpole, *Letters*, ed. Toynbee, vi. p. 172, Walpole to Earl of Hertford, 20 January 1765.

32 Bodleian Library, North Papers, D23, fol. 177, North to Guilford, 15 January 1765.

33 Brougham, *Historical Sketches*, p. 392.

34 *The Diaries of Sylvester Douglas, Lord Glenbervie*, ed. Francis Bickley, 2 vols (London, 1928), i. p. 180.

Chapter 3: Political Apprenticeship

1 Sir Lewis Namier and John Brooke, *The History of Parliament: House of Commons 1754–1790*, 3 vols (London, 1964), i. p. 10.

2 Roger North, *The Lives of the Norths*, ed. Augustus Jessop, 3 vols (London, 1890).

3 Roger North, *Examen, or an Enquiry into the Credit and Veracity of a Pretended Complete History* (London, 1740).

4 Ragnhild Hatton, *George I, Elector and King* (London, 1978), p. 398.

5 Wallingford's title was unrecognised as the House of Lords had disallowed his father's claim to the earldom of Banbury, see A. Beesley, *The Complete History of Banbury* (London, 1841), p. 519.

6 Romney Sedgwick, *The History of the House of Commons, 1715–1754*, 2 vols (London, 1970), i. pp. 302–3.

7 Bodleian Library, North Papers, C11, fol. 71, Guilford to Wallingford, 11 November 1729.

8 Sedgwick, *House of Commons, 1715–1754*, i. p. 303; Bodleian Library, North Papers, C11, fol. 78, Guilford to Corporation of Banbury.

9 Namier and Brooke, *House of Commons, 1754–1790*, i. p. 356.

10 Lilian Dickens and Mary Stanton, eds, *An Eighteenth-Century Correspondence* (London, 1910), Guilford to Sanderson Miller [? November 1752].

11 Namier and Brooke, *House of Commons*, i, introduction, passim.

12 Ian R. Christie, *Wilkes, Wyvill and Reform* (London, 1962), p. 2.

13 Peter D. G. Thomas, *The House of Commons in the Eighteenth Century* (Oxford, 1971), pp. 1, 127, 136.

14 Ibid., pp. 89–92.

15 Ibid., pp. 122–25.

16 Ibid., p. 2.

17 Sir Lewis Namier, *Personalities and Powers* (London, 1955), p. 32.

18 Ibid., p. 25.

19 William, Lord North, 'Lord North the Prime Minister', *North American Review*, 177 (1903), p. 260.

[20] Horace Walpole, *Memoirs of the Reign of George III*, ed. G. F. Russell Barker, 4 vols (London, 1894), ii. p. 67n.

[21] Reginald Lucas, *Lord North*, 2 vols (London, 1913), i. p. 32.

[22] W. Baring Pemberton, *Lord North* (London, 1938), p. 94.

[23] Walpole, *George III*, ed. Barker, i. p. 276.

[24] Reed Browning, *The Duke of Newcastle* (New Haven and London, 1975), pp. 213 et seq.

[25] Ibid., p. 35.

[26] Ibid., p. 213.

[27] W. E. H. Lecky, *History of England in the Eighteenth Century*, 8 vols (London, 1875–90), ii. p. 439; G. M. Trevelyan, *History of England* (London, 1942), p. 534.

[28] Browning, *Newcastle*, p. 79.

[29] Bodleian Library, North Papers, D24, fol. 78, North to Guilford, 20 April 1770.

[30] C. D. Smith, *The Early Career of Lord North the Prime Minister* (London, 1979), p. 268.

[31] Sir Nathaniel Wraxall, *The Historical and Posthumous Memoirs, 1772–1784*, ed. Henry B. Wheatly, 5 vols (London, 1884), i. p. 376; Valentine, *North*, ii. p. 264.

[32] He appointed his eldest son, the future sixth Earl of Guilford, Master of Holy Cross Hospital in Winchester. His depredations in that capacity formed the basis of Trollope's novel *The Warden*.

[33] Bodleian Library, North Papers, D7, fol. 67, Legge to Guilford, 9 November 1756.

[34] Ibid., D23, fol. 63, North to Guilford, 20 December 1757.

[35] Ibid., D23, fol. 54, North to Guilford, 1 February 1758.

[36] Ibid., D23, fol. 79, North to Guilford, 28 January 1758.

[37] Smith, *North*, pp. 282–83.

[38] Ibid., pp. 283–85.

[39] Bodleian Library, North Papers, D23, fol. 77, North to Guilford, 8 July 1758.

[40] North, 'Lord North the Prime Minister', *North American Review*, 176 (1903), p. 782.

[41] *The Letters of Horace Walpole*, ed. Mrs Paget Toynbee, 16 vols (Oxford, 1857–59), iii. p. 264, Walpole to George Montagu, 16 November 1754.

[42] Wraxall, *Memoirs*, i. p. 362.

[43] Walpole, *George III*, ed. Barker, iv. p. 52.

[44] William Cobbett, ed., *The Parliamentary History of England*, 36 vols (London, 1806–20), vol. 15, cols 832 et seq.

[45] North, 'Lord North the Prime Minister', p. 782.

[46] Ibid.

[47] Bodleian Library, North Papers, D23, fol. 57, North to Guilford, 8 December 1757.

[48] Sir Norman Chester, *The English Administrative System, 1780–1870* (Oxford, 1981), p. 45.

[49] Valentine, *North*, i. p. 79; Romney Sedgwick, 'Letters from William Pitt to Lord Bute, 1755–1758', *Essays Presented to Sir Lewis Namier*, ed. Richard Pares and A. J. P. Taylor (London, 1956), p. 147. Sedgwick dates this letter from 'internal evidence' to end of March 1758 but, unless it is assumed Pitt had made an earlier and different offer of an overseas appointment to North, this dating must be wrong as North's letter to his father on the subject is dated in his own hand 17 January.

[50] Bodleian Library, North Papers, D23, fol. 66, North to Guilford, 17 January 1758.

Chapter 4: A Man with a Future

[1] William, Lord North, 'Lord North the Prime Minister', *North American Review*, 176 (1903), p. 782.

[2] William Cobbett, ed., *The Parliamentary History of England*, 36 vols (London, 1806–20), vol. 15, cols 945–46.

[3] Alan Valentine, *Lord North*, 2 vols (Norman, Oklahoma, 1967), i. p. 83.

⁴ BL, Add. MS 32840, fol. 245, Guilford to Newcastle, 21 April 1759, quoted Valentine, *North*, i. p. 82.

⁵ Reginald Lucas, *Lord North*, 2 vols (London, 1913), i. p. 29, Newcastle to Pitt, 24 May 1759.

⁶ Sir Norman Chester, *The English Administrative System, 1780–1870* (Oxford, 1981), p. 43.

⁷ Ibid., p. 234.

⁸ C. D. Smith, *The Early Career of Lord North the Prime Minister* (London, 1979), p. 77.

⁹ Chester, *English Administrative System*, p. 145.

¹⁰ Bodleian Library, North Papers, D23, fol. 136 et seq, North to Guilford, 12 October 1762.

¹¹ Ibid. D23, fol. 133, North to Guilford, 10 October 1762.

¹² Ibid., D23, fol. 136, North to Guilford, 12 October 1762.

¹³ Ibid., Add. C4, fol. 52, North to Guilford, 22 July 1765.

¹⁴ HMC, *Carlisle MSS* (London, 1897), p. 576, George Selwyn to Carlisle, 13 February 1782.

¹⁵ Henry, Lord Brougham, *Historical Sketches of Statesmen who Flourished in the Time of George III* (London, 1839), p. 391.

16 Robert Beatson, *A Political Index*, 3 vols (London, 1806), i. p. 243.

¹⁷ Valentine, *North*, i. p. 87.

¹⁸ Ibid., p. 90.

¹⁹ *Letters from George III to Lord Bute, 1756–1766*, ed. Romney Sedgwick (London, 1939), p. xliii.

²⁰ John Brooke, *King George III* (London, 1985), p. 48.

²¹ Ibid., p. 53.

²² Sedgwick, *Letters from George III to Lord Bute*, passim.

²³ Valentine, *North*, i. p. 106.

²⁴ BL, Add. MS 32933, fol. 183, North to Newcastle, 10 January 1761[2]. North's letter is in fact dated 1761, perhaps because he momentarily forgot the tranposition of the start of the New Year in the 1752 calendar reforms.

²⁵ Ibid., fol. 404, J. West to Newcastle, 19 January 1762.

²⁶ Horace Walpole, *Memoirs of the Reign of George III*, ed. G. F. Russell Barker, 4 vols (London, 1894), i. p. 104.

²⁷ BL, Add. MS 32933, fol. 408, Barrington to Newcastle, 19 January 1762.

²⁸ Ibid., fol. 404, J. West to Newcastle, 19 January 1762.

²⁹ Sedgwick, *Letters from George III to Lord Bute*, p. 109, King to Bute, 19 May 1762

³⁰ Valentine, *North*, i. p. 107.

³¹ BL, Add. MS 32947, fol. 84, North to Newcastle, 24 February 1763.

³² Valentine, *North*, i. p. 108.

³³ Bodleian Library, North Papers, D23, fol. 154, North to Guilford, 4 November 1762.

³⁴ Valentine, *North*, i. p. 111.

³⁵ Bodleian Library, North Papers, D8, fol. 111, Guilford to Bute, 15 July 1761.

³⁶ Ibid., D8, fol. 109, Bute to Guilford, 15 July 1761.

³⁷ Walpole, *George III*, ii. p. 115.

³⁸ Valentine, *North*, i. p. 114.

³⁹ *The Grenville Papers*, ed. William James Smith, 4 vols (London, 1852–53), ii. pp. 208–11.

⁴⁰ Ibid., iv. p. 151, North to Halifax, 30 October 1763.

⁴¹ Peter D. G. Thomas, *Lord North* (London, 1976), p. 11.

⁴² Charles Chevenix Trench, *Portrait of a Patriot* (Edinburgh and London, 1962), p. 17.

⁴³ Ibid., p. 8.

⁴⁴ *Gibbon's Journals*, ed. D. M. Low (London, 1929), p. 145.

⁴⁵ George Rudé, *Wilkes and Liberty* (Oxford, 1962), p. xiii.

⁴⁶ Ibid., p. 193.

[47] Ibid., p. 194.

[48] Chevenix Trench, *Portrait of a Patriot*, p. 56.

[49] Cobbett, *Parliamentary History*, vol. 15, col. 1331.

[50] Ibid., vol. 15, col. 1363.

[51] Chevenix Trench, *Portrait of a Patriot*, p. 116.

[52] *Grenville Papers*, ii. pp. 151–52, North to Halifax, 30 October 1763.

[53] Bodleian Library, North Papers, Add. C4, fol. 50, North to Guilford, 8 November 1763.

[54] North's part in the Wilkes debates of 1763–64 is here largely based on the account in Thomas, *North*, pp. 12–13.

[55] George Martelli, *Jeremy Twitcher* (London, 1962), p. 62.

[56] Valentine, *North*, i. p. 121; Bodleian Library, North Papers, D23, fol. 173, North to Guilford, 10 April 1764.

[57] Walpole, *Letters*, ed. Toynbee, v. p. 385, Walpole to Earl of Hertford, 17 November 1763.

[58] *The Complete Works of William Hazlitt*, ed. P. P. Howe, 21 vols (London, 1930), i. p. 170.

[59] Sir Nathanial Wraxall, *The Historical and Posthumous Memoirs, 1772–1784*, ed. Henry B. Wheatley, 5 vols (London, 1884), i. p. 364.

[60] James Boswell, *Life of Johnson*, ed. Birkbeck Hill, 6 vols (Oxford, 1950), v. p. 409.

[61] *The Autobiography of Edward Gibbon*, ed. Lord Sheffield (London, 1978), p. 178.

[62] Cobbett, *Parliamentary History*, vol. 18, col. 1419.

[63] Smith, *North*, p. 82.

[64] Rudé, *Wilkes*, p. 30

[65] Paul Langford, *The First Rockingham Administration, 1765–1766* (London, 1973), pp. 8–9.

[66] Thomas (*North*, p. 15) states he was the only member of the Treasury Board not to be dismissed; Valentine (*North*, i. p. 125) simply says he left office with Grenville; and Lucas (*North*, i. p. 35), relying on Lecky, maintains he was dismissed. This last view gets possible support from a comment North made in a Commons debate in February 1770: 'I myself was once removed'. Henry Cavendish, *Debates in the House of Commons, 1768–1771*, ed. J. Wright, 2 vols (London 1841–43), i. p. 452.

[67] *Additional Grenville Papers, 1763–1765*, ed. John Tomlinson (Manchester, 1962), pp. 205–6.

[68] *The Correspondence of George the Third, 1760–1783*, ed. Sir John Fortescue, 6 vols (London, 1927), i. pp. 136–37, 142, 153–54.

[69] Smith, *North*, p. 82; Horace Walpole, *The Yale Edition of Horace Walpole's Correspondence*, 48 vols (New Haven, 1937–83), x. p. 197, George Montagu to Walpole, 20 January 1766.

[70] Bodleian Library, North Papers, Add. C4, fol. 56, North to Guilford 25 December 1765. William, Lord North, in 'Lord North the Prime Minister: A Personal Memoir', *North American Review*, 176 (1903), p. 790, transcribed the date of this letter as 1769. As the opening lines convey good wishes to Lady Guilford who died in 1766 that is clearly wrong. This incorrect dating has subsequently been followed in their respective biographies by Valentine, Thomas and Smith, all of whom interpret 'the late offer' as a tentative offer of the premiership during North's interview with the King on the evening of 20 December 1769.

[71] BL, Add. MS 32972, fol. 60, Newcastle to Rockingham, 16 November 1765; fol. 70, Dartmouth to Newcastle, 28 November 1765; fol. 95, Newcastle to Rockingham, 1 December 1765.

Chapter 5: Arrival

[1] John Brooke, *King George III* (London, 1985), p. 122.

[2] Alan Valentine, *Lord North*, 2 vols (Norman, Oklahoma, 1967), i. p. 128.

³ HMC, *Stopford-Sackville MSS*, 2 vols (London and Hereford, 1904 and 1910), i. p. 112, Lord George Sackville to General Irwin, 10 June 1766.

⁴ *The Letters of Horace Walpole*, ed. Mrs Paget Toynbee, 16 vols (Oxford, 1857–59), vii. pp. 3–4, Walpole to George Montagu, 25 May 1766.

⁵ *Memoirs of the Marquess of Rockingham*, ed. Earl of Albemarle, 2 vols (London, 1852), i. p. 345.

⁶ *The Camden Miscellany*, 4th series, 7 (1969), 'The Ryder Diaries', ed. Peter D. G. Thomas, p. 258.

⁷ Ibid., p. 258.

⁸ Paul Langford, *The First Rockingham Administration* (London, 1973), p. 76. The present author acknowledges with thanks that this brief account of the Stamp Act crisis is largely drawn from this book.

⁹ William Cobbett, ed., *The Parliamentary History of England*, 36 vols (London, 1806–20), vol. 16, col. 92.

¹⁰ Valentine, *North*, i. p. 130.

¹¹ Peter D. G. Thomas, *Lord North* (London, 1976), p. 16.

¹² *The Trumbull Papers*, Collections of the Massachusetts Historical Society, 5th series, 9 (1885), p. 246, Johnson to Pitkin, 13 November 1767.

¹³ Rockingham, *Memoirs*, i. p. 269.

¹⁴ HMC, *Dartmouth MSS*, 3 vols (London, 1887–96), ii. p. 36, Earl of Chesterfield to Dartmouth, 20 February 1766.

¹⁵ Cobbett, *Parliamentary History*, vol. 16, col. 178.

¹⁶ Waldershare MSS, North to Guilford, 15 July 1766 (Bodleian Library, MS Eng. c. 3337, fol. 44.). When this book was first planned the present Earl of Guilford held a small collection of family papers which he kindly made available to the present author. Some have subsequently been transferred to the Bodleian Library, whose reference number will be included in brackets.

¹⁷ Bodleian Library, North Papers, Add. C4, fol. 59, North to Guilford, 31 July 1766.

¹⁸ Ibid., Add. C4, fol. 62, Pitt to North, 28 July 1766.

¹⁹ HMC, *Dartmouth MSS*, iii. p. 182, Chesterfield to Dartmouth, 24 May 1766.

²⁰ Bodleian Library, North Papers, Add. C4, fol. 59, North to Guilford, 31 July 1766.

²¹ C. D. Smith, *The Early Career of Lord North* (London 1979), p. 285.

²² *The Diaries of Sylvester Douglas, Lord Glenbervie*, ed. Francis Bickley, 2 vols (London, 1928), i. p. 148.

²³ Ibid., i. p. 231.

²⁴ George Augustus, third Earl; Catherine (Kitty), Lady Glenbervie; Francis, fourth Earl; Anne, Countess of Sheffield; Frederick, fifth Earl. Towards the end of his life Frederick settled in Corfu and founded the Ionian University.

²⁵ Bodleian Library, North Papers, passim.

²⁶ Sir Nathaniel Wraxall, *The Historical and Posthumous Memoirs, 1772–1784*, ed. Henry B. Wheatley, 5 vols (London, 1884), i. p. 361.

²⁷ Waldershare MSS, North to Guilford, 15 July 1766. (Bodleian Library, MS Eng. c. 3337 fol. 44.)

²⁸ Smith, *North*, p. 285.

²⁹ J. E. D. Binney, *British Public Finance and Administration, 1774–92* (Oxford, 1958), p. 151, quoting PRO, 30/8, bundle 231, booklet, *The Business Done in Treasury*.

³⁰ Ibid.

³¹ Sir Lewis Namier and John Brooke, *The History of Parliament: House of Commons, 1754–1790*, 3 vols (London, 1964), ii. pp. 249–50.

³² Glenbervie, *Diaries*, i. p. 170.

³³ *The Grenville Papers*, ed. William James Smith, 4 vols (London, 1852–53), iii. p. 315, Whately to Grenville, 5 September 1766; p. 332, Whately to Grenville, 20 October 1766.

³⁴ Thomas, *North*, p. 18; Reginald Lucas, *Lord North*, 2 vols (London, 1913), i. p. 50.

[35] Valentine, *North*, i. p. 147.

[36] Bodleian Library, North Papers, D24, fol. 21, North to Guilford, 6 December 1766.

[37] Valentine, *North*, i. p. 142.

[38] Waldershare MSS, North to Guilford, 24 April 1767 (Bodleian Library, MS Eng. c. 3337, fol. 53).

[39] Valentine, *North*, i. p. 145.

[40] Waldershare MSS, North to Guilford, 22 December 1766 (Bodleian Library, MS Eng. c. 3337, fol. 48).

[41] J. H. Jesse, *George Selwyn and his Contemporaries*, 4 vols (London, 1882), ii. p. 119, Gilly Williams to Selwyn, 26 December 1766.

[42] *The Last Journals of Horace Walpole*, ed. A. F. Steuart, 2 vols (London, 1910), ii. p. 210.

[43] Bodleian Library, North Papers, B15, fol. 132.

[44] Peter D. G. Thomas, *The Townshend Duties Crisis* (Oxford, 1987), p. 6. Thomas's clear account of the crisis has been the principal source for this section.

[45] Valentine, *North*, i. p. 148.

[46] Peter D. G. Thomas, *British Politics and the Stamp Act Crisis* (Oxford, 1975), pp. 361–62.

[47] Thomas, *North*, p. 20.

[48] *The Correspondence of Edmund Burke*, ed. Thomas W. Copeland et al., 10 vols (Cambridge, 1958–78), x. p. 297n.

[49] Philip Henry Stanhope, Lord Mahon, *History of England, 1713–1783*, 7 vols (London, 1836–54), v, appendix p. xvii.

[50] *The Correspondence of George III, 1760–1783*, ed. Sir John Fortescue, 6 vols (London, 1927), i. p. 459, Grafton to King, 5 March 1767.

[51] Ibid., p. 460, King to Grafton, 5 March 1767.

[52] *Autobiography of Augustus Henry, Third Duke of Grafton*, ed. Sir William R. Anson (London, 1898), p. 123, North to Grafton, 4 March 1767.

[53] William, Lord North, 'Lord North the Prime Minister', *North American Review*, 176 (1903), p. 786.

[54] Valentine, *North*, i. p. 153; *The Grenville Papers*, iv. p. 162, Charles Lloyd to Lord Temple, 10 September 1767.

[55] *Grafton Autobiography*, p. 166, North to Grafton, 6 September 1767.

[56] Ibid.

[57] Ibid., p. 167, North to Grafton, 10 September 1767.

[58] Ibid., pp. 167–68.

[59] Fortescue, *Correspondence*, i. p. 505, King to Grafton, 12 September 1767.

[60] *The Trumbull Papers*, Collections of the Massachusetts Historical Society, 5th series, 9 (1885), p. 246, Johnson to Pitkin, 13 July 1767.

[61] Bodleian Library, North Papers, Add. C4, fol. 101, North to Guilford, 14 October 1767.

[62] *Political and Social Letters*, ed. Emily F. D. Osborn (London, n.d. [1890]), p. 175, Mrs Osborn to John Osborn, 29 September 1767.

[63] Bodleian Library, North Papers, Add. C4, fol. 97, North to Guilford, 12 October 1767.

[64] Thomas, *North*, p. 23.

[65] Horace Walpole, *Memoirs of the Reign of George III*, ed. G. F. Russell Barker, 4 vols (London, 1894), iii. p. 90.

[66] Grafton, *Autobiography*, p. 227.

[67] *Grenville Papers*, p. 304, Whately to Grenville, 4 June 1768.

[68] Valentine, *North*, i. p. 157.

[69] Wraxall, *Memoirs*, i. p. 367.

[70] Glenbervie, *Diaries*, i. p. 326.

[71] Wraxall, *Memoirs*, i. p. 362.

[72] Valentine, *North*, i. p. 160; Lucas, *North*, i. pp. 65–66.

[73] Walpole, *George III*, iii. p. 149.

[74] Brooke, *George III*, p. 147.
[75] Grafton, *Autobiography*, p. 199.
[76] Ibid., p. 201.
[77] Valentine, *North*, i. p. 161.
[78] Fortescue, *Correspondence*, ii. p. 21, King to North, 25 April 1768.
[79] Charles Chevenix Trench, *Portrait of a Patriot* (Edinburgh and London 1962), p. 226.
[80] Thomas, *North*, p. 25.
[81] Bodleian Library, North Papers, D24, fol. 52, North to Guilford, 14 November 1768.
[82] Thomas, *North*, p. 27.
[83] Fortescue, *Correspondence*, ii. p. 76, King to North, 28 January 1769.
[84] Thomas, *North*, p. 27.
[85] Ibid., p. 28.
[86] Fortescue, *Correspondence*, ii. p. 90, King to North, 16 April 1769.
[87] *Sir Henry Cavendish's Debates of the House of Commons*, ed. J. Wright, 2 vols (London, 1841), i. pp. 268 et seq.
[88] H. V. Bowen, *Revenue and Reform: The Indian Problem in British Politics, 1757–1773* (Cambridge, 1991), p. 33.
[89] Ibid., pp. 5 et seq.
[90] Cavendish, *Debates*, i. p. 253.
[91] Cobbett, *Parliamentary History*, vol. 16, col. 609.
[92] Valentine, *North*, i. p. 174.
[93] *Correspondence of John, Fourth Duke of Bedford*, ed. Lord John Russell, 3 vols (London, 1859), iii. p. 408, Rigby to Bedford, 11 April 1769.
[94] Cavendish, *Debates*, i. p. 399.
[95] *Trumbull Papers*, p. 425.
[96] Thomas, *North*, pp. 32–33.
[97] Cavendish, *Debates*, i. p. 84.
[98] Ibid., i. p. 88.
[99] *The Trumbull Papers*, p. 303, Johnson to Pitkin, 18 November 1768.
[100] Cavendish, *Debates*, i. p. 206.

Chapter 6: The King's First Minister

[1] C. D. Smith, *The Early Career of Lord North the Prime Minister* (London, 1979), pp. 155–56.
[2] Bodleian Library, North Papers, Add. C4, fol. 132, North to Guilford, 30 May 1769. In addition to North's son George, Dartmouth's eldest son, also called George, was then at Eton.
[3] *The Correspondence of George III, 1760–1783*, ed. Sir John Fortescue, 6 vols (London, 1927), ii. p. 110, King to North, 20 December 1769.
[4] See Chapter 4, n. 70 above.
[5] The *London Magazine* is quoted in Cobbett, vol. 16, col. 669n. The report in *Parliamentary History* itself was taken from the *Gentleman's Magazine*.
[6] William Cobbett, ed., *The Parliamentary History of England*, 36 vols (London, 1806–20), vol. 16, cols 717 et seq.
[7] Peter D. G. Thomas, *Lord North* (London, 1976), p. 34.
[8] John Brooke, *King George III* (London, 1985), p. 156.
[9] *Autobiography of Augustus Henry, Third Duke of Grafton*, ed. Sir William R. Anson (London, 1898), p. 251.
[10] *Gentleman's Magazine*, vol. 40 (1770), p. 44.
[11] Horace Walpole, *Memoirs of the Reign of George III*, ed. G. F. Russell Barker, 4 vols (London, 1894), iv. p. 34.

244 *Notes to Pages 79–86*

[12] Brooke, *George III*, p. 157.

[13] Grafton, *Autobiography*, pp. 248–49.

[14] Ibid., p. 250.

[15] Walpole, *George III*, iv. p. 44.

[16] HMC, *Eglinton MSS* (London, 1885), p. 420, Robert Thomson to Edward Weston (a retired civil servant), 20 January 1770: 'The Event of this day will hardly be in the evening post, & if it is, you will not believe it ... the Duke of Grafton has resigned ... '

[17] Bodleian Library, North Papers, Add. C4, fol. 132, North to Guilford, 30 May 1769. Mrs Horton's story had a happy ending as she later married the second Viscount Maynard.

[18] *Dictionary of National Biography*, s.n.

[19] Fortescue, *Correspondence*, ii. p. 125, King to North, 22 January 1770.

[20] Ibid., p. 126, King to North, 23 January 1770.

[21] Thomas, *North*, p. 35.

[22] Walpole, *George III*, vi. p. 51.

[23] Fortescue, *Correspondence*, ii. p. 128, King to North, 1 February 1770.

[24] *Letters of the First Earl of Malmesbury*, ed. Earl of Malmesbury, 2 vols (London, 1870), i. p. 189, Mr Harris to his son, 2 February 1770; HMC, *Eglinton MSS* (London, 1885), p. 420, Robert Thomson to Edward Weston, 30 January 1770; *London Chronicle*, 27 (1770), p. 110.

[25] *The Letters of Horace Walpole*, ed. Mrs Paget Toynbee, 16 vols (Oxford, 1857–59), vii. p. 362, Walpole to Mann, 30 January 1770.

[26] Sir Charles Bunbury's suit against against his wife, Lady Sarah Lennox, was heard in the spring of 1769, see Stella Tillyard, *Aristocrats* (London, 1994), p. 283; Lady Francis Arundel, daughter of the second Duke of Rutland, died 29 November 1769, see *Collins's Peerage*, ed. Sir Egerton Brydges, 9 vols (London, 1812), i. p. 484.

[27] Bodleian Library, North Papers, Add. C4, fol. 170, North to Guilford, 1 December [1769].

[28] Ibid., Add. C4, fol. 100, North to Guilford, 14 October 1767.

[29] Thomas, *North*, p. 41.

[30] Fortescue, *Correspondence*, iv. p. 70, North to King, 21 March [1778].

[31] As early as 1775 Thomas Hutchinson, formerly Governor of Massachusetts, noted in his diary: 'Ld Guilford is very old ... and Ld North is not long lived – corpulent etc'. Thomas Hutchinson, *The Diary and Letters*, ed. P. O. Hutchinson, 2 vols (London, 1883 and 1886), i. p. 444, 12 May 1775.

[32] The *Autobiography and Correspondence of Mary Granville, Mrs Delany*, ed. Lady Lanover, 3 vols (London, 1861), 3 vols (London, 1862), 2nd series, ii. p. 476, Delany to Miss Port, 10 October 1779; Alan Valentine, *Lord North*, 2 vols (Norman, Oklahoma, 1967), ii. p. 108.

[33] Henry, Lord Brougham, *Historical Sketches of Statesmen who Flourished in the Time of George III*, (London, 1839), p. 395.

[34] Eric Robson, 'Lord North', *History Today*, 2 (1952), p. 537, quoting William Eden, first Lord Auckland.

[35] BL, Add. MS, 38212, fols 61–62, Robinson to Jenkinson, 16 August 1779, quoted H. Butterfield, 'Lord North and Mr Robinson, 1779', *Cambridge Historical Review*, 15 (1937), p. 268.

[36] Hutchinson, *Diary*, i. p. 404, 14 March 1775.

[37] J. D. Griffiths Davies, *George the Third* (London, 1936), p. 140.

[38] Thomas, *North*, p. 46.

[39] Fortescue, *Correspondence*, ii. p. 130, King to North, 16 February 1770.

[40] N. A. M. Rodger, *The Insatiable Earl: A Life of John Montagu, Fourth Earl of Sandwich* (London, 1993), p. 131.

[41] Fortescue, *Correspondence*, ii. p. 207, King to North, 16 January 1771.

[42] Ibid., p. 251, King to North, 7 June 1771.

[43] Ibid., p. 252, King to North, 9 June 1771.

[44] *Gentleman's Magazine*, 42 (1772), p. 293.

[45] B. D. Bargar, *Lord Dartmouth and the American Revolution* (Columbia, South Carolina, 1965), p. 53.

[46] Fortescue, *Correspondence*, ii. p. 210, North to King, 17 January 1771.

[47] Staffordshire County Record Office, Dartmouth MSS, D(W)1778/1.ii, quoted Smith, *North*, p. 91.

[48] Ibid., p. 92.

[49] Brougham, *Historical Sketches*, p. 392.

[50] Sir Nathanial Wraxall, *The Historical and Posthumous Memoirs, 1772–1734*, ed. Henry B. Wheatly, 5 vols (London, 1884), i, p. 373.

[51] Cobbett, *Parliamentary History*, vol. 20, col. 925.

[52] From a gloss by Dr John Allen included in *Memorials and Correspondence of Charles James Fox*, ed. Lord John Russell, 4 vols (London, 1853–57), ii. p. 38.

Chapter 7: A Confident Start

[1] Sir Lewis Namier and John Brooke, *The History of Parliament: House of Commons, 1754–1790*, 3 vols (London, 1964), iii. p. 554.

[2] *Sir Henry Cavendish's Debates of the House of Commons*, ed. J. Wright, 2 vols (London, 1841), i. p. 438.

[3] *The Letters of Edward Gibbon*, ed. J. E. Norton, 3 vols (London, 1956), i. p. 256, Gibbon to Dorothea Gibbon, 17 February 1770.

[4] William Cobbett, ed., *The Parliamentary History of England*, 36 vols (London, 1806–20), vol. 16 col. 848.

[5] Alan Valentine, *Lord North*, 2 vols (Norman, Oklahoma, 1967), i. p. 195.

[6] Cobbett, *Parliamentary History*, vol. 16 col. 845.

[7] *The Correpondence of George III, 1760–1783*, ed. Sir John Fortescue, 6 vols (London, 1927), ii. p. 132, King to North, 28 February 1770.

[8] Cobbett, *Parliamentary History*, vol. 16 col. 894.

[9] Ibid.

[10] BL, Egerton MS 221, fols 133–34, quoted C. D. Smith, *The Early Career of Lord North the Prime Minister* (London, 1979), p. 229.

[11] Fortescue, *Correspondence*, ii. p. 134, King to North, 16 March 1770.

[12] J. D. Griffiths Davies, *George the Third* (London, 1936), p. 130.

[13] Bodleian Library, North Papers, D24, fol. 79, North to Guilford, 20 April 1770.

[14] Namier and Brooke, *House of Commons, 1754–1790*, i. p. 126.

[15] W. Baring Pemberton, *Lord North* (London, 1938), p. 111.

[16] Namier and Brooke, *House of Commons, 1754–1790*, i. p. 146.

[17] Ibid., p. 147.

[18] In *Personalities and Powers* (London, 1955), ch. 4, 'King George III: A Study of Personality', p. 43, Namier suggests the placemen might have accounted for one-third and the Country Gentlemen for one-fifth of the membership of the House.

[19] John Brooke, *King George III* (London, 1955), p. 158.

[20] Peter D. G. Thomas, *Lord North* (London, 1976) p. 46.

[21] Pemberton, *North*, p. 116.

[22] Thomas, *North*, p. 62.

[23] This view is cogently argued as far as America is concerned by N. A. M. Rodger in *The Insatiable Earl* (London 1993), pp. 212 et seq.

[24] Thomas, *North*, pp. 59 et seq.

[25] Cobbett, *Parliamentary History*, vol. 16, col. 945.

[26] Ibid., cols 950–51.

[27] Cavendish, *Debates*, i. pp. 484, 486.

[28] Peter D. G. Thomas, *The Townshend Duties Crisis* (Oxford, 1987), p. 165.

[29] Cavendish, *Debates*, i. pp. 487–89.

[30] Ibid., p. 492.

[31] Thomas, *North*, p. 71.

[32] Cavendish, *Debates*, i. pp. 497–98.

[33] Thomas, *North*, p. 72.

[34] Cavendish, *Debates*, i. p. 496.

[35] Julius Goebel, *The Struggle for the Falkland Islands* (New Haven, 1982), pp. 1 et seq. The present account of the background to the Falklands Islands crisis is largely drawn from this book.

[36] Cavendish, *Debates*, ii. p. 286; John Aikin, *Annals of the Reign of George the Third*, 2 vols (London, 1816), i. p. 92.

[37] Valentine, *North*, i. p. 20.

[38] Fortescue, *Correspondence*, ii. p. 174. King to North, 28 November 1770.

[39] Cavendish, *Debates*, ii. p. 222.

[40] Goebel, *Falklands Islands*, pp. 300, 337.

[41] Cobbett, *Parliamentary History*, vol. 16, col. 1031.

[42] Margaret Cotter Morison, 'The Duc de Choiseul and the Invasion of England', *Transactions of the Royal Historical Society*, 3rd series, (1910), pp. 104–5,

[43] Valentine, *North*, i. p. 212.

[44] Ibid., p. 207.

[45] Ibid., p. 209.

[46] Horace Walpole, *Memoirs of the Reign of George III*, ed. G. F. Russell Barker, 4 vols (London, 1894), iv. p. 158.

[47] Thomas, *North*, p. 48.

[48] *Trumbull Papers*, p. 457, Johnson to Trumbull, 12 October 1770.

[49] Bodleian Library, North Papers, D24, fol. 93, Lady North to Guilford, 13 November 1770.

[50] Cavendish, *Debates*, ii. p. 51.

[51] Morison, 'Duc de Choiseul', p. 105; Thomas, *North*, p. 50.

[52] Thomas, *North*, p. 50.

[53] Cavendish, *Debates*, ii. p. 304n.; Barré had earlier voiced his suspicions in a letter to Chatham, probably written 22 January, included in *The Correspondence of William Pitt, Earl of Chatham*, ed. W. S. Taylor and J. H. Pringle, 4 vols (London, 1838–40), iv. p. 74.

[54] Cavendish, *Debates*, ii. p. 234.

[55] Rodger, *The Insatiable Earl*, p. 130; Morison, 'Duc de Choiseul', p. 104.

[56] Henry, Lord Brougham, *Historical Sketches of Statesmen* (London 1839), p. 396.

[57] *Morning Herald*, 6 August 1782, quoted *The Complete Peerage*, ed. Hon. Vicary Gibbs et al., 14 vols (London, 1910–40), i. p. 497, appendix H.

Chapter 8: The East India Company

[1] Peter D. G. Thomas, *Lord North* (London, 1976), p. 62.

[2] *Annual Register* (1763), p. 76, quoted H. V. Bowen, *Revenue and Reform: The Indian Problem in British Politics, 1757–1773* (Cambridge, 1991), p. 2.

[3] Bowen, *Revenue and Reform*, pp. 5, 48 et seq.

[4] Ibid., p. 7.

[5] Ibid., p. 104 et seq.

[6] Alan Valentine, *Lord North*, 2 vols (Norman, Oklahoma, 1967), i. p. 296.

[7] *Sir Henry Cavendish's Debates of the House of Commons*, ed. J. Wright, 2 vols (London, 1841), i. p. 87.

[8] Thomas, *North*, p. 61.

[9] Bowen, *Revenue and Reform*, pp. 33 et seq.

[10] Ibid., p. 72.

[11] Thomas, *North*, p. 62.

[12] Bowen, *Revenue and Reform*, p. 8.

[13] Lucy S. Sutherland, *The East India Company in Eighteenth-Century Politics* (Oxford, 1952), p. 141.

[14] Bowen, *Revenue and Reform*, p. 104.

[15] Ibid., pp. 125–28.

[16] Horace Walpole, *Last Journals*, ed. A. F. Steuart, 2 vols (London, 1910), i. p. 72.

[17] Sutherland, *East India Company*, p. 229.

[18] Sir George Forrest, *The Life of Lord Clive*, 2 vols (London, 1918), ii. pp. 379–80, Wedderburn to Clive, 21 October 1771; North to Clive, 29 October 1771. The letters are quoted from Powis MSS, but one of the dates must be wrong as North's letter was written first.

[19] William Cobbett, ed., *The Parliamentary History of England*, 36 vols (London, 1806–20), vol. 17, col 233.

[20] Ibid., col. 237.

[21] Bowen, *Revenue and Reform*, p. 99.

[22] Cobbett, *Parliamentary Reform*, vol. 17, col. 328.

[23] Ibid., col. 454.

[24] Ibid., col. 460.

[25] Bowen, *Revenue and Reform*, p. 100.

[26] *The Correspondence of George III, 1760–1783*, ed. Sir John Fortescue, 6 vols (London, 1917), ii. p. 376, North to King, 4 August 1772; ii. p. 382, North to King, 14 August 1772.

[27] Ibid., pp. 379–80, North to [?Dartmouth], 10 August 1772.

[28] R. D. Bargar, *Lord Dartmouth and the American Revolution* (Columbia, South Carolina, 1965), pp. 56–57; Bodleian Library, North Papers, D24, fol. 197, Dartmouth to Guilford, 12 August 1772.

[29] *The Correspondence of Edmund Burke*, ed. T. W. Copeland et al., 9 vols (Cambridge, 1958–70), ii. pp. 350–51, Burke to William Dowdeswell, 27 October 1772.

[30] Fortescue, *Correspondence*, ii. p. 382, North to King, 24 August 1772.

[31] Forrest, *Lord Clive*, ii. p. 396, North to Wedderburn, 18 September 1772.

[32] Bodleian Library, North Papers, D24, fol. 172, George North to Guilford, 5 October 1772.

[33] Bowen, *Revenue and Reform*, p. 128.

[34] Bodleian Library, North Papers, D24, fol. 177, North to Guilford, 5 October 1772.

[35] Forrest, *Lord Clive*, ii. p. 205.

[36] Ibid., p. 396, quoting Powis MSS, Clive to Strachey, 7 November 1772.

[37] Fortescue, *Correspondence*, ii. p. 407, King to North, 25 November 1772.

[38] Cobbett, *Parliamentary History*, vol. 17, col. 517.

[39] Ibid., cols 529 et seq.

[40] Walpole, *Last Journals*, ii. p. 161.

[41] Cobbett, *Parliamentary History*, vol. 17, col. p. 161.

[42] Ibid., cols 533 et seq; Walpole, *Last Journals*, i. p. 161; Bowen, *Revenue and Reform*, p. 145.

[43] *The Letters of Edward Gibbon*, ed. J. E. Norton, 3 vols (London, 1956), i. p. 352, Gibbon to Holroyd, 11 December 1772.

[44] Sheffield Archives, WWM, Burke Papers, 1/395, Rockingham to Burke, 22 October 1772, quoted Sutherland, *East India Company*, p. 241.

[45] Cobbett, *Parliamentary History*, vol. 17, col. 832.

[46] East India Company Court Book, 81, p. 415, quoted Sutherland, *East India Company*, p. 249.

[47] Fortescue, *Correspondence*, ii. p. 408, King to North, 26 November 1772.

[48] Ibid., pp. 411–12, King to North, 7 December 1772.

[49] Ibid., p. 459, King to North, 9 March 1773.

[50] Ibid., pp. 479–80, King to North, 3 May 1773.

[51] Ibid., pp. 485–86, King to North, 18 May 1773.

[52] Thomas, *North*, p. 53.

[53] Cobbett, *Parliamentary History*, vol 17, cols 883–84; Thomas, *North*, p. 66.

[54] Bowen, *Revenue and Reform*, pp. 166–67, pp. 176 et seq.

[55] Cobbett, *Parliamentary History*, vol. 17, cols 904, 914.

[56] Thomas, *North*, p. 65.

[57] Walpole, *Last Journals*, i. p. 199.

[58] Cobbett, *Parliamentary History*, vol. 17, col. 682.

[59] Fortescue, *Correspondence*, ii. p. 491, King to North, 22 May 1773.

[60] Sutherland, *East India Company*, p. 291.

[61] Bowen, *Revenue and Reform*, p. 187.

[62] Sutherland, *East India Company*, p. 267.

[63] BL, Add. MS 29194, fols 84–85, undated letter to Warren Hastings, quoted P. J. Marshall, *Problems of Empire: Britain and India, 1757–1814* (London, 1968), p. 34.

Chapter 9: The Good Years

[1] Bodleian Library, North Papers, Add. C4, fol. 158, North to Guilford, 6 May 1772.

[2] *Correspondence of William Pitt, Earl of Chatham*, ed. W. S. Taylor and J. H. Pringle, 4 vols (London, 1838–40), iv. p. 332, Chatham to Earl of Shelburne, 6 March 1774.

[3] Peter D. G. Thomas, *The House of Commons in the Eighteenth Century* (Oxford, 1971), pp. 79–81.

[4] Sir Nathaniel Wraxall, *The Historical and Posthumous Memoirs, 1772–1784*, ed. Henry B. Wheatley, 5 vols (London, 1884), i. p. 369.

[5] Peter D. G. Thomas, *Lord North* (London, 1976), p. 58. North's handling of the National Debt and his use of lotteries is here largely based on Thomas, ibid., p. 55 et seq.

[6] Bodleian Library, North Papers, D24, fol. 78, North to Guilford, 20 April 1770.

[7] Ibid., Add. C4, fol. 167, North to Guilford, undated.

[8] Peter Mathias, *The Transformation of England* (London, 1979), p. 125.

[9] Ibid., p. 287.

[10] Ibid., pp. 124, 287.

[11] Alan Valentine, *Lord North* (Norman, Oklahoma, 1967), ii. p. 96.

[12] Ross J. S. Hoffman, *The Marquis* (New York, 1973), p. 287.

[13] BL, 8145 aaa 17, *Letters which Passed in Great Britain Relative to the Absentee Tax*, p. 16, the Duke of Devonshire and others to Lord North, 16 October 1773.

[14] HMC, *Dartmouth MSS*, 3 vols (London, 1887–96), iii. p. 206.

[15] BL, 8145 aaa 17, *Letters which Passed in Great Britain Relative to the Absentee Tax*, p. 11, North to the Duke of Devonshire, 21 October 1773.

[16] *Chatham Correspondence*, iv. pp. 299–308.

[17] *The Correspondence of George III, 1760–1783*, ed. Sir John Fortescue, 6 vols (London, 1927), iii. p. 18, King to North, 22 October 1773.

[18] Valentine, *North*, ii. p. 99.

[19] Fortescue, *Correspondence*, iii. pp. 33–37, four letters each way between the King and North, 17 to 28 November 1773.

[20] Valentine, *North*, ii. p. 99

[21] Henry Roseveare, *The Treasury, 1660–1870* (London, 1973), pp. 61 et seq., pp 83 et seq. The present author is indebted to this book for its clear account of North's Treasury reforms.

[22] Treasury Minute Books, PRO, T.29–45, p. 54, quoted Roseveare, *The Treasury*, p. 182.

[23] Thomas, *North*, p. 123.

[24] Ibid., p. 105.

[25] Roseveare, *The Treasury*, p. 61.

[26] John Cannon, *The Noble Lord in the Blue Ribbon*, Historical Association pamphlet, 74 (London, 1970), p. 24.

[27] Valentine, *North*, i. p. 236; Thomas, *North*, p. 74; Peter D. G. Thomas, *Tea Party to Independence* (Oxford, 1991), pp. 88, 114.

[28] William Cobbett, ed., *The Parliamentary History of England*, 36 vols (London, 1806–20), vol. 17, col. 1357.

[29] Ibid., col. 1367.

[30] W. P. M. Kennedy, ed., *Statutes, Treaties and Documents of the Canadian Constitution, 1713–1929* (Oxford, 1930), p. 95.

[31] Ibid., p. 130.

[32] Cobbett, *Parliamentary History*, vol. 17, col. 1389.

[33] Thomas, *North*, p. 79.

[34] Cobbett, *Parliamentary History*, vol. 17, col. 1074.

[35] Valentine, *North*, i. p. 196.

[36] Cobbett, *Parliamentary History*, vol. 17, col. 1063.

[37] Fortescue, *Correspondence*, iii. p. 75, Suffolk to King, 26 February 1774.

[38] Chatham, *Correspondence*, iv. p. 334, Temple to Countess of Chatham, 8 March 1774; Valentine, *North*, i. pp. 315–16.

[39] Horace Walpole, *Last Journals*, ed. A. F. Steuart (London, 1910), i. p. 314.

[40] Bodleian Library, North Papers, Add. C4, fol. 164, North to Guilford, 18 August 1772.

[41] Ibid., D24, fol. 161, North to Guilford, 21 June [1772].

[42] Ibid., D24, fol. 183, North to Guilford, 24 August 1773.

[43] Valentine, *North*, i. p. 304

[44] *The Letters of Horace Walpole*, ed. Mrs Paget Toynbee, 16 vols (Oxford, 1857–59), viii. p. 391, Walpole to Countess of Upper Ossory, 30 December 1773.

[45] *Letters of the First Earl of Malmesbury*, ed. Earl of Malmesbury, 2 vols (London, 1870), i. p. 311, Mrs Harris to her son, 25 June 1775.

[46] *The Yale Edition of Horace Walpole's Correspondence*, 48 vols (New Haven, 1937–1983), xxiv. p. 63n., Walpole to Mann, 29 November 1774.

[47] Fortescue, *Correspondence*, iii. p. 154, King to Guilford, 5 October 1772.

[48] Ibid., iii. p. 155, King to North, 29 November 1774.

[49] Bodleian Library, North Papers, D24, fol. 177, North to Guilford, 5 October 1772.

[50] Smith, *North*, p. 165.

[51] *The History of the University of Oxford*, v (Oxford, 1986), ed. L. S. Sutherland and L. G. Mitchell, pp. 170–71.

[52] Ibid., p. 166.

[53] Cobbett, *Parliamentary History*, vol. 17, col. 272.

[54] *History of Oxford University*, v. pp. 169–70.

[55] Ibid., p. 171.

[56] Cobbett, *Parliamentary History*, vol. 17, col. 272.

[57] Bodleian Library, North Papers, D25, fol. 140, Lady North to Guilford, Friday [1787].

[58] Ibid., D24, fol. 188, North to Guilford, 24 September 1773.

Chapter 10: The Thirteen Colonies

[1] G. M. Trevelyan, *History of England* (rev. edn, London, 1944), p. 551.

[2] Richard C. Simmons, *The American Colonies from Settlement to Independence* (London, 1976), p. 9.

[3] John Richard Alden, *Pioneer America* (London, 1966), p. 18.

[4] Simmons, *American Colonies*, pp. 14–15.

[5] Alden, *Pioneer America*, p. 21.

[6] F. George Kay, *The Atlantic Ocean* (London, 1954), p. 85.

[7] Simmons, *American Colonies*, p. 24.

[8] Ibid., p. 124.

[9] J. Potter, 'The Growth of Population in America, 1700 to 1860', in *Population in History*, ed. D. V. Glass and D. E. C. Eversley (London, 1965), pp. 636 et seq.

[10] *The Works of John Adams*, ed. Charles Francis Adams, 10 vols (Boston, 1850–56), x. pp. 282–83, Adams to Niles, 13 February 1818.

[11] Kate Hotblack, *Chatham's Colonial Policy* (London, 1917), p. 173, Franklin to Governor Shirley of Massachusetts, 4 December 1754, quoting BL, Add. MS 35911, fols 60–61.

[12] Sir George Otto Trevelyan, *The American Revolution*, 3 vols (London, 1905), i. p. 16, source not given.

[13] HMC, *Various MSS*, 7 vols (London, 1901–14), vi. p. 111, Ellis to Knox, 23 March 1774.

[14] *Correspondence of Edmund Burke*, ed. Earl Fitzwilliam, 4 vols (London, 1844), i. p. 509, Lee to Burke, 16 December 1774.

[15] Alden, *Pioneer America*, p. 48.

[16] John Richard Alden, *A History of the American Revolution* (London, 1969), p. 33.

[17] Simmons, *American Colonies*, p. 274.

[18] Edward McCrady, *The History of South Carolina*, 4 vols (New York, 1897–1902), ii. pp. 254–55, Glen to Newcastle, 6 February 1742/43.

[19] David Duncan Wallace, *The Life of Henry Laurens* (New York, 1915), p. 37, Glen to Bedford, 10 October 1748, quoting W. Roy Smith, *South Carolina: Royal Province* (New York, 1903), p. 297.

[20] Peter D. G. Thomas, *The Townshend Duties Crisis* (Oxford, 1987), p. 88.

[21] Claud H. Van Tyne, *Causes of the War of Independence* (Boston, 1922), p. 60.

[22] Alden, *Pioneer America*, p. 41.

[23] *American Archives: A Documentary History of the Origin and Progress of the North American Colonies*, ed. Peter Force, 4th series, 6 vols (Washington, 1837–46), ii. p. 27, Dartmouth to the Governors of the Colonies, 3 March 1775.

[24] Simmons, *American Colonies*, p. 301.

Chapter 11: The Gathering Storm

[1] Peter D. G. Thomas, *Tea Party to Independence* (Oxford, 1991), p. 14.

[2] Ibid., p. 17.

[3] Ibid., p. 18.

[4] B. D. Bargar, *Lord Dartmouth and the American Revolution* (Columbia, South Carolina, 1965), p. 98.

[5] Thomas Hutchinson, *Diary and Letters*, ed. P. O. Hutchinson, 2 vols (London, 1883 and 1886), ii. p. 101.

[6] Thomas, *Tea Party*, p. 19.

[7] William Cobbett, ed., *The Parliamentary History of England*, 36 vols (London, 1806–20), vol. 18, col. 177.

[8] Thomas, *Tea Party*, pp. 30–32.

[9] Peter D. G. Thomas, *Lord North* (London, 1976), p. 75; Cobbett, *Parliamentary History*, vol. 17, cols 1163 et seq.

[10] *The Correspondence of Edmund Burke*, ed. Thomas V. Copeland et al., 10 vols (Cambridge, 1958–78), ii. p. 528, Burke to Committee of Correspondence, 6 April 1774.

[11] Cobbett, *Parliamentary History*, vol. 17, col 1171.

[12] Ibid., vol. 17, col. 1165.

[13] *The Letters of Richard D. and George Cumberland*, ed. Clementina Black (London, 1912), p. 61, Gooch to George Cumberland, 13 May 1774.

14 HMC, *Dartmouth MSS,* 3 vols (London, 1887–96), i. p. 353, Joseph Reed to Dartmouth, 30 May 1774.

15 Cobbett, *Parliamentary History,* vol. 17, col. 1193.

16 Ibid., vol. 17, col. 1200.

17 Ibid., vol. 17, col. 1202.

18 *The Correspondence of William Pitt, Earl of Chatham,* ed. W. S. Taylor and J. H. Pringle, 4 vols (London, 1838–40), iv. p. 335.

19 Hutchinson, *Diary,* i. p. 285.

20 Alan Valentine, *Lord North,* 2 vols (Norman, Oklahoma, 1967), i. p. 313.

21 Cobbett, *Parliamentary History,* vol. 17, col. 1300.

22 *Burke Correspondence,* ii. p. 534, Burke to Committee of Correspondence, 4 May 1774.

23 Hutchinson. *Diary,* i. p. 213, Hutchinson to friend, 8 August 1774.

24 *The Correspondence of George III, 1760–1783,* ed. Sir John Fortescue, 6 vols (London, 1927), iii. p. 153, King to North, 14 November 1774.

25 Ibid., iii. p. 154, King to North, 18 November 1774; p. 156, King to North, 15 December 1774.

26 Ibid., iii. p. 154, King to North, 18 November 1774.

27 Hutchinson, *Diary,* i. p. 201, Hutchinson to Thomas Hutchinson, 3 August 1774.

28 Ibid., i. p. 293, 12 November 1774.

29 Ibid., i. p. 329, 19 November 1774.

30 Ibid., i. p. 130, 22 November 1774.

31 Thomas, *North,* pp. 83–84.

32 Cobbett, *Parliamentary History,* vol. 18, col. 222.

33 Ibid., vol. 17, col. 1172.

34 Hutchinson, *Diary,* i. p. 297, 19 November 1774.

35 Fortescue, *Correspondence,* iii. p. 134, North to King, 27 September 1774.

36 Hutchinson, *Diary,* p. 298, 19 November 1774.

37 Fortescue, *Correspondence,* iii. pp. 133–53.

38 Ibid., iii. p. 152, North to King, 14 November 1774.

39 Cobbett, *Parliamentary History,* vol. 18, cols 33–34.

40 Ibid., vol. 18, col. 43.

41 Thomas, *Tea Party,* p. 128.

42 Claud H. Van Tyne, *The Causes of the War of Independence* (Boston, 1922), p. 443.

43 Thomas, *Tea Party,* p. 152.

44 Ibid., pp. 149–50.

45 *The Correspondence of General Thomas Gage, 1763–1775,* ed. C. E. Carter, 2 vols (New Haven, 1931–33), i. p. 375, Gage to Dartmouth, 25 September 1774, in which he gave Dartmouth the gist of what he had told Hutchinson.

46 Hutchinson, *Diary,* i. p. 297, 19 November 1774.

47 Fortescue, *Correspondence,* iii. p. 136, King to North, 15 December 1774.

48 HMC, *Dartmouth MSS,* i. pp. 372–73.

49 Bargar, *Dartmouth,* p. 417.

50 Cobbett, *Parliamentary History,* vol. 18, col. 223.

51 Thomas, *Tea Party,* pp. 190–93.

52 Cobbett, *Parliamentary History,* vol. 18, col. 223.

53 *The Letters of Edward Gibbon,* ed. J. E. Norton, 3 vols (London, 1956), i. p. 59, Gibbon to Holroyd, 8 February 1775.

54 Hutchinson, *Diary,* i. p. 375, 9 February 1775.

55 *American Archives: A Documentary History of the Origin and Progress of the North American Colonies,* ed. Peter Force, 4th series, 6 vols (Washington, 1837–46), ii. p. 1519, letter to a gentleman in Philadelphia, 1 July 1775.

56 Bodleain Library, North Papers, D13, fol. 7, Dampier to Guilford, 6 February 1775.

57 Cobbett, *Parliamentary History,* vol. 18, col. 320.

[58] Fortescue, *Correspondence*, iii. p. 178, North to King, 20 February 1775.

[59] Cobbett, *Parliamentary History*, vol 18, cols 329–30.

[60] Ibid., vol. 18, col. 335.

[61] Thomas, *North*, p. 86.

[62] Hutchinson, *Diary*, i. p. 445, 15 May 1775.

[63] Cobbett, *Parliamentary History*, vol. 18, col. 650.

[64] Philip Henry Stanhope, Lord Mahon, *History of England, 1713–1783*, 7 vols (London, 1836–54), vi. p. 103.

[65] *Gage Correspondence*, i. p. 376, Gage to Dartmouth, 25 September 1774.

[66] Ibid., ii. p. 163, Dartmouth to Gage, 27 January 1775.

[67] Thomas, *Tea Party*, p. 226.

[68] Frederick Mackenzie, *A British Fusilier in Revolutionary Boston*, ed. Allen French (Harvard, 1926), p. 51.

[69] Thomas, *Tea Party*, p. 227.

[70] Mackenzie, *British Fusilier*, pp. 54, 57.

[71] John Richard Alden, *History of the American Revolution* (London, 1969), p. 24.

[72] Thomas, *Tea Party*, pp. 227–28.

[73] Bargar, *Dartmouth*, p. 168.

[74] Cobbett, *Parliamentary History*, vol. 18, col. 694.

[75] Hutchinson, *Diary*, p. 460, 31 May 1775.

[76] *Gage Correspondence*, ii. p. 200, Dartmouth to Gage, 1 July 1775.

[77] Fortescue, *Correspondence*, iii. p. 178, King to North, 20 February 1775.

[78] *The Complete Works of Benjamin Franklin*, ed. J. Bigelow, 10 vols (New York and London, 1887–88), v. p. 497.

[79] HMC, *Dartmouth MSS*, i. p. 329, Guilford to Dartmouth, Friday night and Sunday morning [December] 1745.

[80] Force, *American Archives*, ii. p. 30, extract from a letter from London to a gentleman in New York.

Chapter 12: Wartime Prime Minister

[1] *American Archives: A Documentary History of the Origin and Progress of the North American Colonies*, ed. Peter Force, 4th series, 6 vols (Washington, 1837–46), ii. p. 1870.

[2] John Richard Alden, *The American Revolution* (London, 1954), pp. 61–62.

[3] Ibid., p. 29.

[4] *The Correspondence of General Thomas Gage, 1763–1775*, ed. C. E. Carter, 2 vols (New Haven, 1931–1933), ii. p. 191, Dartmouth to Gage, 15 April 1775.

[5] Alden, *American Revolution*, p. 36.

[6] Jeremy Black, *War for America* (Stroud, 1991), p. 38.

[7] Ibid., p. 78.

[8] *The Correspondence of George III, 1760–1783*, ed. Sir John Fortescue, 6 vols (London, 1927), iii. p. 220, Howe to [? Adjutant General], 22 and 24 June 1775.

[9] Black, *War for America*, p. 78.

[10] Alan Valentine, *Lord North*, 2 vols (Norman, Oklahoma, 1967), i. p. 372.

[11] Fortescue, *Correspondence*, iii. pp. 234–35, North to King, 26 July 1775; and King to North, same date.

[12] Ibid., iii. p. 236, King to North, 28 July 1775.

[13] Ibid., iii. p. 237, King to North, 1 August 1775.

[14] HMC, *Abergavenny MSS* (London, 1887), p. 9, North to Burgoyne, 31 July 1775.

[15] Fortescue, *Correspondence*, iii. pp. 238 et seq.

[16] Ibid., p. 247, King to North, 18 August 1775.

[17] Ibid., p. 251, King to North, September 1775.

[18] Valentine, *North*, i. p. 373.

[19] Fortescue, *Correspondence*, iii. p. 248, King to North, 18 August 1775.

[20] B. D. Bargar, *Lord Dartmouth and the American Revolution* (Columbia, South Carolina, 1965), pp. 154–55.

[21] *Autobiography of Augustus Henry, Third Duke of Grafton*, ed. Sir William R. Anson (London, 1898), p. 271, Grafton to North, 31 August 1775.

[22] Ibid., p. 272.

[23] Ibid., p. 273.

[24] William Cobbett, ed., *The Parliamentary History of England*, 36 vols (London, 1806–20), vol. 18, col. 695.

[25] Ibid., vol. 18, col. 710; Bodleian Library, North Papers, D25, fol. 47, Brownlow North to Guilford, 27 October 1775.

[26] Bodleian Library, North Papers, Add. C4, fol. 177, Lady North to Guilford, Friday evening [27 October 1775].

[27] Cobbett, *Parliamentary History*, vol. 18, col. 907.

[28] Grafton, *Autobiography*, p. 274. He implies his resignation was required immediately after the debate on the Address, but this must be mistaken as the King had still not received it a week later (Fortescue, *Correspondence*, iii. p. 276, King to North, 3 November 1775); also see letter from Lady North in text below.

[29] Bodleian Library, North Papers, D25, fol. 57, Lady North to Guilford, 10 November 1775. Her numerous abbreviations of names have been given in full.

[30] Fortescue, *Correspondence*, iii. p. 278, North to King, 7 November 1775; p. 283, King to North, 9 November 1775.

[31] Ibid., p. 279, King to North, 7 November 1775.

[32] Bodleian Library, North Papers, D26, fol. 24, Brownlow North to Guilford, 11 November 1775.

[33] Valentine, *North*, i. p. 397.

[34] W. Baring Pemberton, *Lord North* (London, 1938), p. 243.

[35] Alden, *American Revolution*, p. 64.

[36] Cobbett, *Parliamentary History*, vol. 18, col. 1038.

[37] Ibid., vol. 18, cols 993, 994.

[38] Alden, *American Revolution*, p. 88.

[39] HMC, *American MSS*, 4 vols (London and Hereford, 1904–9), i. p. 47, North to General Howe, 25 June 1776, in which North refers to sending 'provisions to feed your army (computed at 36,000 men) ... '

[40] Ibid., p. 48.

[41] Peter D. G. Thomas, *Tea Party to Independence* (Oxford, 1991), p. 314.

[42] Alden, *American Revolution*, p. 96.

[43] Kenneth Ellis, *The Post Office in the Eighteenth Century* (Oxford, 1969), p. 96.

[44] Piers Mackesy, *The War for America, 1775–1783* (London, 1964), p. 73.

[45] Bodleian Library, North Papers, D25, fol. 92, Lady North to Guilford, 9 September 1776

[46] Thomas Hutchinson, *The Diary and Letters*, ed. P. O. Hutchinson, 2 vols (London, 1883 and 1886), i. p. 445, 12 May 1775.

[47] *Gentleman's Magazine*, 46 (1776), p. 434.

[48] Cobbett, *Parliamentary Papers*, vol. 18, col. 1426.

[49] Bodleian Library, North Papers, D17, fol. 10, St John to Guilford, 24 October 1776.

[50] Horace Walpole, *Last Journals*, ed. A. F. Steuart, 2 vols (London, 1910), ii. p. 13.

[51] *Letters of the First Earl of Malmesbury*, ed. Earl of Malmesbury, 2 vols (London, 1870), i. p. 350, Mr Harris MP to his son, 18 November 1776.

[52] Bodleian Library, North Papers, D25, fols 98–101, North to Guilford, 2 November 1776.

[53] *The Autobiography and Correspondence of Mary Granville, Mrs Delany*, ed. Lady Lanover, 3 vols (London, 1861), 3 vols (London, 1862), 2nd series, ii. pp. 276–77, Frederick Montagu to Delany, 8 November 1776.

[54] Bodleian Library, North Papers, D25, fols 98–102, North to Guilford, 2 November 1776.

[55] Ibid., D25, fol. 107, George North to Guilford, 9 November 1776.

[56] Valentine, *North*, i. p. 426.

[57] Bodleian Library, North Papers, D25, fol. 110, George North to Guilford, undated.

[58] Ibid., D17, fol. 44, Egerton to Guilford, 5 April 1777.

[59] Fortescue, *Correspondence*, iii. pp. 431–32, North to King, 20 March [1777]; King to North, 21 March 1777.

[60] Bodleian Library, North Papers, D25, fol. 116, Brownlow North to Guilford, 7 January 1777.

[61] Fortescue, *Correspondence*, iii. p. 421, King to North, 24 February 1777. Thomas, *North*, p. 107, says the meeting took place on 24 February and that North was present; Valentine, *North*, i. p. 442, suggests that it was a day later and that he wasn't.

[62] Alden, *American Revolution*, p. 116.

[63] Valentine, *North*, i. p. 444.

[64] Colonial Office 5/94, Library of Congress transcripts, Germain to Howe, 18 May 1777, quoted Alden, *American Revolution*, p. 117.

[65] Alden, *American Revolution*, p. 121.

[66] Ibid., p. 132.

[67] Black, *War for America*, p. 134.

[68] Alden, *American Revolution*, p. 134.

[69] Valentine, *North*, i. p. 461.

[70] Black, *War for America*, p. 128.

[71] All North's extant letters during July and August are dated from Downing Street or Bushy.

[72] Valentine, *North*, p. 452.

[73] Walpole, *Last Journals*, ii. p. 27.

[74] Fortescue, *Correspondence*, iii. p. 450, King to North, 4 June 1777.

[75] Bodleian Library, North Papers, Add. C4, fol. 179, North to Guilford, 16 August 1777.

[76] HMC, *Abergavenny MSS*, p. 18, Robinson to King, 19 September 1777.

[77] Fortescue, *Correspondence*, iii. p. 478, King to North, 19 September 1777.

[78] Ibid., vi. p. 7, King to North, 5 May 1782.

[79] John Brooke, *King George III* (London, 1985), p. 209.

[80] Ibid., p. 210.

[81] Richard Pares, *King George III and the Politicians* (Oxford, 1953), p. 172n.

[82] BL, Egerton MS 2232, fol. 11, North to Thurlow, 30 October 1777, quoted Valentine, *North*, i. p. 461.

Chapter 13: After Saratoga

[1] Alan Valentine, *Lord North*, 2 vols (Norman, Oklahoma, 1967), i. p. 467.

[2] BL. Add. MS 34414, quoted Reginald Lucas, *Lord North*, 2 vols (London, 1913), ii. p. 54.

[3] William Cobbett, ed., *The Parliamentary History of England*, 36 vols (London, 1806–20), vol. 19, col. 355.

[4] Ibid., vol. 19, col. 432.

[5] Ibid., vol. 19, col. 430.

[6] *The Correspondence of George III, 1760–1783*, ed. Sir John Fortescue, 6 vols (London, 1927), iii. p. 530, North to King, 30 December 1777.

[7] Ibid., iii. p. 501, Sandwich to King, 2 December 1777.

[8] Ibid., iii. p. 504, North to King, 4 December 1777.

[9] Cobbett, *Parliamentary History*, vol. 19, col. 532.

[10] Ibid., vol. 19, col. 541.

[11] Fortescue, *Correspondence*, iii. p. 503, King to North, 4 December 1777.

[12] See John Brooke, *King George III* (London, 1985), p. 184, for a fuller discussion.

[13] Charles E. Ritcheson, *British Politics and the American Revolution* (Norman, Oklahoma, 1954), pp. 234–35.

[14] Fortescue, *Correspondence*, iv. p. 27, North to King, 29 January 1778.

[15] Ibid., iv. p. 30, King to North, 31 January 1778.

[16] Cobbett, *Parliamentary History*, vol. 19, cols 762 et seq.

[17] Ibid., vol 19, col. 767n.

[18] Valentine, *North*, i. p. 507.

[19] Peter D. G. Thomas, *Lord North*, (London, 1976), p. 110.

[20] Ritcheson, *British Politics*, p. 258.

[21] Ibid., p. 267.

[22] Horace Walpole, *Last Journals*, ed. A. F. Steuart, 2 vols (London, 1910), ii. p. 12.

[23] Ritcheson, *British Politics*, p. 272.

[24] Ibid., p. 277.

[25] Ibid., p. 280.

[26] Fortescue, *Correspondence*, iv. p. 132, King to North, undated.

[27] Ibid., iv. p. 133, King to North, 6 May 1778.

[28] Ibid., iv. pp. 135 and 138, King to North, 7 and 10 May 1778.

[29] Ibid., iv. p. 144, North to King, 17 May 1778.

[30] Ibid., iv. p. 163, King to North, 22 June 1778.

[31] Ibid., iv. p. 145, King to North, 19 May 1778.

[32] Ibid., iv. p. 144, North to King, 17 May 1778.

[33] Ibid., iv. pp. 165 and 167, North to King, 2 and 7 June 1778.

[34] Ibid., iv. p. 144, North to King, 17 May 1778.

[35] Ibid., iv. p. 145, North to King, 19 May 1778.

[36] Ibid., iv. p. 163, King to North, 2 June 1778.

[37] Valentine, *North*, ii. p. 25.

[38] Waldershare MSS, Edward George to Guilford, 30 June 1778. (Not in the Bodleian Library.)

[39] Valentine, *North*, ii. p. 147.

[40] Cobbett, *Parliamentary History*, vol. 19, col. 1119.

[41] Ibid., vol. 19, col. 1126; Thomas, *North*, p. 118.

[42] Thomas, *North*, p. 122.

[43] John Richard Alden, *The American Revolution* (London, 1954), pp. 181 et seq.

[44] Fortescue, *Correspondence*, iv. p. 211, North to King, 25 October [1778].

[45] Ibid., iv. p. 213, King to North, 2 November 1778.

[46] Ibid., iv. p. 215, North to King, 10 November 1778.

[47] Ibid., iv. p. 217, King to North, 10 November 1778.

[48] Ibid., iv. p. 219, North to King, 14 November 1778.

[49] Ibid., iv. p. 220, King to North, 14 November 1778.

[50] Ibid., iv. p. 222, North to King, 16 November 1778.

[51] Herbert Butterfield, 'Lord North and Mr Robinson, 1779', *Cambridge Historical Review* (1937), p. 275.

[52] Fortescue, *Correspondence*, iv. pp. 262 and 263, King to North 29 January, and King to North, 29 January 1779.

[53] Valentine, *North*, ii. p. 113.

[54] Brooke, *George III*, p. 199.

⁵⁵ *The Private Papers of John, Fourth Earl of Sandwich*, ed. G. R. Barnes and J. H. Owen, Navy Records Society, 3 (1936), p. 25, memorandum dated 21 June 1779, quoted Valentine, *North*, ii. p. 110.

⁵⁶ Fortescue, *Correspondence*, iv. p. 350, King to North, 21 June 1779.

⁵⁷ *Sandwich Private Papers*, iii. p. 26, King to Sandwich, 21 June 1779, quoted Valentine, *North*, ii. p. 211.

⁵⁸ Valentine, *North*, ii. p. 109.

⁵⁹ Fortescue, *Correspondence*, iv. p. 360, King to North, 18 June 1779.

⁶⁰ J. H. Jesse, *George Selwyn and his Contemporaries*, 4 vols (London, 1843–44), iv. p. 202, Carlisle to Selwyn, 18 June 1779.

⁶¹ Cobbett, *Parliamentary History*, vol. 20, cols 926–27. This story is also supported by Thomas Hutchinson, *The Diaries and Letters*, ed. P. O. Hutchinson, 2 vols (London, 1883 and 1886), ii. p. 262, 22 June 1779.

⁶² Fortescue, *Correspondence*, iv. p. 377, Jenkinson to King, 25 June 1779.

⁶³ Valentine, *North*, ii p. 118.

⁶⁴ Fortescue, *Correspondence*, Sandwich to King, 16 August 1779.

⁶⁵ Valentine, *North*, ii. p. 68.

⁶⁶ Walpole, *Last Journals*, ii. p. 226.

⁶⁷ HMC, *Abergavenny MSS* (London, 1887), p. 24, Robinson to King and King to Robinson, 13 March 1779.

⁶⁸ BL, Add. MS 38212, fol. 59, Robinson to Jenkinson, 11 August 1779, quoted Butterfield, 'Lord North and Mr Robinson', p. 275.

⁶⁹ BL, Add. MS 38212, fols 248–53, Robinson to Jenkinson, 25 November 1779, quoted Butterfield, 'Lord North and Mr Robinson', p. 275.

Chapter 14: The Road to Yorktown

¹ John Richard Alden, *The American Revolution* (London, 1954), p. 206.

² Ibid., p. 228.

³ Ibid., p. 231.

⁴ William Cobbett, ed., *Parliamentary History of England*, 36 vols (London, 1806–29), vol. 21, col. 361.

⁵ Horace Walpole, *Last Journals*, ed. A. F. Steuart, 2 vols (London, 1910), ii. p. 296.

⁶ Cobbett, *Parliamentary History*, vol. 21, col. 363.

⁷ *The Correspondence of George III, 1760–1783*, ed. Sir John Fortescue, 6 vols (London, 1927), v. p. 40, King to North, 7 April 1780.

⁸ Ibid., v. p. 43, Jenkinson to King, 14 April 1780; ibid., iv. p. 505, Jenkinson to King, 1 December 1779.

⁹ Ibid., v. p. 42, King to North, 11 April 1780.

¹⁰ Cobbett, *Parliamentary History*, vol. 21, cols 497 and 522.

¹¹ W. Baring Pemberton, *Lord North* (London, 1938), p. 119.

¹² Cobbett, *Parliamentary History*, vol. 21, col. 655.

¹³ Fortescue, *Correspondence*, v. p. 73, King to North, 6 June 1780.

¹⁴ Ibid., v. p. 71, King to North, 5 June 1780; Valentine, *North*, ii. p. 217.

¹⁵ Sir Nathanial Wraxall, *The Historical and Posthumous Memoirs, 1772–1784*, ed. Henry B. Wheatley, 5 vols (London, 1884), i. pp. 267 et seq.

¹⁶ Fortescue, *Correspondence*, v. p. 95, King to North, 3 July 1780.

¹⁷ Valentine, *North*, ii. p. 220.

¹⁸ Fortescue, *Correspondence*, v. p. 87, Jenkinson to King, 17 June 1780.

¹⁹ Valentine, *North*, ii. p. 220; I. R. Christie, 'The Marquis of Rockingham and Lord North's Offer of a Coalition, June–July 1780', *English Historical Review*, 69 (1954), p. 388 et seq.

²⁰ Fortescue, *Correspondence*, v. pp. 95–98, King to North, 3 July 1780.

[21] Christie, 'North's Offer of a Coalition', p. 392.

[22] Valentine, *North*, pp. 224 et seq.

[23] I. R. Christie, *The End of North's Ministry, 1780–1782* (London, 1958); Sir Lewis Namier and John Brooke, *The History of Parliament: House of Commons, 1754–1790*, 3 vols (London, 1964), i. p. 2.

[24] *The Diaries of Sylvester Douglas, Lord Glenbervie*, ed. Francis Bickley, 2 vols (London, 1928), i. p. 2.

[25] HMC, *Abergavenny MSS*, p. 33, North to Robinson, 13 August 1780.

[26] Christie, *North's Ministry*, pp. 42–43.

[27] Quoted Cobbett, *Parliamentary History*, vol. 21, col. 767.

[28] Christie, *North's Ministry*, pp. 102, 104.

[29] Ibid., pp. 98–99.

[30] Ibid., pp. 161–62.

[31] Valentine, *North*, ii. p. 236.

[32] HMC, *Buckinghamshire MSS*, Papers of Lord Emly (London, 1895), p. 160, Lord Lucan to E. S. Perry, 3 October 1780.

[33] *The Letters of Horace Walpole*, ed. Mrs Paget Toynbee, 16 vols (Oxford, 1857–59), xi. p. 299, Walpole to Countess of Upper Ossory, 10 October 1780.

[34] Cobbett, *Parliamentary History*, vol. 21, col. 795.

[35] *Walpole Letters*, ed. Toynbee, xi. p. 313, Walpole to Mann, 2 November 1780.

[36] BL, Add. MS 37835, fol. 186, King to Robinson, 2 November 1780; fol. 188, King to Robinson, 4 November 1780.

[37] *The Journal of Samuel Curwen*, ed. Andrew Oliver, 2 vols (Cambridge, Massachusetts, 1972), ii. p. 821, 29 March 1782.

[38] See chapter 7, n. 56 above.

[39] Thomas Hutchinson, *The Diaries and Letters*, ed. P. O. Hutchinson, 2 vols (London, 1883 and 1886), i. p. 445, 12 May 1774.

[40] Christie, *North's Ministry*, p. 238.

[41] Valentine, *North*, ii. p. 243.

[42] Bodleian Library, North Papers, Add. C4, fol. 202, North to Guilford, 25 April 1781.

[43] Christie, *North's Ministry*, pp. 240 et seq.

[44] Ibid., pp. 251–52.

[45] Fortescue, *Correspondence*, v. p. 184, North to King, 14 January 1781.

[46] Christie, *North's Ministry*, p. 251.

[47] Ibid., p. 253.

[48] Jeremy Black, *War for America* (Stroud, 1991), pp. 206 and 219.

[49] Christie, *North's Ministry*, p. 262.

[50] Ibid.

[51] Black, *War for America*, pp. 220–21.

[52] Alden, *American Revolution*, pp. 239 et seq.

[53] Black, *War for America*, pp. 28–29.

[54] Ibid., pp. 224–25.

[55] Ibid., pp. 227–28.

[56] Ibid., pp. 228 et seq.

Chapter 15: The End of an Era

[1] According to Horace Walpole, *Last Journals*, ed. A. F. Steuart, 2 vols (London, 1910), ii. p. 278, the news was first learnt from a French 'Gazette' imported via Dover. Sir Nathaniel Wraxall, *The Historical and Posthumous Memoirs, 1772–1784*, ed. Henry B. Wheatly, 5 vols (London, 1884), ii. p. 138, talks of 'official intelligence' arriving via Falmouth. In *Correspondence of Charles, First Marquis Cornwallis*, ed. Charles Ross, 3 vols (London, 1859), i. p. 129n., it

is pointed out that the official despatch did not report the fact of the capitulation, only its strong probability.

[2] Wraxall, *Memoirs*, ii. p. 138.

[3] Bodleian Library, North Papers, D26, fol. 28, Brownlow North to Guilford, undated.

[4] HMC, *Carlisle MSS* (London, 1897), p. 539, Loughborough to Carlisle, 30 November 1781.

[5] Alan Valentine, *Lord North*, 2 vols (Norman, Oklahoma, 1967), ii. p. 274.

[6] Ibid., ii. p. 275.

[7] William Cobbett, ed., *The Parliamentary History of England*, 36 vols (London, 1806–20), vol. 22, cols 636–37.

[8] *The Correspondence of George III, 1760–1783*, ed. Sir John Fortescue, 6 vols (London, 1927), v. p. 304, King to North, 28 November 1781.

[9] Cobbett, *Parliamentary History*, vol. 22, col. 729.

[10] Ibid., vol. 22, col. 716.

[11] Fortescue, *Correspondence*, v. p. 312, King to North, 13 December 1781.

[12] Cobbett, *Parliamentary History*, vol. 22, col. 829.

[13] Ibid., vol. 22, cols 808 et seq.

[14] Wraxall, *Memoirs*, ii. p. 160.

[15] Valentine, *North*, ii. pp. 298–99.

[16] Fortescue, *Correspondence*, v. p. 313, King to Germain, 15 December 1781; p. 314, Germain to King, 16 December 1781.

[17] I. R. Christie, *The End of North's Ministry* (London, 1958), pp. 291–92.

[18] Fortescue, *Correspondence*, v. pp. 32–35, Stormont to King and King to Stormont, 23 December 1781.

[19] Ibid., v. p. 326, King to North, 26 December 1782.

[20] Ibid., v. pp. 324–25, King to North, 21 January 1782.

[21] Ibid., v. p. 336, North to King, 21 January 1782.

[22] Ibid., v. p. 337.

[23] HMC, *Carlisle MSS*, p. 576, Selwyn to Carlisle, 13 February 1782.

[24] BL, Add. MS 34429, fols 330–31, Loughborough to Eden, 29 January 1782.

[25] Cobbett, *Parliamentary History*, vol. 22, cols 930–31.

[26] Ibid., cols 932–46.

[27] Fortescue, *Correspondence*, v. p. 365, King to North, 21 February 1782.

[28] Cobbett, *Parliamentary History*, vol. 22, col. 1030.

[29] Ibid., vol. 22, col. 1049.

[30] Ibid., vol. 22, col. 1071

[31] Fortescue, *Correspondence*, v. p. 374, King to North, 26 February 1782.

[32] Cobbett, *Parliamentary History*, vol. 22, col. 1077.

[33] Fortescue, *Correspondence*, v. p. 374, North to King, [28 February] 1782.

[34] Ibid., v. p. 375, King to North, 28 February 1782.

[35] Cobbett, *Parliamentary History*, vol. 22, col. 1149.

[36] Fortescue, *Correspondence*, v. p. 381, North to King, 9 March 1782.

[37] Ibid., v. p. 382, King to North, 9 March 1782.

[38] Cobbett, *Parliamentary History*, vol. 22, cols 1191 and 1193.

[39] Fortescue, *Correspondence*, v. p. 391, King to North, 16 March 1782.

[40] Ibid., v. p. 392, King to Thurlow, 18 March 1782.

[41] Peter D. G. Thomas, *Lord North* (London, 1976), p. 131.

[42] Ibid., p. 132.

[43] Fortescue, *Correspondence*, v. p. 395, North to King, 18 March 1782. The full text of this letter is given in the Appendix, pp. 229–31, to this book.

[44] Ibid., v. p. 397, King to North, 19 March 1782.

[45] Ibid., v. p. 398, North to King, 19 March 1782.

[46] Christie, *North's Ministry*, p. 368.

[47] Wraxall, *Memoirs*, ii. pp. 241–42.

[48] Walpole, *Last Journals*, ii. p. 422.

[49] Wraxall, *Memoirs*, ii. p. 242.

[50] Christie, *North's Ministry*, p. 368.

[51] Valentine, *North*, ii. p. 315.

[52] *Memorials of Charles James Fox*, ed. Lord John Russell, 4 vols (London, 1853), i. p. 296.

[53] Cobbett, *Parliamentary History*, vol. 22, col. 1217.

[54] Wraxall, *Memoirs*, ii. p. 247.

[55] Cobbett, *Parliamentary History*, vol. 22, col. 1217.

[56] Fox, *Memorials*, i. p. 296.

[57] Ibid., i. p. 295; Valentine, *North*, ii. p. 316.

[58] See p. 177 above.

[59] John Brooke, *King George III* (London, 1985), pp. 214–15.

[60] Ibid., p. 113.

[61] Ibid., pp. 201 et seq.

[62] Fortescue, *Correspondence*, iii. p. 237, King to North, 30 July 1775.

[63] Ibid., p. 237, King to North 1 August 1775; p. 238, North to King, 3 August 1775.

[64] Ibid., p. 237, King to North, 28 July 1775.

[65] See p. 157 above.

[66] Ibid.

[67] Fortescue, *Correspondence*, p. 248, King to North 18 August 1775; Valentine, *North*, i. p. 373.

Chapter 16: The Coalition and the Last Decade

[1] Peter D. G. Thomas, *Lord North* (London, 1976), p. 135.

[2] *Journal and Correspondence of William, Lord Aukland*, ed. Bishop of Bath and Wells [Robert, second Lord Aukland], 4 vols (London, 1861–62), i. p. 25, Lord Loughborough to William Eden, 18 August 1782.

[3] *The Autobiography and Correspondence of Mary Granville, Mrs Delany*, ed. Lady Lanover, 3 vols (London, 1861), 3 vols (London, 1862), 2nd series iii. p. 108, Montagu to Delany, 10 September 1782.

[4] *The Letters of Edward Gibbon*, ed. J. E. Norton, 3 vols (London, 1956), ii. p. 23, Gibbon to Lord Sheffield, 29 September 1782.

[5] John Brooke, *King George III* (London, 1985), p. 224.

[6] *The Correspondence of George III, 1760–1783*, ed. Sir John Fortescue, 6 vols (London, 1927), vi. p. 97, King to North, 7 August 1782.

[7] Ibid., vi. p. 98, North to King, 10 August 1782.

[8] Ibid., v. p. 405, King to North, 22 March 1782; p. 407, North to King, 22 March 1782.

[9] Ibid., v. p. 421, King to North, 27 March 1782; p. 422, North to King, 27 March 1782.

[10] Ibid., v. p. 481n.

[11] Ibid., vi. p. 27, North to King, 16 May 1782.

[12] *The Later Correspondence of George III*, ed. A. Aspinall, 5 vols (Cambridge, 1962–70), i. p. 42, King to Henry Drummond, 22 March 1784 and subsequent letters; i. p. 105, King to Drummond, 24 October 1784.

[13] William Cobbett, ed., *The Parliamentary History of England*, 36 vols (London, 1806–20), vol. 23, col. 207.

[14] Ibid., vol. 23, col. 256.

[15] Ibid., vol. 23, col. 322.

[16] Thomas, *North*, p. 135.

[17] Alan Valentine, *Lord North*, 2 vols (Norman, Oklahoma, 1967), ii. p. 342.

[18] Ibid., ii. p. 347.

[19] *Memorials and Correspondence of Charles James Fox*, ed. Lord John Russell, 4 vols (London, 1853), ii. p. 38.

[20] Cobbett, *Parliamentary History*, vol. 23, col. 487.

[21] Sir Nathaniel Wraxall, *The Historical and Posthumous Memoirs, 1772–1784*, ed. Henry B. Wheatly, 5 vols (London, 1884), iii. p. 49.

[22] Cobbett, *Parliamentary History*, vol. 23, col. 557.

[23] Thomas, *North*, p. 138.

[24] Brooke, *George III*, p. 236.

[25] BL, Add. MS 38218, fol. 156, William Adam to Jenkinson, 3 January 1773, quoted Valentine, *North*, ii. p. 345.

[26] Wraxall, *Memoirs*, ii. p. 237; Reginald Lucas, *Lord North*, 2 vols (London, 1913), ii. p. 210.

[27] Lord Edmund Fitzmaurice, *Life of William, Earl of Shelburne*, 3 vols (London, 1875–76), iii. p. 154.

[28] Kent County Records Office, North Papers, U471 C23/3. Valentine, *North*, reprinted the whole document in its short-hand form, as appendix C, and deciphered a number of passages for his main text, ibid., pp. 355–66. Quotations here are from that source.

[29] Present author's rendering from Valentine's appendix.

[30] Kent County Record Office, North Papers, U471 C23/10, North to Guilford, undated.

[31] *The Diaries of Sylvester Douglas, Lord Glenbervie*, ed. Francis Bickley, 2 vols (London, 1928), i. p. 180, 23 February 1798.

[32] Thomas, *North*, p. 138.

[33] Fortescue, *Correspondence*, vi. p. 257, King to Thurlow, 2 March 1773.

[34] Ibid., vi. p. 258, King to Thurlow, 3 March 1773.

[35] Ibid., vi. p. 273, King to North, 12 March 1773; Thomas, *North*, p. 139.

[36] Fortescue, *Correspondence*, vi. p. 329, King to Lord Temple, 1 April 1783.

[37] Ibid., vi. pp. 288–90, King to North and North to King, both 18 March 1783.

[38] Ibid., vi. p. 309, King to Pitt, 25 March 1783.

[39] Ibid., vi. p. 309, Pitt to King and King to Pitt, both 25 March 1783.

[40] Ibid., vi. p. 331, King to North, 2 April 1783.

[41] Ibid., vi. p. 330 King to Temple, 1 April 1783.

[42] Reginald Lucas, *Lord North*, 2 vols (London, 1913), ii. p. 240.

[43] Cobbett, *Parliamentary History*, vol. 23, col. 851.

[44] Valentine, *North*, ii. pp. 379, 381.

[45] Cobbett, *Parliamentary History*, vol. 23, col. 1306; vol. 24, col. 61.

[46] Ibid., vol. 23, col. 1284.

[47] Valentine, *North*, ii. p. 385.

[48] Brooke, *George III*, p. 253.

[49] Cobbett, *Parliamentary History*, vol. 24, cols 160, 196.

[50] Ibid., vol. 24, col. 203.

[51] Fortescue, *Correspondence*, vi. p. 476, King to North, 18 December 1783.

[52] Brooke, *George III*, p. 256.

[53] Cobbett, *Parliamentary History*, vol. 24, cols 589, 591.

[54] Valentine, *North*, ii. p. 412.

[55] Thomas, *North*, p. 147.

[56] Cobbett, *Parliamentary History*, vol. 24, cols 987 et seq.

[57] Ibid., vol. 26, cols 818, 823; Bodleian Library, North Papers, D21, fol. 114, Dr Lamb to Guilford, 1 April 1787.

[58] Thomas, *North*, p. 146.

[59] Bodleian Library, North Papers, D26, fol. 73, George North to Guilford, 25 September 1785.

[60] Valentine, *North*, ii. p. 436.

[61] Bodleian Library, North Papers, D26, fol. 77, North to Guilford; fol. 82, Lady North to Guilford, both 17 October 1785.

[62] Waldershare MSS, North to Guilford, 24 November [1786] (Bodleian Library, MS Eng. c. 3337, fol. 58).

[63] Henry, Lord Brougham, *Historical Sketches of Statesmen Who Flourished in the Time of George III* (London 1839), p. 395, letter from Lady Charlotte Lindsay.

[64] Wraxall, *Memoirs*, iv. p. 437.

[65] HMC, *Rutland MSS*, iii. 1894 (London), p. 380, David Pultney to Duke of Rutland, 31 March 1787.

[66] Bodleian Library, North Papers, D26, fol. 122, Lady North to Guilford, 10 May 1787.

[67] Brougham, *Historical Sketches*, p. 395.

[68] *The Yale Edition of Horace Walpole's Correspondence*, 48 vols (New Haven, 1937–83), xxxiii. p. 580, Walpole to Countess of Upper Ossory, 4 October 1787.

[69] Thomas, *North*, p. 149.

[70] Ibid., p. 151.

[71] Cobbett, *Parliamentary History*, vol. 29, col. 93.

[72] Ibid., vol. 29, cols 855 et seq.

[73] Brougham, *Historical Sketches*, p. 396.

[74] PRO, 30/29/6, Edward Legge to Lord Granville Leveson-Gower, 13 August [1792], quoted Aspinall, *Later Correspondence*, vi. p. 604n.

[75] *Memoirs of Richard Cumberland Written by Himself*, 2 vols (London, 1807), ii. pp. 349–50.

[76] Brougham, *Historical Sketches*, pp. 391–97.

[77] Glenbervie, *Diaries*, i. p. 247.

[78] *Life and Letters of Sir Gilbert Elliot, First Earl of Minto*, 3 vols (London, 1754), i. p. 235.

[79] Leonard Mills, *Ceylon under British Rule* (Oxford, 1933), pp. 27 et seq.

[80] Z. D. Ferriman, *Some English Philhellenes* (London, 1919), p. 101.

Chapter 17: Conclusion

[1] *The Diaries of Sylvester Douglas, Lord Glenbervie*, ed. Francis Bickley, 2 vols (London, 1928), i. p. 61.

[2] William Lecky, *History of England in the Eighteenth Century*, 8 vols (London, 1878–82), iii. p. 127.

[3] G. M. Trevelyan, *British History in the Nineteenth Century and After* (London, 1937), p. 41.

[4] Dorothy Marshall, *Eighteenth-Century England* (London, 1962), p. 405.

[5] J. H. Plumb, *The First Four Georges* (London, 1957), p. 114.

[6] Sir Nathaniel Wraxall, *The Historical and Posthumous Memoirs, 1772–1784*, ed. Henry B. Wheatley, 5 vols (London, 1884), i. p. 373.

[7] Horace Walpole, *Memoirs of the Reign of George III*, ed. G. F. Russell Barker, 4 vols (London, 1894), iv. p. 55.

[8] C. D. Smith, *The Early Career of Lord North the Prime Minister* (London, 1979).

[9] Peter D. G. Thomas, *Lord North* (London, 1976).

[10] John Brooke, *King George III* (London, 1985), p. 196.

[11] *The Letters of Philip Dormer Stanhope, Earl of Chesterfield*, ed. Lord Mahon, 5 vols (London and Philadelphia, 1892), ii. pp. 473–74.

Bibliography

Manuscripts

Dartmouth Papers, Staffordshire County Record Office.
Newcastle Papers, British Library.
North Papers, Bodleian Library.
North Papers, Kent County Record Office.
North Papers, Waldershare Park, Dover.

Printed Works

Adams, John, *The Works of John Adams*, ed. Charles Francis Adams, 10 vols (Boston, 1850–56).

Aikin, John, *Annals of the Reign of George III*, 2 vols (London, 1816).

Alden, John Richard, *A History of the American Revolution* (London, 1969).

——, *Pioneer America* (London, 1966).

American Archives: A Documentary History of the Origin and the Progress of the North American Colonies, ed. Peter Force, 4th series, 6 vols (Washington, DC, 1837–46).

Aukland, Lord, *Journal and Correspondence of William, Lord Aukland*, ed. Bishop of Bath and Wells [Robert, second Lord Aukland], 4 vols (London, 1861–62).

Baker, Kenneth, *The Prime Ministers: An Irreverent Political History in Cartoons* (London, 1995).

Bargar, D. B., *Lord Dartmouth and the American Revolution* (Columbia, South Carolina, 1965).

Beatson, Robert, *A Political Index*, 3 vols (London, 1806).

Bedford, Duke of, *Correspondence of John, Fourth Duke of Bedford*, ed. Lord John Russell, 3 vols (London, 1859).

Binney, J. E. D., *British Public Finance and Administration, 1774–1792* (Oxford, 1958).

Black, Jeremy, *War for America* (Stroud, 1991).

Bowen, H. V. *Revenue and Reform: The Indian Problem in British Politics, 1757–1773* (Cambridge, 1991).

Brooke, John, *King George III* (London, 1985).

Brougham, Henry, Lord, *Historical Sketches of Statesmen Who Flourished in the Time of George III* (London, 1839).

Browning, Reed, *The Duke of Newcastle* (New Haven and London, 1975).

Brydges, Sir Egerton, ed., *Collins's Peerage*, 9 vols (London, 1812).

Burke, Edmund, *The Correspondence of Edmund Burke*, ed. T. W. Copeland et al., 9 vols (Cambridge, 1958–70).

Butterfield, H., 'Lord North and Mr Robinson, 1779', *Cambridge Historical Journal*, 5 (1937), pp. 155–279.

——, *George III, Lord North and the People* (London, 1949).

——, *The Fox-North Coalition: Crisis of the Constitution* (Cambridge, 1969).

Cannon, John, *Aristocratic Century* (Cambridge, 1984).

——, *Lord North: The Noble Lord in the Blue Ribbon* (London, 1970).

Cavendish, Sir Henry, *Debates in the House of Commons, 1768–1771*, ed. J. Wright, 2 vols (London, 1841).

Chatham, Earl of, *Correspondence of William Pitt, Earl of Chatham*, ed. W. S. Taylor and J. H. Pringle, 4 vols (London, 1838–40).

Chester, Sir Norman, *The English Administrative System, 1780–1870* (Oxford, 1981).

Chevenix-Trench, Charles, *Portrait of a Patriot* (Edinburgh and London, 1962).

Christie, Ian R., *The End of North's Ministry, 1780–1782* (London, 1958).

——, *Wilkes, Wyvill and Reform* (London, 1962).

Cobbett, William, ed., *The Parliamentary History of England*, 36 vols (London, 1806–20).

Cornwallis, Marquis, *Correspondence of Charles, First Marquis Cornwallis*, ed. Charles Ross, 3 vols (London, 1859).

Cumberland, Richard, *Memoirs of Richard Cumberland Written by Himself*, 2 vols (London, 1807).

Cumberland, Richard and George, *The Letters of Richard D. and George Cumberland*, ed. Clementina Black (London, 1912).

Curwen, Samuel, *The Journal of Samuel Curwen*, ed. Andrew Oliver, 2 vols (Cambridge, Massachusetts, 1972).

Davies, J. D. Griffiths, *George III* (London, 1936).

Delany, Mrs, *The Autobiography and Correspondence of Mary Granville, Mrs Delany*, ed. Lady Llanover, 3 vols (London, 1861), 3 vols (London, 1862).

Dodington, George Bubb, *The Political Journal of George Bubb Dodington*, ed. John Carswell and Lewis Arnold Dralle (Oxford, 1965).

Donoughue, Bernard, *British Politics and the American Revolution: The Path to War, 1773–1775* (London, 1964).

Fitzmaurice, Lord Edmund, *Life of William, Earl of Shelburne*, 3 vols (London, 1875–76).

Forrest, Sir George, *The Life of Lord Clive*, 2 vols (London, 1918).

Fox, Charles James, *Memorials and Correspondence of Charles James Fox*, ed. Lord John Russell, 4 vols (London, 1853–57).

Franklin, Benjamin, *The Complete Works of Benjamin Franklin*, ed. J. Bigelow, 10 vols (New York and London, 1987–88).

Gage, General Thomas, *The Correspondence of General Thomas Gage, 1763–1775*, ed. C. E. Carter, 2 vols (New Haven, 1931–33).

George III, *Letters from George III to Lord Bute, 1756–1766*, ed. Romney Sedgwick (London, 1939).

——, *The Correspondence of George III, 1760–1763,* ed. Sir John Fortescue, 6 vols (London, 1927).

——, *The Later Correspondence of George III,* ed. A. Aspinall, 5 vols (Cambridge, 1962–70).

George, Mary Dorothy (ed.), *Catalogue of Political and Personal Satires Preserved... in the British Museum,* v (London, 1978).

Gibbon, Edward, *Gibbon's Journals,* ed. D. M. Low (London, 1929).

——, *The Autobiography of Edward Gibbon,* ed. Lord Sheffield (London, 1978).

——, *The Letters of Edward Gibbon,* ed. J. E. Norton, 3 vols (London, 1956).

Gibbs, Vicary et al., eds, *The Complete Peerage,* 14 vols (London, 1910–40).

Glenbervie, Lord, *The Diaries of Sylvester Douglas, Lord Glenbervie,* ed. Francis Bickley, 2 vols (London, 1928).

Goebel, Julius, *The Struggle for the Falkland Islands* (New Haven, 1982).

Grafton, Duke of, *Autobiography of Augustus Henry, Third Duke of Grafton,* ed. Sir William R. Anson (London, 1898).

Grenville, *The Grenville Papers,* ed. William James Smith, 4 vols (London 1852–53).

——, *Additional Grenville Papers, 1763–1765,* ed. John Tomlinson (Manchester, 1962).

Harcourt, *Harcourt Papers,* ed. E. W. Harcourt, 14 vols (privately printed, 1880–1905).

Hatton, Ragnhild, *George I, Elector and King* (London, 1978).

Hervey, John, Lord, *Memoirs of the Reign of George II,* ed. Romney Sedgwick, 3 vols (London, 1931).

Historical Manuscripts Commission (HMC):

——, *Abergavenny MSS,* 4 vols (London, 1887).

——, *American MSS,* 4 vols (London and Hereford, 1904–9).

——, *Buckinghamshire MSS* (London, 1895).

——, *Carlisle MSS* (London, 1897).

——, *Dartmouth MSS,* 3 vols (London, 1887–96).

——, *Eglinton MSS* (London, 1885).

——, *Egmont MSS,* 3 vols (London, 1920–23).

——, *Hastings MSS* (London, 1934).

——, *Rutland MSS,* 4 vols (London, 1888–1905).

——, *Stopford–Sackville MSS,* 2 vols (London and Hereford, 1904 and 1910).

——, *Various MSS,* 7 vols (London, 1901–14).

Hoffman, Ross J. S., *The Marquis: A Study of Lord Rockingham, 1780–1782* (New York, 1973).

Hosmer, James K., *The Life of Thomas Hutchinson* (Boston and New York, 1896).

Hotblack, Kate, *Chatham's Colonial Policy* (London, 1917).

Hughes, Edward, 'Lord North's Correspondence, 1766–83', *English Historical Review,* 62 (1947), pp. 218–38.

Hutchinson, Thomas, *Diary and Letters,* ed. P. O. Hutchinson, 2 vols (London 1883 and 1886).

Jesse, J. H., *George Selwyn and his Contemporaries,* 4 vols (London, 1982).

——, *Memoirs of Celebrated Etonians,* 2 vols (London, 1901).

Kay, F. George, *The Atlantic Ocean* (London, 1954).

Langford, Paul, *A Polite and Commercial People* (Oxford, 1989).

——, *The First Rockingham Administration, 1765–1766* (London, 1973).

Lecky, William, *History of England in the Eighteenth Century*, 8 vols (London, 1878–82).

Leeds, Duke of, *The Political Memoranda of Francis, Fifth Duke of Leeds*, ed. Oscar Browning, Camden Society, new series, 35 (1884).

Lucas, Reginald, *Lord North*, 2 vols (London, 1913).

McGrady, Edward, *The History of South Carolina*, 4 vols (New York, 1897–1902).

MacKenzie, Frederick, *A British Fusilier in Revolutionary Boston*, ed. Allen French (Freeport, New York, 1926).

Mackesy, Piers, *War for America* (London, 1964).

Mahon, Philip Henry Stanhope, Lord, *History of England, 1713–1783*, 7 vols (London, 1836–54).

Malmesbury, Earl of, *Letters of the First Earl of Malmesbury*, ed. Earl of Malmesbury, 2 vols (London, 1870).

Marshall, Dorothy, *Eighteenth-Century England* (London, 1962).

Martelli, George, *Jeremy Twitcher* (London, 1962).

Mathias, Peter, *The Transformation of England* (London, 1979).

Namier, Sir Lewis, *Personalities and Powers* (London, 1955).

Namier, Sir Lewis and Brooke, John, *The History of Parliament: House of Commons, 1754–1790*, 3 vols (London 1964).

North, Roger, *The Lives of the Norths*, ed. Augustus Jessop, 3 vols (London, 1890).

North, William, Lord, 'Lord North the Prime Minister', *North American Review*, 176 (1903), pp. 778–91; 177 (1903), pp. 260–77.

Owen, John B., *The Eighteenth Century, 1714–1815* (New York and London, 1974).

Oxford, *The History of the University of Oxford*, v. ed. L. S. Sutherland and L. G. Mitchell (Oxford, 1986).

Pares, Richard, *King George III and the Politicians* (Oxford, 1953).

Pemberton, W. Baring, *Lord North* (London 1938).

Plumb, J. H., *The First Four Georges* (London, 1957).

——, 'British Attitudes to the American Revolution', *The Light of History* (London, 1972).

Potter, J., 'The Growth of Population in America, 1700 to 1860', *Population in History*, ed. D. V. Glass and D. E. C. Eversley (London, 1965).

Ritcheson, Charles E., *British Politics and the American Revolution* (Norman, Oklahoma, 1954).

Robson, R. J., *The Oxford Election of 1754* (Oxford, 1962).

Rockingham, Marquis of, *Memoirs of the Marquis of Rockingham*, ed. Earl of Albemarle, 2 vols (London, 1852).

Rodger, N. A. M., *The Insatiable Earl: A Life of John Montagu, Fourth Earl of Sandwich* (London, 1993).

Roseveare, Henry, *The Treasury, 1660–1870* (London, 1973).

Rudé, George, *Wilkes and Liberty* (Oxford, 1962).

Ryder, Nathaniel, 'The Parliamentary Diaries of Nathaniel Ryder, 1764–1767', ed. Peter D. G. Thomas, *Camden Miscellany*, 4th series, 7 (1969).

Sandwich, Earl of, *The Private Papers of John, Fourth Earl of Sandwich*, ed. G. R. Barnes and J. H. Owen, Navy Records Society, 3 (1936).

Sedgwick, Romney, *The History of the House of Commons, 1715–1754*, 2 vols (London, 1970).

Simmons, Richard C., *The American Colonies from Settlement to Independence* (London, 1976).

Smith, C. D., *The Early Career of Lord North the Prime Minister* (London, 1979).

Sutherland, Lucy, *The East India Company in Eighteenth-Century Politics* (Oxford, 1952).

Thomas, Peter D. G., *British Politics and the Stamp Act Crisis* (Oxford, 1975).

——, *Lord North* (London, 1976).

——, *Sources for the Debates of the House of Commons, 1768–1774* (London, 1959).

——, *Tea Party to Independence* (Oxford, 1991).

——, *The American Revolution* (Cambridge, 1986), from the series The English Satirical Print, 1600–1832.

——, *The House of Commons in the Eighteenth Century* (Oxford, 1971).

——, *The Townshend Duties Crisis* (Oxford, 1987).

Tillyard, Stella, *Aristocrats* (London, 1994).

Trevelyan, George Macaulay, *History of England* (London, 1994).

Trevelyan, Sir George Otto, *The American Revolution*, 3 vols (London, 1905).

Trumbull, *The Trumbull Papers*, Collections of the Massachusetts Historical Society, 5th series, 9 (1885).

Valentine, Alan, *Lord North*, 2 vols (Norman, Oklahoma, 1967).

Van Tyne, Claud H., *Causes of the War of Independence* (Boston, Massachusetts, 1922).

Wallace, David Duncan, *The Life of Henry Laurens* (New York, 1915).

Walpole, Horace, *Last Journals*, ed. A. Francis Steuart, 2 vols (London, 1910).

——, *Memoirs of King George II*, ed. John Brooke, 3 vols (New Haven, 1985).

——, *Memoirs of the Reign of George III*, ed. G. F. Russell Barker, 4 vols (London, 1894).

——, *The Letters of Horace Walpole*, ed. Mrs Paget Toynbee, 16 vols (Oxford 1857–59).

——, *The Yale Edition of Horace Walpole's Correspondence*, 48 vols (New Haven, 1937–83).

Wraxall, Sir Nathaniel, *The Historical and Posthumous Memoirs, 1772–1784*, ed. Henry B. Wheatley, 5 vols (London, 1884).

Index

Illustrations are shown in italics